Arms, Defense Policy, and Arms Control

Essays by

Franklin A. Long
Abram Chayes
Richard A. Falk
Marshall D. Shulman
Paul Doty
Harvey Brooks
Graham T. Allison
Frederic A. Morris
John Steinbruner
Barry Carter
Les Aspin
R. James Woolsey
Thomas C. Schelling
George W. Rathjens

Arms, Defense Policy, and Arms Control

Edited by FRANKLIN A. LONG *and* GEORGE W. RATHJENS

 W · W · NORTON & COMPANY · INC · *New York*

ISBN–0–393–05573–6 (Cloth Edition)
ISBN–0–393–09188–0 (Paper Edition)

1 2 3 4 5 6 7 8 9 0

CONTENTS

ACKNOWLEDGMENTS

A debt of gratitude is owed to a number of institutions and several foundations for making this volume possible. The idea for a major study of arms control in the seventies originated with the American Academy of Arts and Sciences Committee for Pugwash Conferences. Funds for the study—for preliminary meetings and for a 1973 summer study—were generously provided by the Ford Foundation, the Johnson Foundation, the Rockefeller Foundation, The Rockefeller Brothers Fund, the Alfred P. Sloan Foundation, and the Carnegie Endowment for International Peace. Special thanks are owed the Johnson Foundation, and its President, Leslie Paffrath; they entirely supported the Academy's pioneering arms-control studies in 1960, and they have been equally helpful this time. Two vital planning meetings at Wingspread and a subsequent conference were made possible by their very generous support. Thanks are due also to the Aspen Institute for Humanistic Studies and its President, Joseph Slater, for providing an incomparable setting and essential "housekeeping" assistance for the work of the summer study group. Given the importance of the effort, the Academy made an appropriation from its own research funds to advance the study; John Voss, the Academy's Executive Officer, is owed thanks for helping in numerous ways. Finally, we are greatly indebted to Franklin Long and George Rathjens, who were not only generous with their time, but took seriously their many obligations as editors of a volume that seemed constantly to call for their attention.

for the American Academy of Arts and Sciences
Stephen R. Graubard

Arms, Defense Policy, and Arms Control

FRANKLIN A. LONG

Arms Control from the Perspective of the Nineteen-Seventies

THE PUBLICATION at this time of a *Dædalus* book on arms control, fifteen years after the initial, widely influential *Dædalus* volume on the same subject,[1] leads us almost unavoidably to ask what has happened in the field during the intervening years. Enough has happened, it turns out, to make an answer to this question the principal focus of this introductory article, although it is also both surprising and gratifying to discover that a large majority of the general principles and programs that were laid down in the 1960 volume retain their validity today. The problem of nuclear war, which appeared then to be of almost overriding concern, remains high on the list of international problems, and nuclear deterrence continues to be as central a concept as it appeared to be in 1960. Verification of arms-control and disarmament agreements remains a problem, though one that has been alleviated technically by the development of space-orbiting reconnaissance satellites and improved seismic detection of underground nuclear explosions. Negotiation of arms-control agreements and the problem of agreements between the two superpowers, the United States and the Soviet Union, remain key issues. Even the 1960 definition of 'arms control' remains entirely adequate today; paraphrasing Thomas Schelling slightly, it is: *a*) to reduce the probability of war, *b*) to reduce the costs of preparations for war, and *c*) to reduce the death and destruction if control fails and war comes.

What, then, has changed? A general answer is that arms control and disarmament now appear to be politically more complex than they did in 1960, while the technical aspects (of verification and the like) appear somewhat less complicated and perhaps therefore less consequential. The growing appreciation of the interconnections between arms control and such problems as international political relations, crisis stabilization, and military weapons development has decreased the likelihood that arms control will develop into a separate intellectual (or even political) discipline, capable of justifying, for example, distinct academic departments in universities or specialized professional journals.[2]

Of the many changes in emphasis and understanding of the subject of arms control, there are at least half a dozen that merit explicit identification and more detailed analysis:

1. Although a few simple, occasionally "cosmetic," arms-control measures can be discussed and negotiated in the absence of broader considerations, virtually all substantive arms-control discussions turn out to be intimately and often intricately linked to broader political issues and to such other foreign-policy objectives as trade, alliances, relief of political tensions, and increased crisis stabilization.

2. The world political scene within which arms-control possibilities are to be

1

viewed has become more complicated. The "bilateral world" of the nineteen-fifties has become increasingly multilateral. The less developed nations of the world, particularly China and those nations with large supplies of critically needed natural resources, have assumed greater importance. Finally, other types of problems have grown in significance, for example, shortages of energy and food, and economic stability in the face of inflation and recession.

3. The very considerable difficulties and delays that have arisen in recent years in negotiating and obtaining acceptance for substantive arms-control measures have forced a recognition that the world urgently needs better negotiation procedures, notably improved mechanisms for restraining weapons developments during the negotiation period.

4. There is increased appreciation of the need for more effective international organizations and mechanisms for developing and monitoring arms-control and disarmament agreements, for settling disputes among nations, and for carrying out other peace-keeping activities.

5. There is a greater realization, especially in the United States, but, it is to be hoped, elsewhere as well, that world stability, in the form of specific military and political responses of other nations, is greatly influenced by decisions on military force levels and weapons procurement of any single nation; in a very real sense, "arms control begins at home."

6. The costly and often destabilizing impacts of new military technology, so dramatically illustrated by the atom bomb of 1945, have continued, perhaps even accelerated. The resulting new and improved military systems complicate arms-control negotiations and make us realize that, unfortunately, there can be both qualitative and quantitative arms races.

1. The Interactions between Arms Control and Other Political and Social Issues

To illustrate this first point, let us hypothesize an ideal sequence of actions of a "pure" arms-control negotiation: A group of nations, concerned over the costs of their military programs and the danger of arms competition, becomes persuaded that their individual national securities would be maintained, or even enhanced, by the negotiation of an appropriate arms-control measure. The measure might include one of several provisions: for example, mutual budget reductions for military programs; broad or specific reductions in military force levels; or prohibition or elimination of particular categories of military weapons. The nations convene a conference to identify those arms-control measures that, in the belief of the negotiators, they could all support. These measures are then embodied in a treaty to be signed and ratified by the nations concerned.

Only very occasionally does an arms-control negotiation actually proceed as straightforwardly as this, although the negotiations leading to the prohibition of a relatively unattractive—and not yet developed—weapons system, e.g., No Bombs in Space Orbit, is perhaps one such case. The more frequent situation is far more complicated, especially where control of existing and important weapons systems is involved. There will be vehement debates within each nation, during which the broad implications of an arms-control measure will be argued. Its effect on relative military capabilities will receive major attention, of course, but strong voices will also debate its impact on broad foreign-policy objectives, on the national budget, on the international balance of trade, on domestic politics, and on any major technological problems. The complex interplay of these several groups of participants will continue into the negotiation process itself, as nations place different weights on these several factors and hence arrive at different negotiating positions.

The current SALT negotiations between the United States and the Soviet Union for mutual limitations on strategic nuclear-weapons systems provide a good example of the interdependence of arms control and other political and social factors. The negotiations themselves are fairly sharply focused, but closely linked to them have been questions of detente, trade arrangements, and the emigration policies of the Soviet Union. The geopolitical situations of the two nations are different; so, consequently, are their foreign-policy objectives.

In 1972 many analysts questioned whether the final SALT I agreements, as announced at the Nixon-Brezhnev summit meetings, needed to be so inextricably bound up with such a large package of other detente-oriented measures—exchange of scholars, trade agreements, and the like. However, informed accounts by Newhouse and others[3] of these negotiations strongly suggest that this complex package was probably unavoidable. The continuous Soviet statements that progress toward broad accommodations should accompany progress toward arms control suggest a confirmation of this theory. On the other hand, an implicit corollary is that, over time, changing political circumstances can modify the utility and viability of any international agreement, including those for arms control and disarmament. An explicit recognition of this possibility is the provision of the 1963 Limited Nuclear Test Ban Treaty, which permits a nation to withdraw, ninety days after notification, on grounds that "extraordinary events . . . have jeopardized the supreme interests of the country."

What all this means is that arms-control efforts can never stand alone. While the notion of an "arms-control community" does have a limited validity, in that there are now groups of scholars and government officials whose main professional concern is arms control and disarmament, this community must maintain strong ties with the related political activities if their work is not to become sterile or disjointed.

2. Implications of the Increasingly Complex World Scene

The loss of influence of the superpowers and the tendencies toward political multipolarity, the increased expectations and needs of the less developed nations, the growing world competition for scarce natural resources, the continuing build-up of military forces and the spread of modern military weapons, the increased world vulnerability to air and water pollution, and misuse by various nations of the world's oceans all have direct relevance to prospects for world order and freedom from war. Negotiating arms control and disarmament is only one of many areas where the impact of these complexities is felt. Because the ongoing SALT negotiations are limited to strategic nuclear-weapons systems that are very largely in the hands of the United States and the Soviet Union, it has been possible to limit these negotiations to just the two nations. Nevertheless, the outcome of these negotiations may significantly affect the security interests of allied NATO and Warsaw Pact nations, leading to the need for frequent consultations, especially within NATO. More generally, and for most other weapons systems and questions of foreign policy, the world is far less dominated by the two superpowers than it was a couple of decades ago. Among the larger nations, France, China, and India all now pursue relatively independent foreign policies, and all three have also successfully tested nuclear explosive devices which they have independently developed. The former colonial nations of Africa and Asia are now fiercely independent and especially prone to suspicions of attempted domination by the big powers. The Middle East, now including Cyprus, remains volatile, with most of its countries increasingly resentful of big power pressures, and with many of them, especially the rich oil-producing countries, increasingly able to take an independent political line. These developments of separatism and independent action are not surprising, but they do complicate the successful negotiation of significant arms control, whether by formal negotiation or informal agreement.

The Nuclear Non-Proliferation Treaty (NPT) is a case in point. The essential aim of this treaty—to limit the spread of nuclear weapons among the nations of the world—is at least theoretically widely approved. Nevertheless, the NPT has never been fully accepted and may already, before it is five years old, be seriously weakened. Partly it is a question of big power/small power antagonism, including unwilling- ness on the part of the non-nuclear nations to accept their implied second-class status and broad resentment on their part in the "I'm-all-right-Jack-and-business-as-usual" attitudes of the United States and the Soviet Union. But the difficulties go well be- yond these generalities. Many nations, which are contemplating possible use of nuclear weapons and which have not yet carried out the sober analyses of nuclear military effectiveness that have already been made by the United States, the Soviet Union, and the United Kingdom, can hardly help but see in these weapons potent additions to their own military programs. The continued preoccupation of the super- powers with more and newer nuclear weapons can only offer support to this belief and increase skepticism about the NPT. A different concern that some nations have about the NPT relates to the possible economic utility of peaceful nuclear explosions for earth-moving and for development of natural resources. Both the superpowers have continually touted the potential benefits of these uses, but neither of them has seriously attempted detailed economic analyses or has presented definite plans to make peaceful nuclear explosive devices widely available. One can be sure that these and other aspects of the Non-Proliferation Treaty will be given sharp analysis at the first five-year review of the treaty in 1975.[4] But even if the NPT survives and gains in- creased acceptance, the basic problem remains of a world in flux, with independent nation-states intent on maximizing their military position vis-à-vis their neighbors.[5]

In the meantime, important new world problems have appeared on the horizon that may just possibly divert nations from their preoccupation with the military aspects of "national security." The immediate ones are inflation and recession and their potential impact on international stability; over the longer pull, the most threatening are the supplies of energy and food. After a period of euphoria, caused in part by the new technologies of the Green Revolution, the world has returned to a shocked realization of the slender margin between adequate food production and mass starvation and of its vulnerability to climatic variations, be it drought in the United States or the failure of a monsoon in Africa or India. Will this realization, or even the totality of all these non-military problems, be reflected in decreased expenditures for military programs? This is at the moment anything but certain, but some readjustment of priorities seems almost inescapable, and large military expenditures will surely be vulnerable.[6]

3. Difficulties in the Negotiation Process

The years since the 1960 *Dædalus* volume was published have seen active international negotiation on measures for arms control and disarmament. The United Nations established in 1961 what was to become the Eighteen Nation Disarmament Committee. This, with modifications, still continues as the Conference of the Committee on Disarmament (CCD). The important bilateral SALT discussions between the Soviet Union and the United States were initiated in 1969 and still continue. And there have been concrete accomplishments: SALT I in 1972, the Limited Nuclear Test Ban of 1963, the Non-Proliferation Treaty, a Latin American Nuclear Free Zone, and others. The overall record, however, remains one of very modest, often peripheral, progress, which has occurred during a period dominated by a virtually worldwide and continuing buildup of military forces. By any plausible reckoning, one would have to characterize the arms-control and especially the disarmament accomplishments of the past decade or two as disappointing. The world has, it is true, avoided nuclear war, but that is about all that can be said.

Successful international negotiation is immensely difficult. Even bilateral negotiations are delicate and tedious; significant multilateral negotiations are more complicated still. First, there is no adequate forum—the Conference of the Committee on Disarmament, for example, has degenerated into a debating club, and the United Nations has so far been an inadequate sponsor for other serious negotiation. But the problem goes well beyond structure: nations inevitably differ in their capabilities, priorities, problems, and interests. Political and military imbalances between nations are often great, and mutual suspicion is commonplace. Only occasionally, then, will there be the confluence of interests that makes substantial arms-control agreements possible, i.e., a situation where agreements will be of *mutual benefit,* where, in other words, a "non-zero sum game" is at least conceivable. The wonder is that any arms-control agreements at all have been negotiated. It can be hoped, since some have, that nations do at least recognize the danger, expense, and sheer destructive potential of the current extensive militarization.

The record of recent SALT negotiations between the United States and the Soviet Union illustrates many of the difficulties of serious arms-control negotiations. Here was a simple bilateral negotiation, carefully restricted to strategic nuclear weapons, a comparatively simple group of military systems. Negotiations were serious and confidential and apparently enjoyed broad support from each side. Even then, however, the process was slow and difficult. The proposal for the negotiations came from President Lyndon Johnson in early 1967 and was accepted by the Soviets about a year later. The first session, scheduled for late 1968, was cancelled by the Soviet occupation of Czechoslovakia. Negotiations finally began in November, 1969. The proposed SALT I agreements were reached in 1972, roughly five years after the first invitation to negotiate was issued.

When they were announced in May, 1972, by Brezhnev and Nixon, it was clear that the SALT I agreements were only part of a larger set of agreements involving trade, cultural and scientific exchange, and technology transfer. Fortunately for arms control, the SALT agreements were still of major importance: a treaty restricting mutual deployment of anti-ballistic missile systems, a five-year interim "freeze" on numbers of major types of delivery systems for strategic nuclear weapons, and the legitimization of space-orbiting satellite flights for unilateral intelligence gathering. But what of the military buildup that continued both in the United States and in the Soviet Union during these negotiations, and what of the aftermath? A pattern of mutual restraint, which might have been expected to accompany serious negotiations, simply did not appear. During the 1967-72 period, the Soviet Union deployed ICBMs and SLBMs at a high rate, and the United States developed and began the deployment of MIRVed nuclear warheads. Nor did the signing and ratifying of the 1972 SALT agreement slow the buildup in armaments. The Soviet Union embarked on new ICBM systems to replace older ones; the United States continued its MIRV deployment and accelerated its new and expensive (roughly one billion dollars per boat) Trident submarine missile system. Thus it is that, in spite of the benefits of the 1972 treaty for ABM restriction, there are thoughtful analysts who argue that SALT I and its protracted negotiations were, on balance, of very doubtful utility.

There are also important possibilities for arms-control negotiation between the United States and the Soviet Union, or between both of them and their allies, untouched by SALT, which lie in the area of conventional military forces, including weapons and troop levels. For both superpowers, this area accounts for roughly two thirds of their military expenditures, and it must be addressed if one of the objectives of negotiation is a sizable reduction in military budgets. But here the active participation of other nations, e.g., East Germany and Poland, West Germany and France, is an almost essential requirement, and for this sort of complex multinational negotiation, the lack of a suitable forum is particularly troublesome. The CCD is probably too ineffectual to be useful. As of now, the best plan would appear to be the organization of an ad hoc arrangement as was done for SALT. But the problems of continuity and of provisions for technical and analytical support for the negotiations would be formidable. Finally, as the current Mutual Balanced Force Reduction negotiations illustrate, there very probably needs to be some procedure to limit the negotiators to a reasonable number. Since these will be continuing problems, one can only hope that the United Nations, or some other established international body, can supply the forum and provide the expert analysis that will be needed.

4. The Need for More Effective International Organizations

The discussions and negotiations on disarmament that have taken place during the past two decades have utilized two principal avenues of communication: normal diplomatic channels (mostly bilateral discussions) and the United Nations (mostly multinational discussions), the latter principally in the CCD. Most nations clearly prefer the diplomatic channel for serious negotiations. Almost all of the important American-Soviet discussions have wholly or partially taken this path. It was also used to spectacular effect by Henry Kissinger in his series of Middle East talks.

Particularly for the major powers, the United Nations has usually seemed an uncomfortable arena for discussions of issues where national security is seriously in-

the other developed nations assign a very high priority to a stable posture of mutual nuclear deterrence. Strategic nuclear forces for deterrence, however, take less than a third of their military budgets. The remainder goes to maintenance of extensive conventional military forces. For the Soviet Union, some fraction of these conventional forces is used to maintain hegemony over its East European satellites and to oppose Chinese forces on the long China-Soviet border. Other conventional forces are presumably available for support of more distant allies or associates, for example, in the Middle East.

In the case of this country, which has generally friendly border states and only a remote concern for enemy invasion by either land or sea, the *raison d'être* for virtually all of the conventional military forces must necessarily be the support of distant allies and more generally the furthering of American foreign-policy objectives. Given the fact that this country is now not at war and has established at least a partial detente with the Soviet Union and China, one can seriously question whether all the currently available military forces are really required. To put the question another way, are there not more effective, as well as less expensive, ways to develop favorable relations with foreign governments than by giving such great weight to military programs?

Unhappily, this sort of broad questioning of our programs of national security raises as many problems as it solves. Let us assume, by way of illustration, that American relations with the developing nations would improve if we were to take ten billion dollars per year (roughly ten per cent) from our military budgets and utilize these funds for such sensible programs as food and technical assistance. How would we go about implementing such a program? Can Congress do it? Not likely. Military programs and international technical assistance programs are dealt with by separate Congressional committees, each of which has negligible consideration for the problems of the other. No effective mechanism exists in Congress for considering the essential components of national security, broadly defined.

What about the Office of the President? Broad analysis is more likely to be accomplished, but, even here, national security issues are parceled out to half a dozen agencies (Defense, State, National Security Council, Atomic Energy Commission, Arms Control and Disarmament Agency, Treasury, Commerce, to name the most obvious) so that a balanced overall assessment is again difficult. Furthermore, the participants come to a conference table with different degrees of power. The Department of Defense is far larger than all the other agencies put together; it alone spends about six per cent of the entire gross national product of the nation. The Arms Control and Disarmament Agency (ACDA), in contrast, has been so weakened that it probably ought now to be viewed as an appendage to the State Department rather than as an independent agency. Organizationally, the National Security Council is the obvious Executive office to conduct broad analyses and recommend national security priorities, and occasionally it has so operated, e.g., under Henry Kissinger during Richard Nixon's first term. But the size, the political clout, and especially the continuity of the Department of Defense virtually insure it a dominant voice in national-security discussions. The consequence is that non-military programs tend to get rather short-changed.

Consider, for example, the problem of the spread of nuclear weapons to other nations. Until India's recent announcement of a "peaceful" nuclear explosion, the number of nuclear powers had for over a decade held constant at five: China, France, the United Kingdom, the United States, and the Soviet Union. But the possibility still existed that nuclear weapons would be developed by many other countries, including ones in such politically turbulent areas as the Middle East and Southeast Asia. Over time, the probability that the activities of these nations would provide the trigger for a nuclear war appeared at least as high as the probability that it would be triggered by one of the original five.[9] Surely this argued for intensive efforts on the part of the United States to minimize nuclear proliferation. In fact, however, American efforts have been both belated and half-hearted. The Nuclear Non-Proliferation Treaty was finally developed, perhaps two years later than it might have been, at the Eighteen Nation Disarmament Committee. In the subsequent program to obtain widespread acceptance and ratification of the treaty, neither this country nor the Soviet Union appeared willing to expend much political capital. Nor did either appear willing to set examples by exercising restraint in its own nuclear-weapons programs. As a consequence, world acceptance of the NPT has been only partial, and many nations, e.g., Japan and Egypt, that signed the NPT have yet to ratify it. It is hard to examine this history without becoming persuaded that American analysis of its national security was at best inadequate and, more probably, wrongheaded.

6. The Impacts of New Military Technology and the Qualitative Arms Race

Looking back over the three decades since the end of World War II, we realize that the world has witnessed three recent major revolutionary developments in military technology as well as a host of other developments of almost equal importance. The three major revolutionary changes are: nuclear bombs with their megaton potency for destruction, ICBMs with their capability for fast and accurate delivery of nuclear bombs to distant continents, and space-based reconnaissance satellites with their power rapidly to survey immense areas of the globe. The impact of these three developments on military programs and on political stability has been, and continues to be, very great.

The importance of the third of these—space-based reconnaissance satellites—is not widely recognized, presumably because details of their capabilities and use remain (foolishly) concealed by a blanket of secrecy imposed by military classification. However, it is easy to appreciate the importance of being able to maintain continuous photographic surveillance of the territory of one's military opponents by "national technical means" (which is the current euphemistic phrase for satellite surveillance). And to those who were aware of satellite capabilities, it was of great significance that the ABM treaty, which the United States and the Soviet Union negotiated in 1972, provided that "each party shall use national technical means of verification at its disposal in a manner consistent with generally recognized principles of international law," with the further stipulation that "each party undertakes not to interfere with the national technical means of verification of the other party."[10] Here, then, is one item of new military technology which, by improving verification capabilities, has greatly aided the prospects for significant measures of arms control and disarmament.

The overwhelming destructive power of nuclear weapons, the first of the recent revolutionary developments, continues to inhibit their use in war and to press the nuclear-armed nations into postures of nuclear deterrence, all the more since their deadliness has been increased by the second revolutionary development—the ICBMs. (Remember that a megaton-sized nuclear bomb, weighing only several hundred pounds and deliverable by rockets to almost any spot in the world, has the explosive potential of *one million tons* of TNT, which itself was an explosive that, through most of World War II, was good enough to be the world's basic weapon.) The concept of nuclear deterrence is increasingly seen as awkward and troublesome,[11] but it is still true that for three decades nuclear deterrence has "worked," i.e., there has been no nuclear war and no military conflict between the nuclear superpowers.

The gloomy obverse of this posture of restraint in use of nuclear weapons is the lack of restraint in their procurement. The number and complexity of nuclear weapons continue to rise, as does the number of countries that have deployed them. The problem for the world remains the same: For how long will it be able to keep the nuclear scorpion in the bottle?

If one looks at the full spectrum of recently developed military technology, the most impressive aspects are the breadth, importance, and continuing flow of the new weapons and support equipment, to the degree that the word "revolutionary" is now being applied to virtually every phase of modernized warfare. In recent years, we have seen the development of nuclear-armed cruise missiles for naval use, of supersonic aircraft, of "smart bombs" for precision aerial bombardment, of guided anti-tank weapons, of air-to-ground and ground-to-ground guided missiles for "stand-off" warfare. A different point (developed in detail in this volume by Harvey Brooks) is that a continuing set of apparently modest qualitative improvements can ultimately produce almost revolutionary change. A good example is the steady increase in accuracy of ICBMs to the point where the average miss-distance will soon be only a few hundred feet, and the counterforce capability of the weapon will again be greatly enhanced. It is the impact of these continuing improvements that has led to the significance of the phrase "qualitative arms race," measuring a race, not in numbers, but in degree of technical sophistication. The 1972 SALT I interim agreement led to a "freeze" in numbers of superpower ICBMs. But the qualitative arms race goes on and has perhaps even been accelerated by the restriction in numbers.

These developments have implications well beyond the nations that produce the improvements. Proliferation of nuclear weapons has been minimal, it is true, but with conventional weapons the world arms trade has flourished, and even the poor nations can obtain sophisticated and deadly modern weapons—Phantom-jet aircraft, SAM-6 missiles, and the like. In a very real sense, technology itself, by presenting a continuing stream of new weapons options to decision-makers, has become a major generating element of the arms race.

The importance of new military technology and the continuing threat that, due to advances in technology, existing weapons or defenses will become obsolete, raise major dilemmas for the technologically advanced nations. Military technology is ever more sophisticated and costly, and the maintenance of effective and competitive programs of research and development (to say nothing of procurement) is increasingly burdensome. Thus, for this country, the total expenditure for military and space research and development is approaching fifteen billion dollars per year and constitutes almost half of the *total* American research and development effort, public and private. Part of the dilemma is that this is an immense diversion of technical effort away from pressing civilian needs into what (from a civilian standpoint) are relatively unproductive activities. Another part of the dilemma is that this immense military research and development effort inevitably produces pressures to procure and deploy some of the interesting new military products that result from it, often regardless of need or even, occasionally, desirability.[12]

The third and especially painful part of the dilemma (for supporters of arms control and reduced military budgets) is that there are persuasive arguments for the encouragement and support of military research and development. One argument has been that it is essential to maintain up-to-date information on the possible new military weapons and tactics that technology offers, partly to anticipate moves by opponents, and partly to obtain control of such weapons before they can be deployed. It is this sort of rationale that explains why, in the United States, research and development on anti-ballistic missile systems continue in the face of the American-Soviet treaty that restricts ABM deployment. Indeed, almost every governmental discussion of an arms-control measure tends to be accompanied by exhortations to "increase R&D."

The problem, of course, is one of control. How can we have an effective system of military research without employing half of the nation's technical manpower resources? How can we maintain control over weapons procurement in the face of "technically sweet" new products from research? How can we negotiate stable and useful measures of international arms control and disarmament, in spite of the destabilizing potential of new technology? Here are some major problems for the next generation of arms controllers.

Concluding Remarks

The more general question, which inescapably arises from this list of the new directions and new understandings of arms control, is what do we do next? Since most of the papers in this volume address this question in one way or another, it would be presumptuous indeed to attempt here to anticipate their responses, but it does at least seem safe to say that there is no single answer. We must surely continue to negotiate for broader, more effective, international measures for arms control. We should try to build detente to alleviate political tensions and military rivalries. We need to do a better job of controlling our own military programs and reaching a consensus on what constitutes national security. This is not a new or surprising list of directions for action; all of it could have been said (and most of it was) in the 1960 *Dædalus* discussion. But in the intervening fifteen years there has been some progress. We have negotiated a few significant arms-control measures; we have incorporated into our negotiations useful and supportive measures leading to a relaxation of tension and to detente; we have developed some important unobtrusive means of verification. With these and other accomplishments behind us, we may hope for greater progress in the future.

REFERENCES

[1] *Dædalus*, Winter issue, 1960. Most of the essays also appeared in *Arms Control, Disarmament, and National Security*, ed. D. G. Brennan (New York, 1961).

[2] The majority of scholarly publications on arms control and disarmament is to be found in journals with a broad concern for international affairs, e.g., *Foreign Affairs, Foreign Policy,* and *Orbis.* Somewhat surprisingly, another significant journal is *Scientific American,* where articles on the subject tend to emphasize the scientific and technical aspects. Over the past two decades, numerous new journals have appeared, specifically devoted to arms control and disarmament; few have survived. It is also noteworthy that the United States Arms Control and Disarmament Agency, whose establishment in 1961 seemed much in line with the *Dædalus* recommendations, has not managed to acquire a central position in this country's development and negotiation of arms-control agreements. At one time or another in recent years, the Department of State, the National Security Council, and even the Department of Defense have appeared to be more centrally involved than the Agency in the development of American positions on arms control and disarmament.

[3] John Newhouse, *Cold Dawn* (New York, 1973); Mason Willrich and John Rhinelander, *SALT: The Moscow Agreements and Beyond* (New York, 1974).

[4] By mid-1973 there were seventy-eight parties to the Non-Proliferation Treaty, although many of the nations that had signed had not yet ratified; many militarily significant and near-nuclear states, including Israel, India, and Brazil, have not yet even signed.

[5] Statistics on the level of world military expenditures illuminate the problem. These expenditures now amount to around $250 billion per year, which is approximately equal to the *total* GNP for the poorer half of the world. American and Soviet military expenditures are roughly three quarters of this amount.

[6] One can take a wry satisfaction in the fact that a very common reaction to the recent test of a nuclear explosive by India was to comment on the singular inappropriateness of large expenditures on this sort of sophisticated system by such a desperately needful nation.

[7] Leonard Beaton, *The Reform of Power* (New York, 1972). See also review by Alistair Buchan in *Survival,* 14:6 (1972), 301.

[8] In this connection, one thinks of the generally collaborative relations among the nations of South America, as contrasted to the turbulence of a century ago. Thus the once common border disputes among Venezuela, Colombia, Ecuador, and Peru (countries that now are all members of the Andean Pact) have virtually disappeared; consequently, there is a greatly reduced requirement for military forces in those countries. An even more spectacular example is Japan, whose national-security requirements involve a comparatively miniscule military force.

[9] Robert Heilbroner in *An Inquiry into the Human Prospect* (New York, 1974), postulates the eventual development of another sort of nuclear-weapons threat from the under-developed countries, namely, nuclear-weapons blackmail to force the developed nations to discharge some of their wealth.

[10] For a fuller discussion of the importance of satellite reconnaissance, see Herbert Scoville, Jr., in Willrich and Rhinelander, *op. cit.,* pp. 160-182.

[11] See, for example, the Iklé-Panofsky exchange in *Foreign Affairs,* January and October, 1973.

[12] A reason that has frequently been advanced to explain why MIRVed nuclear warheads were developed and deployed by the United States, in the face of strong arguments that they were destabilizing and therefore undesirable, is that they gave a "technically sweet" solution to a military desideratum, that is, obtaining a wider coverage of enemy targets at moderate cost.

ABRAM CHAYES

Nuclear Arms Control After the Cold War

THIS PAPER REPRESENTS an attempt to envision the general character of arms-control problems and some of the specific issues that would arise in an international setting radically different from the one that has existed for the past twenty-five years. That era was dominated by a nuclear confrontation between two superpowers in an atmosphere of intense political hostility and what was perceived on both sides to be a severe threat. The "radically different" setting projected here assumes that this sharp confrontation is over, that the SALT agreements and the subsequent series of summits, the successful West German *Ostpolitik,* and the end of the Vietnam war are evidence of the willingness of the two powers to settle the Cold War more or less on the basis of the status quo. It assumes also that competition and rivalry between the two powers will continue, although not with the previously constant overtones of the threat or use of force. I have characterized this state of affairs simply as the "end of the Cold War"—rather than "detente" or some such term—to indicate a marked change from the atmosphere of the post-war decades, but with a degree of caution as to how far the amelioration is likely to go.

I. Arms Control and the Ending of the Cold War

The Strategic Arms Limitation Agreements (SALT), signed in May 1972, can be taken as a convenient mark for the end of the Cold War. They were also the culmination of a series of treaties on nuclear weaponry between the United States and the Soviet Union that began a decade earlier with the Limited Test Ban Treaty. The series includes agreements prohibiting nuclear deployment in outer space and on the seabed, as well as the Non-Proliferation Treaty (NPT). The significance of these agreements can be appraised from several different perspectives.

In one sense, the series of treaties is wholly unprecedented. There is no comparable historical example of two leading powers carrying out far-ranging negotiations, extended in time and resulting in mutual agreements regulating the testing, deployment, and force levels of their most important weapons systems. The closest parallel is the Naval Disarmament Agreements after World War I. But in that case, although there was a nascent rivalry between the United States and Japan, the participants were not avowed adversaries, each regarding the other as a present danger to its security. Equally unprecedented is the degree to which issues of arms control and strategic-force posture have been drawn into the main arena of political controversy in the United States. Even in the Soviet Union, it appears that strategic weaponry is a subject of debate not only within the government, but also, at least to some extent, in those scientific and intellectual circles that have some influence on policy.

From the perspective of their impact on military spending and the force postures of the parties, a more skeptical evaluation of these agreements seems warranted. The Outer Space and Sea Bed Treaties prohibited deployments in which there was in any case not much military interest. The Limited Test Ban came at a time when atmospheric testing had reached a point of diminishing returns for the two superpowers. Although the NPT imposed genuine constraints on the non-nuclear parties, it gave the pre-existing policies of the United States and the Soviet Union the sanction of international law. Finally, even regarding SALT, it can be argued that the pressures for ABM deployment in both countries had already been blunted on technical and economic grounds and that the force ceilings imposed by the Interim Agreement on Strategic Offensive Arms have not interfered significantly with planned or programmed weapons systems on either side. The SALT follow-on at Moscow in June, 1974, and at Vladivostok in November reveals like characteristics. The "threshold" in the proposed Threshold Test Ban Treaty and the "ceiling" projected for strategic nuclear launchers seem ample enough to accommodate the existing programs of both powers with ease.

At most, it has been said, the arms-control treaties of the last decade placed additional psychological and political barriers in the way of outcomes that were unlikely in any case. By giving formal legal sanction to a set of mutual expectations, the agreements made action (or inaction) on the basis of those expectations more comfortable and reliable for both sides. Set against these benefits are the side effects of the negotiation and agreement process that exacerbated the arms race: the proliferation of "bargaining chips"; the tendency of the parties to assume a hostile and adversary tone for negotiating purposes; and the pressures generated to build up to treaty limits or to intensify efforts in areas not covered by the agreement.

From still a third perspective, these agreements can be seen as a part—and perhaps an essential part—of the political process of devolution from the harshest phases of the Cold War. The last direct confrontation between the United States and the Soviet Union involving the threat of force was the Cuban missile crisis in October, 1962. The Limited Test Ban followed within a year. A principal dimension of the Cold War—the one that accounted for much of its danger and terror—was the strategic face-off between the two parties. It was inevitable, therefore, that any process of recession from the Cold War would center in large part on the effort to regulate that relationship and bring it under control. The importance of the arms-control issues was enhanced because discussions about them provided a basis— sometimes the only basis—for dialogue between the parties, even in the periods of bitterest hostility.

The agreements are all products of essentially bilateral negotiations, and, with the exception of NPT, the obligations they impose are, in a practical sense, also bilateral. All had great political visibility and were solemnized by the most formal available processes of ratification in each state. The SALT agreements, at the culmination of ten years of this dialogue on strategic nuclear matters, more or less explicitly recognized the military—and presumably political—"parity" between the parties.

Elsewhere in this volume there is an extended assessment of the significance and permanence of the new departure in United States-Soviet relations that began in May, 1972. From today's vantage point, the high hopes for "detente" that blossomed after the Moscow summit seem to have been inflated. The arms race goes on. Both parties have continued to increase and refine their strategic arsenals, except where the express prohibitions of the SALT agreements operate. In the Soviet Union, strategic expansion has been accompanied by a continuing conventional build-up. For the Soviets, the anticipated economic benefits have been slow to materialize and might not live up to expectations, even if Congress were to be more cooperative. For the United States, the October War put a considerable crimp in whatever hopes were entertained for political cooperation. The Soviet performance in that affair suggests a continued willingness to take risks with the peace for the sake of political gains. At a minimum, the promised cooperation and consultation in the event of threatening situations worked a good deal less smoothly than advertised.

More fundamental for the Soviet leadership, in my view, is the difficulty, already manifesting itself, of maintaining intellectual and cultural control within the Soviet Union and discipline in Eastern Europe in an international atmosphere of steadily ameliorating or even stable relations with the West. If these problems become too great, it is possible that Soviet authorities might resort to the tactic of reactivating external threats to insure internal cohesion. It is probably well to assume that for the time being, and for some time into the future, the Soviet leadership will have considerable capacity to modify and even reverse the present policy of broad accommodation with the United States, and there are readily conceivable occasions when they might wish to do so.

I suggest, however, that, whatever cautions and caveats one may wish to make, a condition of continuing stability between the United States and the Soviet Union without sharp military confrontation is a more plausible prediction than the opposite. At least it is sufficiently plausible to make some forecast of the international setting on such a premise profitable and to draw some implications from it for arms-control activities over the years ahead.

II. *The International System in the Wake of the Cold War*

A. *The Developed Countries*

In the developed world, with security and territorial issues between East and West muted, what is likely to emerge is a rather unorganized situation in which actors will tend to pursue a variety of national objectives by a variety of means. The absence, on the one hand, of any clearly perceived and credible military threat and, on the other, of any concretely defined common interest means that unified or even coordinated policies will be difficult to attain or sustain. Thus, even though the organizing concept of a five-power balance must be rejected as too simple, one feature that characterizes balance-of-power politics is very likely to be realized: a milieu of shifting alignments, with each party pursuing its own interests as it sees them, ready to join forces with others for particular forays that may seem profitable, but not, on the whole, prepared to take on enduring new military, economic, or political commitments. In short, relaxation of the harsh discipline of the Cold War is likely to provide considerable freedom of action for a number of states, large and small, to pursue a variety of purposes.

All the prophets agree that Western Europe is not likely to attain significant political unity in the next decade or so. The first item on the European agenda is the full incorporation of Britain (and Ireland and Denmark) into the Common Market and, beyond that, the perfection of the Market as an economic community. Although

major obstacles have been overcome and a great deal of experience gained over the
past fifteen years, these remain formidable tasks, more than sufficient to absorb
governmental energies for a considerable time to come. Sharp divisions of outlook and
interest on economic questions—money, agriculture, and now energy are only the
most prominent—must be accommodated.

Meanwhile, relations within Western Europe will be marked by an intricate pattern of maneuvers for influence and position both within and vis-à-vis the developing European institutions, each with varying memberships and jurisdictions.
Often these moves will be responses to tactical situations rather than informed by a
coherent and purposeful pattern. And those grander strategies that may emerge are
likely to be dominated by national and European considerations rather than by the
requirements of military security or wider international relations.

Less thought has been given to the probable evolution in Eastern Europe. But
here, too, stability between the superpowers implies a loosening of ties and controls
between Eastern European countries and Moscow as radical as that in the West, and
perhaps more so. A prolonged and uninterrupted period without military confrontation is likely to be marked by increasingly independent attitudes and policies in these
countries. Rumania and, to a lesser extent, Hungary have already been quite bold in
seeking to exploit the possibilities of the European Security Conference for extending
the tolerances within which they can operate. In a situation of relatively peaceful and
relaxed coexistence, it is not unreasonable to expect that Eastern European states will
exercise somewhat greater influence or constraint on political and economic decisions
in international Communist institutions and will discreetly take advantage of opportunities for economic and other kinds of relations with Western countries.

Again, one should expect a complex pattern of maneuver, sensitive to tactical
nuances. As in Western Europe, this will no doubt express itself in intricate and not
necessarily consistent sets of bilateral relationships, both among Eastern European
countries themselves and across the East-West boundary. The net result will be an
increasingly more diffuse and complicated picture in Eastern Europe, assuming there
is no major crisis between the United States and the Soviet Union and that the cen-
trifugal forces can be controlled at a level that does not invite Soviet intervention.

The overriding confrontation of the Cold War implied relations of deep hostility
between East and West, but relative camaraderie and cooperation within each camp.
"Detente" is likely to eliminate both the hostility and the camaraderie and replace
them with generalized, relatively muted adversary relationships.

One recalls that the build-up to World War II was marked by the loss of a sense of
common fate and purpose among industrialized countries and by increasing recourse
to autarchic and retaliatory economic policies. I would not exclude completely the
possibility of a re-run of this scenario, particularly if anything like the general depres-
sion of the nineteen-thirties should recur (brought on, perhaps, by the inability to
manage the multifarious problems of continued growth). After all, large military
forces, amply provided with nuclear weapons, remain arrayed against one another
both in Europe and, less prominently, in the Pacific. But for the present, given the
stake the developed countries have in the status quo and the memory of the costs of
previous efforts at military settlement, one may hope and even predict that the
developed countries are not likely to resort to the threat or use of force in an attempt
to resolve the conflicts of economic interest and demand among them.

B. The Third World

By contrast, in the developing countries, there is explosive potential for the international politics of the next generation. Indeed, a good case can be made that for the rest of this century, and even beyond, the principal threats to the peace will be generated in the Third World.

In the immediate post-war period, this area was dangerous primarily because it was an arena for the struggle between the superpowers. Events in the Middle East emphasize that this danger has by no means subsided. In addition, new sources of conflict will derive in the future from relations among the developing countries themselves and from interaction between the Northern and Southern hemispheres, between the rich and the poor.

The volatility of these relationships is increasingly recognized by traditional foreign-policy analysts, although usually without acknowledging a military dimension to the problem. But attitudes in these countries seem to be hardening. There is intensified, almost automatic skepticism and hostility over pronouncements and initiatives coming from the developed countries, particularly from the United States. And added to the sense of economic grievance and deprivation are overtones of racial indignity. This amalgam has traditionally been one in which men have risked violence and death to change the state of things. The emergence of China into the world community, with ideological and practical reasons for assuming a role as champion of Third World interests, does nothing to soften these prospects.

The Third World, to be sure, is hardly more than a convenient and perhaps misleading catchall for a group of very diverse countries. Differences of size, of available resources, of economic level, geography, history, and culture separate India from, say, Botswano even more than from the United States. In a sense, this very diversity is part of the problem. A unified "Third World" arrayed implacably against the North might seem formidable and menacing. But it would represent the emergence of another bipolarity, and we would at least understand the structure of the problem, as well as some of the ways of dealing with it. As it is, in the face of the complex heterogeneity of the Third World, the techniques and strategies we have developed over the past generation for maintaining some stability in a hostile and threatening environment— for example, much of our theory of deterrence—seem almost irrelevant.

Moreover, granting the vast diversity within the Third World, we can still identify some fairly pervasive conditions that make for severe instability and thus increase the prospects for large-scale international violence in the decades ahead. The first of these is growing poverty. There has been considerable economic growth in these countries, rather more thus far in the nineteen-seventies than in the last decade. Nevertheless, the gap between the rich and poor is widening. The very poorest have made the least progress of all, and in many countries, the economic progress that has been made is put at risk by the drastic increase in oil prices.

Moreover, the benefits of economic growth have been spread very unevenly within individual developing countries. For the most part, they have been confined to relatively small educated and urban groups. Economic development and demographic pressure have been accompanied by large-scale urbanization. Millions of people are moving from peasant and tribal villages, where some kind of subsistence and the supports of a traditional society were available, to cities both economically and socially unprepared to receive them. Without jobs, homes, or food, in city after city the newcomers become a turbulent, uprooted, and increasingly desperate mass.

It is not clear that a response from the developed world, even at the outer limits of imaginable wisdom and generosity, could have much impact on this series of intractable and interrelated problems. But, perhaps in part because of this sense of futility, no such response has been forthcoming. The Northern countries have fallen far below the target they themselves established of one per cent of their gross national product for assistance to the developing world. The terms for economic aid have hardened; much of this aid comes in less flexible and less useful forms. A great deal of it is offset by payments on earlier loans or investments, to the extent that in the past few years some developing countries have become net capital exporters. There is no sign in the United States or elsewhere in the Northern Hemisphere of a significant political constituency for changing these policies.

It is true that, in recent years, exports of manufactured goods from the developing countries have been increasing, and the terms of trade in natural resources may be shifting in their favor. But the distribution of these gains bears little relation to the centers of population and need. In fact, it seems fairly clear that one major consequence—perhaps the most important one—of the perceived scarcity of oil and other raw materials will be a devastating increase in the costs and difficulties of development in most of the poorer countries.

A second important factor in the situation is that, although it has had limited impact on the economic condition of the general population, development *is* taking place, and a number of countries are acquiring a considerable scientific and technological capability in the process. The ominous potential of this development is sufficiently prefigured by India's explosion of a nuclear device—the first new state to do so in almost a decade.

But India is not alone in this potential. Among the countries thought likely by the Stockholm International Peace Research Institute (SIPRI) to have nuclear power reactors by 1977 are at least eight developing countries. Of fifteen "key" states, not yet bound by the NPT, but possessing to some degree the potential for developing a nuclear capability, five are in the less-developed category. A sixth, South Africa, is also a source of concern because of its relation to the racial problems of Africa. If the horizon were further extended, say, to the end of the century, the list of developing countries capable of producing nuclear weaponry would be lengthened considerably. By that time, a good many of them would have been able to build on a domestic peaceful-uses industry. Nuclear energy will have become an old established technology, quite openly available to those who want it. Even for states that adhere to the NPT, the contemplated levels of production of nuclear material from power reactors will strain the capacities, such as they are, of the International Atomic Energy Agency (IAEA) safeguards system. Many developing countries, moreover, have civil or military air fleets that could readily be converted to provide a sizeable organized delivery capability for nuclear weapons. SIPRI has cited cost estimates suggesting that a number of developing countries would be able to field a small missile force over a ten-to-twenty-year period.

Such speculations are dour enough in themselves, but they take on an even darker coloration in the light of political developments in the Third World. It seems probable that in most of these countries the effort to transplant the institutions and practices of Western liberal democracy will not succeed. Perhaps India, alone among them, has political institutions in the Western tradition, and even India is for all practical purposes a one-party state. In Latin America, which has a long tradition of political independence and European parliamentarianism, the trend is strongly in the direction of various forms of military and totalitarian rule.

Quite apart from the forms of their political institutions, the new countries, as was to be expected during the early stages of independence and establishment of national identity, have displayed a high degree of political instability. This generally includes frequent turnover of governments, participation by the military in making and unmaking regimes, rule by a single individual or small clique, and not infrequently by demagoguery and the elevation of personally erratic individuals to positions of power. The traditions of public accountability and responsibility for the exercise of power have been slow to develop in some newer countries. This is a formidable catalogue— especially since the United States and the Soviet Union, even with relatively stable governments, have not found it easy to manage their nuclear weaponry in a responsible manner.

In recent years, moreover, there is a growing recognition that the developing countries, though poor and weak, are not devoid of some kinds of retaliatory capacity against even the largest states. In Algeria and Indo-China, indigenous forces have given a good account of themselves against sophisticated modern armaments. Although these performances have taken place in rather special "defensive" situations, they have served to dispel the illusion of invincibility of the military forces of the "advanced" states. The political and economic dividends from the cohesion of the OPEC countries have led to efforts at emulation by producers of other primary products. More ominously, a series of hijackings, kidnappings, and similar events has demonstrated the vulnerability of modern societies to terrorism. Without becoming overly alarmist, it is still possible, in the absence of a response to the problems of the developing world that is in some sense "adequate" (and this seems unlikely), to foresee a growing legitimation in those countries of the use of extreme and high-risk measures for the redress of perceived political and economic grievance.

It should be sufficient simply to call attention to the combination of widespread poverty and grievance, spreading nuclear capability, endemic political instability, and increasing legitimation of terror. The explosive possibilities of the mix should be apparent enough, without the need to specify the ways in which it might lead to military trouble with a nuclear dimension. But it is often assumed that these developments, no matter how aggravated, cannot culminate in a serious military threat to the developed countries, given the existing disproportion of military and, more important, technological power. The assumption is comforting, but one wonders whether it is wholly warranted.

In the first place, there is little basis for complacency about the continued technological superiority of the industrialized countries, at least in the relevant military technologies. The Indian explosion underscored the inevitable spread of nuclear knowledge to Third World countries over the next quarter of a century. More broadly, although the Arab-Israeli conflict is properly seen as an engagement between client states armed and supplied by superpowers, it has another dimension as well. Israel is a modern, unified, highly organized, and technically advanced society. Its adversaries are backward and fragmented, but much more numerous, and they feel themselves deeply aggrieved. In the October War, the technological superiority with which Israel had kept the Arabs at bay for a generation could be seen for the first time to be a wasting asset. The difference between the first three Middle East wars and the fourth was not in the quantity or quality of the Arab armament, but in the fact that Arab soldiers were beginning to learn how to use these complex and technically advanced weapons under battle conditions. Although, in the end, Israel regained military ascendancy on both fronts, the Arabs' performance leaves little doubt that they can sooner or later master the technology of desert war and that the uniting effect of political and ideological grievance can offset the disorganization and diversity of concrete interests that tend to drive the Arab states apart. Israel seems already to have drawn the conclusion that it cannot base its policy on the assurance of continuing military superiority. It would be wrong to assume that there are no warnings in this experience for the other industrialized countries as well.

If one asks for specific examples of how a military threat might develop in the Third World, again the Middle East war heads the list. For it reminds us that, despite the amelioration of bilateral relations between the superpowers, the lively possibility remains that they can be drawn into confrontation in controversies between their respective clients. The dangers are not confined to arenas where the interests of the United States and the Soviet Union are already strongly committed. Struggles within the developing world have marked the last two decades, and they can be expected to continue, if not to increase in frequency and intensity, over the years ahead. They may take the form of civil strife, as in Indo-China; boundary disputes, as in parts of Africa; contests for regional hegemony, as some fear in the case of Brazil; or conflicts growing out of the situation of beleaguered states such as South Africa and Israel. With or without superpower intervention, any one of these could eventuate in the use of force. Given the conditions of widespread nuclear dissemination that we have posited, any use of force could include, or lead to, the use of nuclear force, which by itself would have serious consequences for the rest of the world. In such circumstances, it is hard to see how the United States or the Soviet Union could remain uninvolved.

To the foregoing list of occasions for the use of nuclear weapons must be added the possibilities of conflict over increasingly scarce natural resources, most of them located in the Third World, of recourse to nuclear terror as a tactic of frustration and despair, and of accident, failure of control, or miscalculation in relatively primitive command and control systems.

It is unlikely that any particular one of these possibilities will materialize in the form envisioned, and, even taking the list as a whole, the probability of nuclear trouble is, perhaps, not very high. But the firing of a nuclear weapon in anger in some such situation seems at least as probable (though possibly not so apocalyptic) as did a nuclear exchange between the United States and the Soviet Union in the nineteen-fifties and sixties and much more likely than such an exchange in the nineteen-seventies and eighties. If this prognosis is at all accurate, it calls for a major redirection of arms-control efforts in the years ahead.

C. International Organizations

National sovereignty, whether we like it or not, persists as the central organizing concept of the international system, and it is likely to do so for some decades to come.

ing to perform routine, primarily housekeeping tasks, without credibility, direction, or capacity for action. Their very presence will inhibit new organizational departures. Since institutional growth is slow, we can expect that these conditions will continue for a considerable period, even if contrary forces should begin to operate.

D. Some Qualifications

The foregoing pages, in the well-established tradition of arms controllers, present something of a "worst-case" analysis. Though to my mind it is by no means implausible, there are hopeful elements in the current situation, and to provide a more balanced picture the principal ones should be noted.

First, the new relations between the United States and the Soviet Union enhance the potential for managing and containing clashes of interest between them. One may read the events of October and November, 1973, in the Middle East as a demonstration of this possibility. Although the execution was clumsy, there is reason to hope that the parties will acquire greater finesse with the passage of time.

Second, it is possible that the developed countries will learn to perform better in dealing cooperatively with their economic interrelations than I have suggested. Some observers predict a relatively quick and smooth transition in the European Community. Negotiations under the aegis of the International Monetary Fund (IMF) for the reform of the monetary system seem to be making progress. Preparations for another round of trade negotiations are going forward, though somewhat haltingly. Even the unwillingness to deal with the realities of agricultural trade problems may give way in the face of the growing concern over world food needs.

Progress made on these economic questions should yield spill-over benefits for the developing countries. Moreover, the interests and voices of the developing countries are by no means being universally disregarded. For the first time, for example, they are participating in the IMF monetary negotiations alongside the "Group of Ten" major monetary powers. Indeed, major oil producers will now sit in these councils as a matter of right rather than grace. Intensive and largely successful efforts were made to involve them in the preparatory work for the Stockholm Conference on the Human Environment. They are taking a dominant role in the revision of the law of the sea. Other instances could be cited. Although there is little comfort to be drawn from the recent performance of the oil producing states, it is still conceivable that in time access to the raw materials of developing countries under conditions of scarcity could provide a basis for much larger transfers of natural resources than would be forthcoming by way of "foreign aid."

Finally, the imperatives for international management of new technologies and of common environmental problems may be recognized more readily or may assert themselves more urgently than now seems likely. If so, we may look for international organizations to assume renewed importance and perhaps for new departures in structure and techniques to make them more effective in developing policy and making decisions.

Some or all of these possibilities, and perhaps others, may materialize. But even if they do not, the world could, and probably will, manage to muddle through without major breakdown, as it has for the past generation. Thus, even marginal contributions may have an unexpectedly large impact. Arms-control issues are related to most of the problems and possibilities touched on in this section. It is time to examine these issues more directly, though necessarily briefly.

III. Implications for Arms Control

Nuclear arms-control issues for the years ahead seem to group themselves naturally under three main headings. First is the continuing effort to control and reduce the strategic nuclear arsenals of the two superpowers. Second are the problems of forces in Europe and of European military security now being addressed in the negotiations for Mutual and Balanced Force Reduction (MBFR). Third are the prevention and control of other, probably rather fragmentary, nuclear capabilities in a setting of generalized international instability and diffusion of effective power. These problems can be summed up under the rubric of "non-proliferation."

Before discussing each of these groups in turn, there is a preliminary and more general point to be considered. The admittedly limited arms-control successes of the past decade depended heavily upon the bilateral configuration of the enterprise. First, the bilateral matrix simplified the negotiations themselves. There was elaborate internal bargaining in the United States government and probably in the Soviet Union as well. But in their external aspect, the negotiations were fairly straightforward, two-party games without the complications introduced by the need to coordinate or adjust to a variety of divergent interests.

Secondly, the bilateral setting was the key to the issues of compliance and enforcement that have plagued United States arms-control doctrine and policies. The Baruch plan, the first post-war American arms-control proposal, would have established elaborate international machinery for verification and enforcement of the agreement. The treaty was seen as establishing a precise legal norm. Charges of violation would be investigated by an independent organization with broad access to the "facts." If the investigation warranted, the evidence would be presented before an independent body, which would resolve controversies and make determinations in the manner of a judicial tribunal. The model was the process by which alleged violations of the criminal law are investigated and punished in the United States. This proposal set the pattern for all American arms-control proposals throughout the decade of the fifties.[2]

Despite this well-developed and well-known American position, none of the treaties concluded in the last decade (with the qualified exception of NPT) contains any such enforcement machinery. Because of the bilateral character of the agreements and the focus on strategic weaponry, it was possible to remit verification to "national means," tacitly in most of the agreements, but expressly in SALT.

Moreover, none of the agreements in the series provides any formal sanction for violation. By accident, however, and to some degree over the objection of the United States, the Limited Test Ban Treaty included a clause permitting withdrawal by either party "if it decides that extraordinary events, related to the subject matter of the treaty, have jeopardized [its] supreme interests. . . ." The identical clause has been incorporated into the NPT and the SALT agreements. In the bilateral context of these agreements, this withdrawal clause operates as a sanction, since withdrawal by either party would inevitably portend a far-reaching adjustment across the entire range of relationships between them. In the absence of a fundamental change in policy, neither party wishes to contemplate such a readjustment. Thus breach of the agreement, where it might appear to promise some specific short-term gain, is inhibited by the risk that it will provide justification for the other party to withdraw, with all the broader consequences that would entail.[3]

The simplifying focus on major strategic weapons systems deployed against each other by the superpowers as bilateral adversaries will be blurred to a greater or lesser degree in all of the arms-control negotiations that lie ahead.

A. Strategic Arms Limitation

Whatever the tactical permutations of the continuing SALT talks at any particular time, the primary objective should be to halt the qualitative and quantitative strategic arms race and, in addition, to achieve a significant reduction in strategic weaponry on both sides. The answer to the question whether Vladivostok makes a positive contribution to arms control depends on whether the high numerical ceilings agreed upon there can be converted promptly into a basis for negotiations leading to real reductions and qualitative restraints. No doubt this process must take place within a framework that can be fairly seen as reflecting a parity of force between the two powers, but issues of precise technical or numerical equality should not be permitted to dominate the negotiations. It is widely recognized that, at least with anything like present force levels and configurations, numerical differences in strategic nuclear forces are devoid of direct military significance in the event of nuclear, or even conventional, war. The efforts of strategic analysis to demonstrate that numerical superiority remains meaningful or that present force levels can be justified in terms of plausible missions—for example, damage limitation or war fighting capability—have become increasingly labored and unconvincing. Countries should have little difficulty in drawing the political conclusions. The political value of weapons is ultimately derived from their military significance. If numerical or technical advantage at present levels does not convey the one, it will soon lose the other. It should be a prime objective of arms-control policy to reinforce rather than to obscure this conclusion.

The political atmosphere of the SALT negotiations has already been subtly altered by the Moscow and Washington summits. Now that bipolar strategic confrontation is no longer *the* defining and organizing feature of the international system, arms control is no longer the only, or even the most important, channel for dialogue and mutual adjustment of relations between the two nations. One may predict that the SALT II and SALT III negotiations will have rather less political visibility and importance than their predecessor.

In these circumstances, it is appropriate carefully to consider unilateral measures for shaping and reducing force levels and structures, as an alternative to formal arms-control negotiations. Internal pressures on resources on both sides, in the context of sharply altered perceptions of the international setting, may begin to operate much more powerfully to reduce military budgets than do international agreements. We may already be seeing these forces at work in a more exacting Congressional scrutiny of military budget requests. It may continue to be valuable in some circumstances to give unilaterally determined force postures the sanction of international agreement. But it may also be that, in such a setting, the dissonant side effects of arms-control negotiations will come to outweigh the gains.

China, unlike the other lesser nuclear powers, will in time have the capacity to operate as a significant independent political and military force. In fact, it is a potential third superpower, and other countries will be increasingly prepared to anticipate the event. Moreover, after a certain point, China's nuclear capability will severely complicate the problem of further reductions in strategic weapons by the United States and the Soviet Union. For these reasons, it is particularly important to begin to engage China in the network of existing agreements on nuclear weapons and as a participant in the continuing discussions on their limitation and control. China's willingness to sign the agreement establishing a Latin American nuclear free zone may be a harbinger of a more receptive attitude.

For the present, however, China is pressing forward with its weapons program, having conducted its most recent thermonuclear tests in June, 1974, in the megaton range. The acquisition of an intercontinental delivery capability has been slower. The United States' estimate of the date when China will have an operational ICBM continues to recede. China has MRBMs, however, capable of reaching many targets in the Soviet Union.

The new relationship between the United States and the Soviet Union does not relieve China's security concerns. The concomitant improvement of relations between China and the United States, coupled with the end of the Vietnam War and other withdrawals of United States forces from the approaches to China, may diminish some Chinese anxieties. But it has been clear for a long time that China sees the chief threat to her security as coming from her Soviet neighbor—and apparently the feeling is reciprocated. For this reason, as well as for the requirements of prestige and, perhaps, internal considerations, the Chinese strategic-weapons program is likely to continue for a considerable time, that is, until China has achieved a substantial intercontinental nuclear capacity. The questions are how long a time and how substantial a capacity.

It seems unlikely that, under these circumstances, the Chinese government would agree to limitations on testing, at least for a considerable period. The question of what kind of force ceiling China might accept, given her sense of her own needs, is difficult to answer, especially since we know very little in detail about the considerations underlying China's nuclear program. It is hard to see why, except for the mystical significance of numerical parity, China should need to reach anything approaching the strategic-force levels embodied in the Interim Offensive Weapons agreement or in the Vladivostok accord. This is the more true since the ABM Treaty insures that Soviet cities will be held hostage to China's strategic retaliatory power, as well as that of the United States. In short, China, even on a fairly generous evaluation of the threat, "ought" to be content with something approaching a minimum deterrent.

It may be that resource constraints or good sense will tend to keep Chinese forces at these levels anyway and that there is little to be gained, and perhaps some risk, in trying to induce her to agree to limits numerically inferior to those applicable to the United States and the Soviet Union. If one asks, "What's in it for the Chinese?" the answer has to be, "Not very much." If, as I believe, there would be considerable value in bringing China into the formal arms-control community, it is worth exploring how the prospect could be encouraged.

Two possibilities suggest themselves, perhaps in some combination. The first is a significant reduction in American and especially Soviet strategic arsenals. The importance of such a reduction in China's view—and, as we shall later note, that of other nuclear and potentially nuclear powers as well—lends additional urgency to what should in any case be the prime objective of the ongoing SALT talks.

The second possibility raises greater difficulties. It is a tripartite "no-first-use" agreement. China has favored this for some time; the Soviets have pressed for it periodically. It would seem to have some value for China—and perhaps for the Soviet Union—in connection with their worries vis-à-vis each other. The problem for the United States is the familiar one of the relation of such an agreement to Western European defense. The United States seems warily to have moved somewhat closer to the possibility during the Brezhnev visit in June, 1973. And it may be that, as force-reduction talks in Europe proceed, a way can be found to reconcile a no-first-use undertaking with the needs of European security. If a universal no-first-use agreement is not feasible, more limited arrangements might be considered, perhaps on a geographical basis, or bilaterally between the United States and China.

B. European Security

Here, too, the overriding objective should be a significant reduction in force levels. Although discussion thus far has focused on manpower, it is even more important to cut back the number of nuclear weapons available to both sides in the European theater. An agreement for force reduction, if it can be achieved, could in general rely on bilateral compliance and enforcement mechanisms similar to those contained in the treaties dealing with strategic arms. The negotiating process itself, however, is anything but straightforwardly bilateral. Important conflicts of interest and perspective have already been revealed among the Western allies. And they obviously exist among Warsaw Pact members as well.

The situation, particularly on the Western side, is akin to a two-party parliamentary system with moderately strong party discipline. The party leadership can always enforce the whip on a vote if the matter is important enough. But there are limits on how long the leadership can withstand the resistance of many and/or important members. And there is considerable opportunity for self-expression for the member who knows how to use it. Studies of the dynamics of these systems might shed a good deal of theoretical light on interalliance bargaining.

To date, in MBFR, it has been possible to surmount the divergencies within, as well as between, the two camps on procedural matters, such as representation and the geographical scope of the negotiations. But the conflicts are bound to re-emerge in even sharper form in the consideration of substantive issues. Moreover, the connection between MBFR and the SALT talks—because of the ambiguous character of Western forward-based systems (FBS) capable of reaching the Soviet Union—means that some of these negotiating complexities may reappear in the SALT forum, despite the agreement to disregard them at Vladivostok. For the Western alliance, there is a further difficulty in the domestic political pressure for early results within the United States. This has already exacerbated differences among the allies, and it may well compromise the efficacy of any agreement that is reached.

Under these circumstances, the risks are high for a protracted or aborted negotiation, with the possibility in either case of a more embittered and unstable situation in Europe. Here, too, then, there are strong reasons for considering in some detail unilateral alternatives to multilaterally negotiated arms control. 'Unilateral' in this case does not refer to the United States alone, but to the Western alliance. Re-examination of doctrine, strategy, and technology for the defense of Western Europe is long over-due, and there is good reason to believe that it would lead to significantly reduced re-quirements, especially for nuclear weapons.

If it is thought that manpower reduction must be reserved as a bargaining chip for the MBFR, there is surely no need to await the outcome of these negotiations before starting to withdraw some of the seven thousand United States nuclear warheads now deployed in Western Europe. The purpose of these weapons is ill-defined. Some con-template their use in combat to redress an asserted Western deficit in conventional strength in the event of a ground war in Western Europe. The Germans, and other al-lies on whose territory the explosions would take place, are understandably not very enthusiastic about the prospect. Others see the tactical weapons as contributing to the credibility of the United States' nuclear guarantee of Europe by insuring that any conflict will inevitably and quickly move to the nuclear level. And still others cannot conceive any rational occasion for use of nuclear weapons in an area of such concentrated population and rich human heritage. But there is no immediate need to choose from among these viewpoints. Whatever doctrinal flag one flies, present deployments are excessive and dangerous. They can and should be substantially reduced without regard to any reciprocal action on the Soviet side.

C. Proliferation

Strategic nuclear weapons and European security have been the staples of arms-control analysis for a generation. If the problems are far from being solved, they are, on the whole, fairly well understood. Moreover, one consequence of a more stable relationship between the United States and the Soviet Union is the alleviation of some of the pressure for international action on these problems and the direction of atten-tion to the possibilities of unilateral approaches. These have never been excluded from the province of arms control, but the heart of the subject, in both theoretical and diplomatic terms, has been concerted action of various kinds to achieve results that the parties acting separately would not have chosen.

If there are new problems of a fundamental order, they lie in the effort to control the military (and perhaps paramilitary) implications of the inevitable spread of nuclear knowledge and technology. The Indian explosion, the emphasis on nuclear power as the long-range solution to the energy crisis, and the rapid developments in nuclear technology already noted combine to make this a matter of great practical urgency, indeed of the first priority for those interested in arms control. For the likely seed-bed for international violence in the years ahead will be claims to a "fair share" of the world's goods—as well as prestige and influence—pressed with increasing stridency by countries that have not, heretofore, figured largely in strategic calcula-tions.

The setting does not, on the face of it, seem conducive to effective international arms-control measures, and what possibilities there may be are not well understood. The features that facilitated agreement between the superpowers are conspicuously absent. The primacy of economic rather than strategic issues in relations between developed and developing countries will make it difficult to achieve visibility for arms-control efforts and to focus political pressure on them. The setting is anything but bilateral. International action will have to take into account a wide range of divergent interests and outlooks, in all probability shifting radically over time. There is not even the confrontation of coalitions that to some extent disciplines the diversity in MBFR. More intrusive inspection procedures seem to be needed to police a non-proliferation regime. Much more important, at a given moment the political consequences of a breakdown in the regime for any particular party may not be very great; it might well be prepared to accept those consequences in return for what are perceived to be the gains of withdrawal or violation.

Until the spring of 1974, it was possible, despite these formidable difficulties, to take comfort from the existence of the Non-Proliferation Treaty, adhered to by 84 countries. But the Indian explosion must place the continued viability of the treaty in doubt. Many of the countries with important nuclear capability remain outside the agreement—Japan, Israel, Egypt, and South Africa. Even West Germany, although it has gone through all the necessary internal procedures, has not yet deposited its instrument of ratification. It seems unlikely now that most of these can be persuaded to adhere to the treaty in the absence of some important change of circumstance. If so, countries now parties to the agreement can be expected to grow uneasy, especially since the NPT lacks many of the attributes needed for a stable treaty regime. There are some substantive deficiencies in the provisions of the Treaty. The IAEA safeguards system, despite important loopholes and the prospect that it will be seriously overburdened as the use of nuclear energy grows, is nevertheless regarded as excessively intrusive. The treaty has always been seen as discriminatory against non-nuclear powers. Many of the participants signed up reluctantly to begin with and have never displayed very great enthusiasm for the commitment.

In these circumstances, the overriding priority must be to rescue and revitalize the existing treaty regime. With all its deficiencies, it is the essential basis for any general effort to control the spread of nuclear weapons. The policies pursued by the superpowers to date, in their efforts to maintain and extend the coverage of the NPT, can be characterized as the nth country approach. It consists in concentrating diplomatic efforts and pressures on those few countries thought to be the most likely to opt for nuclear weapons. In a sense, this approach reflects the definition of the problem as the nth-country problem—the potential acquisition of nuclear capability by one or more of a relatively small and identifiable group of states. I have argued above that this concept of the problem has been outrun by events. But in any case, the Indian performance exposes the inadequacies of the policy approach heretofore pursued.

The essential problem of the NPT is that the superpowers have not themselves accepted any significant limitation on their own actions, either in the treaty itself or in other arms-control agreements. Until they do, appeals to the non-nuclear powers to accept a self-denying ordinance will sound increasingly hollow. Thus the first and inescapable responsibility in any future effort to halt the spread of nuclear weapons rests on the superpowers themselves. They must give up something real and tangible if the NPT is to have a good chance of remaining viable. What can they give up? Before the Indian explosion, it is possible that the conclusion of a Comprehensive Test Ban Treaty would have been enough, at least as an earnest declaration of intentions. It would still be important, but, I think, no longer sufficient.

There must be a significant reduction of American and Soviet strategic arsenals, preferably by binding international agreement. This much is implicit in Article VI of the NPT, calling for the parties ". . . to pursue negotiations in good faith on effective measures regarding cessation of the nuclear arms race and disarmament." And if the superpowers fail to meet this minimal obligation, it is hard to see how other countries can be brought to accept more onerous ones.

A third possibility for action by the superpowers is to encourage and accept nuclear free-zone agreements where countries in the regions involved want them. So far the record on this score has been spotty. The Soviet Union has not adhered to the Treaty for the Prohibition of Nuclear Weapons in Latin America, and, although the United States has signed, it has reserved its right to deploy nuclear weapons on territory under its control (including the Panama Canal Zone) within the zone.

Even if the Non-Proliferation Treaty can be kept alive and can be strengthened, much else remains to be done, especially in a period of increasing emphasis on nuclear power. Among the most important is a new approach to the international nuclear-power industry. The time has long since passed when the United States, or the United States and the Soviet Union together, could control and police the spread of nuclear technology. Reactors are now supplied on a competitive basis by manufacturers in France, West Germany, Italy, and Japan. The United Kingdom, West Germany, and the Netherlands have undertaken a joint project to develop a centrifuge technology for fuel enrichment that promises to be simpler and cheaper than the gaseous diffusion method presently employed. An even simpler and cheaper process using lasers is just over the horizon.

International trade in nuclear power equipment seems to be conducted on a purely commercial, "hard-sell," competitive basis, with little reference to the impact on non-proliferation objectives. Presumably manufacturers and their governments rely on the IAEA safeguards to insure against diversion of nuclear materials. But it is fairly generally agreed that the IAEA system will simply be unable to cope with the amounts of nuclear fuel that are anticipated in the next decade or so.

The time has come for a much stricter regulatory policy enforced by the suppliers to supplement IAEA safeguards. This will require agreement at least among manufacturing concerns and probably among the governments involved. Concerted action of this kind could encompass a wide range of measures. Among the most significant would be the improvement of the national safeguard systems of the purchaser countries. The IAEA relies on these national systems for its own monitoring work. Equally important, most, if not all, of the national control systems are now vulnerable to unauthorized withdrawal by non-governmental groups.

Conclusion

The foregoing is hardly more than a truncated checklist of matters that remain active on the arms-control agenda, despite the moderation of relations between the United States and the Soviet Union. Almost all of them have been seen before. But the familiarity of the topics should not obscure an important shift of priority and emphasis. The control of superpower confrontation through nuclear arms-control measures has declined in relative importance as the confrontation has moderated in intensity. In the confused and still dangerous world to come, the main effort must be directed to the problems of nuclear weapons actually or potentially in hands other than those of the superpowers. The foregoing discussion emphasizes the significance in the new context of arms limitation between the superpowers—a Comprehensive Test Ban, significant reductions in strategic and tactical nuclear weapons, and the like. Beyond that, the problems of controlling nuclear arms in a world of widely diffused nuclear capability have been given relatively little systematic attention at the theoretical or operational level. That balance must now be redressed.

REFERENCES

[1] The vote of the Security Council in helping to achieve an initial cease-fire in the Middle East is not necessarily an exception to this generalization for, in that case, Security Council action did not impinge on the perceived national interest of either of the superpowers, and it did not come until that circumstance was itself perceived by them.

[2] In one sense, the on-site inspection controversy derived, or at least gained intensity, from this conception of enforcement. The criminal investigator, it was assumed, should as a matter of course have untrammelled access to the facts needed for his investigation. Failure to agree to this was seen as an indication of deviousness and untrustworthiness. That was not necessarily so. It may simply have involved an insistence that there are important political elements in the enforcement process, and that, to the extent that there are legal aspects, they cannot be dealt with by a literal translation of domestic judicial institutions to the international plane.

[3] The SALT agreements further elaborate the structural features of this compliance mechanism, making explicit many of the elements that were implicit in the earlier agreements. Thus, under SALT, it is expressly forbidden to interfere with the other party's national means of verification or to use new methods of concealment, although it is fairly clear that such acts would have been "extraordinary events" justifying withdrawal from the earlier agreements. Similarly the agreements provide for a Standing Consultative Committee to clarify ambiguous situations and the like. This institutionalizes the informal procedures for exchange of information that have grown up, for example, in connection with venting incidents under the Limited Test Ban. Refusal to respond to reasonable inquiries in such cases might very well have been considered an "extraordinary event." And under SALT, even though provision of information is expressly stipulated to be voluntary, the possibility of withdrawal will tend to insure that both parties are reasonably forthcoming in response to requests.

RICHARD A. FALK

Arms Control, Foreign Policy, and Global Reform

I. A Critique of the Prevailing Approach

RECENT EMPHASIS IN ARMS CONTROL has centered upon the control of the arms race and the prevention of nuclear war.[1] These objectives are obviously interrelated, as some weapons deployments and strategic attitudes present more of a threat than others to the goal of avoiding nuclear or large-scale conventional warfare. Some features of the arms race have even been consistent with overall prevention goals. Particularly where international tension has a strong ideological component, adversaries premise their security on possessing sufficient unilateral capabilities to inflict unacceptable damage and on being perceived as having the will and capability to do so. As ideological tensions wane or disappear, technical considerations grow more prominent, and actual and potential weapons capabilities are viewed in more interactive and even cooperative fashion. During the Nixon-Ford-Brezhnev tenure, bipolar relations have become generally more cooperative, and this development has certainly been reflected in a continuing search for bipolar arms-control agreements.[2] But, at the same time, bipolarity has also been significantly eroded and even superseded by emergent multipolarity and interdependence in such domains as trade, money, and natural resources. China's independent path in foreign policy, India's acquisition of nuclear status, the enormous currency surpluses of the main oil producers, the weakness of the dollar, the shaky domestic political conditions prevailing in most of the principal non-Communist states, and the increasing tactical skill and bargaining leverage displayed by Asian, African, and Latin American countries are all elements that complicate the setting within which arms-control negotiations must now take place.

In part the complexity arises from the widely held suspicion that diplomatic cooperation is included in the secret agenda of Soviet-American arms negotiations, often masquerading (or appearing to do so) under the ritual affirmation of alliance loyalties. The resulting situation is best understood as being ambiguous rather than sinister, although the evidence is such that either perception can seem reasonable;[3] it is doubtful that either Soviet or American leaders have themselves fully sorted out their true schedule of priorities with regard to acknowledged arms-control objectives and unacknowledgeable ambitions for geopolitical management. In any event, in both countries these schedules are bound to be unstable because the ranking of priorities also depends on interactions that are difficult to assess—Soviet governance being such a secretive operation and American governance having been for so long substantially immobilized by the combined impact of Watergate and Vietnam.[4]

35

Furthermore, there are also indications that neither leadership group has fully decided on a clear geopolitical course of action for the years ahead.

Perhaps it has been Henry Kissinger, more than any other commentator on Soviet-American relations, who has over the years counseled both doves and hawks against an overly ideological approach to arms-control negotiations.[5] Kissinger's argument is that American leaders should make "a serious endeavor to resolve concrete issues" rather than become sidetracked by discussions of Soviet intentions or by prospects for liberalizing the harsh Soviet system of domestic rule.[6] Because Kissinger is pessimistic about the latter two issues, he does not want them to become stumbling blocks to the concrete bargains that the superpowers can and should reach to reduce the prospect of nuclear conflagration. To strike a bargain does not require friendship, although a lessening of tensions and increased cordiality among leaders do help sustain a negotiating atmosphere and encourage popular expectations that agreements can, will, and should be reached.

Despite ambiguities and complexities, certain features of the recent American approach to arms-control negotiations can be discerned with sufficient clarity to enable reflection and analysis. Richard Nixon, in his fourth annual report on foreign policy issued in early 1973, expressed the basic character of the recent Soviet-American approach to arms control:

There is mutual agreement that permanent limitations must meet the basic security interests of both sides equitably if they are to endure in an era of great technological change and in a fluid international environment. There obviously can be no agreement that creates or preserves strategic advantages.[7]

Of course, some of this language can be discounted as propaganda; each side would gladly accept whatever advantages the other side was willing to "negotiate away." But it is a significant assertion, because it discloses a parity-oriented rather than a superiority-oriented approach.

The report went on to specify that any acceptable arms-control agreements would have to accomplish the following five objectives:

—establish an essential equivalence in strategic capabilities among systems common to both sides;
—maintain the survivability of strategic forces in light of known and potential technological capabilities;
—provide for the replacement and modernization of older systems without upsetting the strategic balance;
—be subject to adequate verification;
—leave the security of third parties undiminished.[8]

These five requirements express mainstream opinions and conventional wisdom about national security in the nuclear age; they also illustrate the extent to which prenuclear statecraft continues to dominate arms-control thinking. If these requirements are a checklist of critical considerations that any responsible government would take into account, then they are unexceptionable. But if they represent conditions regarded as sufficient in themselves, then they provide opponents of disarmament with authoritative arguments for resistance. Indeed, it is the inherent and readily discernible ambiguity of these requirements that arouses concern and invites suspicion, especially given the "hard-line" background of Richard Nixon and Gerald Ford and their support within military and business circles. The first requirement emphasizes the extent to which "balance" or "equivalence" is relied upon to maintain peace between states with possibly conflicting foreign-policy goals; if one takes this approach, the mutual deterrence of nuclear war becomes nothing more than an important special case in the standard nation-state approach to national security.[9] The second and third requirements listed by Mr. Nixon seek to sustain "equivalence" through time, despite the dynamism of modern weapons technology and asymmetries in relative military capabilities and concepts; they are thus elaborations of the first requirement. The fourth requirement, of "assured verification," can only mean either normal prudence or a kind of generalized Machiavellian reminder that trust and good faith have no place in serious diplomacy. The fifth requirement, which may be the most questionable in terms of real—as distinct from proclaimed—policy, seeks to reconcile superpower diplomacy with alliance diplomacy. Both the United States and the Soviet Union have provided frequent elaborate, but not altogether convincing, reassurances to their allies on this subject, but there is an inevitable ambiguity of intention that arises from ending the Cold War (or appearing to end it, at least provisionally) at a time when there is considerable economic rivalry among advanced industrial states with market economies and intense hostility among various strands of the world Communist movement.[10] It is not clear, and perhaps there is as yet no internal consensus in either superpower, whether this new form of bipolarity is duopolistic in spirit and designed primarily to keep secondary states under control, or whether the earlier bloc rivalry continues to dominate their geopolitical maneuverings, but in muted form. In either case, Nixon's fifth requirement acknowledged the alliance side of geopolitics in the state system and sought to reconcile alignment interests with arms-control policy, both allegedly to contribute to "balance" within the system as a whole.

The other side of this view on arms control is a strong emphasis on the continuing usefulness of force, and of its threatened use, to attain American foreign-policy goals other than those of national defense. Mr. Nixon's words and policy made this clear. He contended, "In a period of developing detente, it is easy to be lulled into a false sense of security," and further,

... military adequacy is never permanently guaranteed. This Nation cannot afford the cost of weakness. Our strength is an essential stabilizing element in a world of turmoil and change. Our friends rely on it; our adversaries respect it. It is the essential underpinning for our diplomacy, designed to increase international understanding and to lessen the risks of war.[11]

More concretely, such an orientation implies a special role for the United States in the state system: "The United States cannot protect its national interests, or support those of its allies, or meet its responsibilities for helping safeguard international peace, without the ability to deploy forces abroad."[12] These so-called "forward deployments" are associated with the main global security missions that the United States undertook in the Cold War—to protect countries in Western Europe and East Asia against Communist expansion or Communist-led insurgencies.

... the American presence in Europe and Asia is essential to the sense of security and confidence of our friends which underpins all our common endeavors—including our joint efforts in the common defense. Our forces are deployed to provide a responsive and efficient posture against likely threats.[13]

In the aftermath of Vietnam, such global foreign-policy aims encourage the development and deployment of non-nuclear weapons that can strike at a distance and thus minimize the risk to American combat personnel. The Nixon Doctrine—applied "in its purest form," we were told by the President (news conference, November 12, 1971), in the air war in Cambodia waged up through August 15, 1973—was a *doctrinal* expression of this posture; the electronic battlefield, "smart bombs," defoliation campaigns, meterological warfare, and saturation bombing were among its *technological* embodiments.

The problem of interpretation is formidable. Are we confronted by a situation in which American (and Soviet) leadership is so wary of the other side that the risks of agreement generally outweigh the risks of virtually unrestrained competition in arms development? Or is the element of wariness mainly a pretext for refusing to curtail freedom of choice in foreign policy and to cut back on military-industrial influence at home? Or, more likely, is there a bewildering mixture of these mutually reinforcing attitudes? It should be emphasized that SALT I, like other arms-control agreements since World War II, had no effect whatsoever on "deployed levels of armaments." Indeed, as the Associate Director of the Livermore Laboratory observed, "Both sides agreed to retain what they had and to do without systems that they did not want."[14]

Despite the general impression that conflict among principal states in the world has entered a moderate phase, it is difficult to discern any modification of foreign-policy objectives and world-order design implicit in the Nixon-Ford/Kissinger-Brezhnev diplomacy. For reasons I hope to make clear, this essential continuity is unfortunate and has had a particularly dampening and distorting effect on the prospects for arms control. There are two principal themes in American thinking:

1) *Foreign policy continuity:* Despite the spirit of detente, the drift of Cold War diplomacy remains unchanged and continues to include massive forward deployments of military capabilities in Europe and Asia, as well as an occasional willingness to undertake counter-insurgency missions in the Third World.[15]

2) *World order continuity:* Despite the new ecological awareness and the prominence of economic interdependence, deference to statist logic remains the cornerstone of analysis and planning for the future of world politics.[16]

In my view, these persistent features have been too little stressed in most recent arms-control literature. I believe that the presumed adequacy of the state system is dangerous to national and global well-being and that arms-control analysis needs to be guided by viable conceptions of foreign policy and world order that are more responsive to our national situation and to the world historical context. Otherwise, ambitious proposals for arms control are inherently unconvincing because they fail to question the underlying dynamics of the war system as it is manipulated by what are now the most powerful and ambitious governments.

II. The Relevance of Foreign-Policy Perspectives

An appropriate foreign policy for the United States ought to satisfy four requirements:

1) It must provide for national defense in all plausible contingencies where the United States or its principal allies could be the victim of direct military attack.[17] In the nuclear age, this requirement entails some form of credible deterrent. The acceptable form and reach of such deterrent capabilities are properly the central issues of

arms-control policy, and their resolution depends on the approach that the principal adversaries take to these same issues.

2) Its main precepts must generate a bipartisan consensus, so that they will not be subject to the vagaries of party politics. Mr. Nixon and Secretary Kissinger were generally successful in generating a new bipartisan consensus for their geopolitical initiatives, especially their effort to mute the Cold War and to replace it with an active form of detente, but they were not able to generate a consensus on the need to sustain extensive alliance commitments in the Third World.[18]

3) It must embody the revered norms and traditions of the society. In particular, the United States government cannot hope to endorse and support anti-democratic governments abroad while endorsing the means and ends of democracy at home. Precisely those Americans most directly in touch with the values our society is supposed to stand for will perceive the immorality of interventions on behalf of undemocratic regimes. This, I believe, is the most important lesson of the anti-war movement generated by the Vietnam War. And it is the fear of such opposition that led in the past to secrecy, deceit, manipulation, and finally outright repression, when that, too, was felt to be necessary. Any stable political system resorts to a certain amount of hypocrisy to reconcile contradictory pulls of policy and to meet emergency pressures, but, if carried very far, either the government is led to repress its domestic opponents or the society becomes so badly split that an effective foreign policy is impossible.

4) It must generally respond to the minimum requirements of world order. These requirements have long been set by the logic of the state system, and have traditionally been satisfied by relying on costly processes of readjustment. The search for balance or control presents alternative ways for a principal government to maintain world order. Even the appearance of nuclear weaponry has not undermined this system. Indeed, the prospect of nuclear war raises the stakes of security so high that the search for "balance" is more intense than it has ever been before.[19] What has imperiled the traditional quest for minimum world order is a combination of factors arising from the growing interdependence of all phases of global activity and from a series of dangerous pressures on the biosystem associated with what might be called "the ecological challenge." We do not yet possess enough information on the increasing interdependence or the seriousness of the ecological challenge to know whether minimum world order can be maintained by a continuing reliance on the state system, or whether some more centralized system of authority will prove essential. But ominous warnings suggest that we should no longer take for granted a world order based on present statist foreign-policy dynamics.

The acceptance of these four conditions would determine the orientation of United States foreign policy, but the conditions themselves do not constitute a program. Specific applications would still have to be worked out in the face of complex and often inconsistent domestic and international considerations.

The suggested reorientation might have profound consequences for arms control, although conjecture is difficult because so much depends upon how we perceive the behavior of principal foreign adversaries and on the relative influence of the military within national policy-making arenas. Nevertheless, a new impetus in arms control could be confidently expected from such a reorientation, even if progress is at first confined to a series of unilateral initiatives and negotiated bargains designed to cut down surplus capacity of various kinds. I believe that rising ecological awareness will make governing groups everywhere (but especially in the United States, because of its disproportionate demands on the world's resources) sensitive to the present waste of resources and the fundamental importance of adopting conservation strategies. Effective arms control is a particularly attractive conservation strategy for a number of reasons, and it offers enterprising politicians many opportunities.

The superpowers might agree to undertake a series of parallel unilateral steps that would proceed in mutually reinforcing directions. These steps would in turn create an appropriate context for negotiating proposals to minimize the scale and scope of deterrence and to limit, at least to some extent, its awesome orbit of devastation, while sustaining its relative safety, enhancing its reliability, and even increasing its flexibility.[20] Arms-control efforts by nuclear superpowers could appropriately concentrate upon securing the cheapest, safest, most reliable, and least inhumane form of deterrent capability. To sustain this objective it would also be necessary to pursue vigorously, and on a global scale, arms-control policies designed to restrict the role of nuclear weapons to the narrowest possible situation, namely, nuclear response to nuclear attack. In the absence of effective global protection for international boundaries (for example, through permanent, internationally supervised buffer zones and retaliatory military capabilities[21]), this objective would not provide adequate security for states such as Israel, Taiwan, and South Africa, which feel threatened by vigorous and widely supported revisionist strategies. Such a security system—unconditionally acknowledging the international legitimacy of state boundaries—would be an unacceptable endorsement of the status quo unless it was combined with an international toleration of the internal dynamics of self-determination (including small-scale and covert cross-border support activities) and with effective procedures for peaceful change.[22] The reformist logic on security here set forth need not be tested by its capacity to control these most troublesome of all international situations, where the local stakes of conflict are irreconcilable and where the beleaguered government is committed to an all-out struggle for survival. Our main concern over the next several decades is to improve international relations in situations where conflict is negotiable or its stakes marginal. It is in such situations that the diplomacy of denuclearization, including such declaratory steps as non-aggression pacts and renunciation of first-use options, might be expected to achieve a desirable reorientation of arms policy.[23]

III. The Relevance of World-Order Perspectives

Arms-control policies since World War II have done little to mitigate the horrors of the war system, to reduce arms spending, or to inhibit the proliferation of non-nuclear weapons technologies. Arms-control measures have served mainly to ratify the bipolar dominance of international politics and to maximize the stability of this dominance from a managerial standpoint. Agreements have simply expressed, in treaty form, those steps that the respective governments were prepared to take on a unilateral basis in any case. So-called "disarmament proposals" were propaganda exercises, cast in terms never intended to gain adversary acceptance; indeed, if acceptance had been forthcoming, the proposals would probably have been reformulated by the original sponsor. In essence, the traditional centrality of the war system in international politics has not been challenged by arms control, but has only been adapted somewhat to certain special characteristics of nuclear technology and to the participation in international affairs of many more centers of independent authority. This adaptation of the war system to new realities has been a generally beneficial process, given the widespread acceptance and inevitable persistence of the state system as it operated from the Peace of Westphalia (1648) to the end of World War II.

The most fundamental challenge to this apparent continuity has to do with the cluster of considerations that can be subsumed under the rubric "the ecological challenge." The limits-to-growth debate and related developments have given potency to a serious world-wide discussion of this problem. In essence, the ecological crisis, if accepted as genuine, requires an adjustment of much more fundamental proportions than that necessitated by the nuclear threat, although the character and timing of this adjustment remain controversial and in doubt.[24] There are two main lines of coherent response: coercive/imperial centralization (i.e., a global structure of authority brought about and maintained by force) and voluntary/contractual centralization (i.e., a global structure of authority brought about by agreement and basically sustained by consent of national governments). There is also a third—and incoherent—response, which is to sustain the fragmented, nationalistic world-order system that operates in accordance with statist logic.[25] This third line of response continues to dominate most of our thinking, although there are some signs that its inadequacy is beginning to be more widely recognized.

These three analytic conceptions are ideal types, whereas concrete situations in the world elicit intermingled strategies, especially during the present period of transition, when the extent of the ecological challenge and its links to the structure of world order are themselves the subjects of vigorous debate in which relatively strong evidence can be adduced to support conflicting views.[26] A minimum expectation during this period of uncertainty would be the initiation of a serious study of comparative systems of world order.[27] Within the confines of this essay, it is only possible to sketch the prospects for global reform in general terms. We should take note of three constructive strategies of global reform, each of which is appropriate to certain conditions of public understanding and great power attitudes, and inappropriate to other conditions. The scholar concerned with policy should attempt to clarify the contexts in which each of the following three reform strategies could constructively be applied.

1) *Reforms within the state system:* If optimistic assessments of technological prospects prove to be correct—including the development of cheap, abundant, and non-polluting energy sources, and given sufficient willingness to suppress or regulate tactics that disrupt complex technology, it may be possible to defer almost indefinitely any fundamental world-order changes which might otherwise have been necessitated by the ecological challenge. However, such reformist potentialities of the state system will depend upon enlightened leadership in the governments of the world on matters of population policy and economic development. The implementation of such potentialities will also require effective compromise among states with vastly diverse interests, technological capacities, and socio-economic status, and on matters as crucial as allocating ocean resources and sharing many of the fruits of new technologies. Earth-resource satellite surveys, weather surveying, information storage and dispersal, and nuclear power are only some of the areas in which it

will be important to spread the benefits of technological advances. To create and sustain such an atmosphere of international cooperation would require, in my view, a substantial dismantling of the war system, as well as a far more successful mobilization of national resources to meet human needs than we have seen to date. To some degree, the multinationalization of business operations, with its claims to represent a "new globalism" rather than a "new *imperium*," might provide some of the inspiration needed for achieving drastic global reform.[28] Also of some importance is the rapid growth of international private (i.e., nongovernmental) institutions in a wide variety of areas (e.g., the German Marshall Fund, the Japan Fund, Amnesty International, the International Commission of Jurists, the Club of Rome, and so on).

2) *Coercive/imperial centralization as a new world-order system:* Pressure brought about by increasing scarcity of land and resources could easily induce national leaders to adopt imperial methods in their efforts to stabilize the world situation. Indeed, such a trend may already be operating at the present time, as the rich and powerful seek to harmonize their own interests and relationships, while policing the poor and weak—but numerous and desperate—with various counterinsurgency techniques. From this perspective, a bipolar detente (with the possible inclusion of other power centers) could be regarded as the incubus for a domineering world-state structure. The control of nuclear weaponry would probably require that the system have at least two capitals, but a limited number of existing governments could seek to centralize global policy on resource use and to achieve minimum conservationist and environmental-quality goals without jeopardizing existing patterns of privilege and stratification. The severity of the scarcity and the ethos of the controllers would determine the extent to which the new world order became openly despotic and repressive. If a spirit of humanity (i.e., a stress on peace and equity in human relations) were to prevail and be sustained by favorable technological developments, such a new *imperium* could perhaps be made acceptable, especially if it relied on indirect rule and minimal governance.[29] Perhaps such a consolidated world-order system could limit itself to policing the technological capacities of the world against misuse or disruption.

Unfortunately, such an eventuality is not very likely to materialize. The formation of this kind of *imperium* is only likely to come about in a time of acute scarcity and in an atmosphere of ecological alarm. It may also be abetted, or even caused, by expectations that rise faster than the domestic capacities to meet them; such a gap between expectations and capacities has already often led to domestic repression and abrupt changes in international relations. Coercion and repression seem integral to the process of establishing and maintaining a system of global supervision based on great-power domination.

In any case, the most powerful states may come to feel extremely vulnerable to disruption by escalating terror tactics. In this eventuality, such governments may undertake actively to disarm the weaker and poorer regions of the world, subjecting them at the same time to rigorous forms of imperial administration, including surveillance and suppression of any threatening mode of deviance.[30] It seems likely that such a global strategy, by its very character, would necessarily be preceded by the destruction of democracy in the United States. Such a precedent is already being set in an increasing number of countries where consensual government has been forcibly replaced by repressive forms of policy and military rule (e.g., Brazil, Chile, South Africa, and Rhodesia). In such circumstances, governance would involve protracted counter-revolutionary warfare on a global scale, since popular sentiment would be strongly aligned with insurgent goals. To offset its universal unpopularity, the constituted authorities would come to rely on terror and military repression, both at home and abroad.

3) *Voluntary/contractual centralization:* This third response to the ecological challenge seems the least likely to come about but also the most desirable. Its prospects depend on a long period of preparation that would allow the necessary value changes to occur in the principal societies of the world. The foreign-policy proposals outlined earlier in this essay are partly intended to facilitate this necessary development of public awareness, at least in the United States. The sooner a transnational movement for voluntary global reform takes shape, the better the prospects for a gradual, nonviolent transition to some variant of voluntary/contractual centralization; in other words, intergovernmental agreements will provide the foundation for a program of drastic global reform.

There are some signs that such a movement is emerging and will be strengthened in the years ahead:

—a growing awareness of the fundamental character of the ecological challenge;

—a growing effort by transnationally-oriented groups—the Club of Rome, editorial board of *The Ecologist,* Institute for World Order—to devise both systematic and politically serious responses to the ecological challenge;

—a realization that world poverty is endangering the well-being of hundreds of millions of people, many of whom are unable to obtain even enough food to sustain basic health;

—widespread disillusionment with the state system arising from the horror of modern war and the vulnerability of all societies to military attack;

—the growth of a global cultural perspective associated with the greater mobility of people, things, and ideas, and the dissemination of the "Apollo Vision" of the earth as an island spinning in space;

—the economic organizational drive to create a single all-embracing market with minimal distortion from national policies, and the technological capacities (e.g., computers and jet travel) to administer such a system;

—strong functional pressures for global patterns and structures of cooperation in relation to environmental policy, ocean-resource development, suppression of terrorism using satellite broadcasting;

—a movement by politically moderate, medium-sized national governments to make it more generally understood that a coercive global tyranny is likely to emerge unless a voluntary system of central guidance is made effective.

IV. Arms-Control Policy and World-Order Reform

Two premises underlie my approach to arms-control and world-order reform:

1) the ecological challenge has been sufficiently substantiated to warrant the serious study of world-order options;

2) any given option is worthy of endorsement only if it can be brought into being through voluntary and contractual means.[31]

In the light of these major premises, I propose that we consider arms-control objectives as though we were operating late in the life of the state system. The first issue is not whether there will be a new world-order system, but whether the one that emerges will come about convulsively (by catastrophe), coercively (by conquest and domination), or voluntarily (by a consensus of opinion). The second issue concerns the design of a future world-order system that can both meet the ecological challenge and allow the human species to overcome the forces that now appear to threaten its well-being, even its survival.[32] I would like here to stress the importance of designing voluntary transition plans and world-order models with a normative consensus on the primacy of minimizing war, poverty, oppression, and environmental decay.[33] At the very least, such a program for global reform should eliminate the more serious drawbacks of the present world-order system, but it could also include more positive goals. However, at this point any emphasis on far-reaching goals (such as individual and group realization) would be both premature and distracting. Global reform should be a continuous process; any reformist success should serve to extend the horizon and bring new goals to the fore.

This approach to the analysis of global prospects can be briefly depicted in schematic terms: Let S_1 represent the existing world-order system, S_2 and S_3 future world-order systems, and S_0 the present point of origin; the location of S_0 near to the end of S_1 expresses a personal judgment as to the relative durability of S_1.

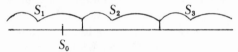

The interval from S_0 to S_2 is denoted as the transition interval, and for convenience this transition period is divided into three stages:

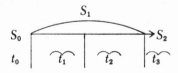

T_1 will be characterized primarily by changes in political awareness in the leading centers of existing power and authority, i.e., domestic arenas of principal sovereign states; t_2 is associated with mobilization for action; t_3 with institutional transformation. This transition sequence is intended only to convey an expected pattern of emphasis; the transition process in real time will be overlapping and cyclical, most likely resembling a spiral rather than the linear form that this analytical scheme suggests.

An effort should be made in t_1 to build public understanding and support for global reform on the basis of the four minimization goals and on the premise that the existing world-order system must be changed by voluntary means within the next several decades. Even given these design constraints, there is an array of S_2 options, ranging from a highly differentiated federal structure to a loose confederation. These various options cannot be discussed in detail here, but in my judgment a preference model for S_2 would rely on a form of "central guidance" that meets the demands of the ecological challenge while involving a minimal bureaucratic buildup and a maximal dispersal of power and authority.[34] This preference model of S_2 would try to combine functional specialization with elaborate checks and balances in political super-vision.[35] The potentialities of information and communications technology would make it possible to develop efficient structures of authority during the transition process (from S_0 to S_2) that have a minimal dependence upon a hierarchical organization.[36]

Within such a movement for drastic global reform there would be a specific role for arms-control advocacy within the United States, a role shaped also by the foreign policy assessments made in Section II. The principal opportunity to promote global reform during t_1 lies in awakening public consciousness to the need, feasibility, and character of a positive S_2. There are also other reform missions in t_1, including the stabilization of relations among governments in S_1 to allow more time for the transi-tion and for the emergence of a global consensus on the nature of peace, justice, and governance in S_2.

In t_1, arms-control advocates can help build the sort of public awareness needed in this country by supporting specific policies and lines of approach, including:

—declaratory measures of weapons renunciation, especially first-use options with respect to nuclear weapons;

—redesign of second-use deterrence systems to minimize damage and civilian casualties, vulnerability to accident and miscalculation, and waste of scarce resources;

—creation of standby war-prevention and conflict-confinement capabilities, partly under international auspices; such capabilities would not be dependent upon ad hoc inter-governmental consensus;

—adoption of unilateral measures to initiate and accelerate a reverse arms race at the strategic level and to negotiate arms-spending ceilings throughout the world;[37]

—declaratory and negotiated restraints on the sale of arms;

—strengthening procedures for dispute settlement and peaceful change so that legislative alternatives to war begin to gain strength.

My point is that, from the perspective of world order, arms control has a major educational role to play. Global reform, engineered by voluntary planning and rein-forced by popular and leadership support, depends upon what is essentially a learning process that will be characterized in its early stages by value changes and altered states of political awareness. A great deal of debate will be necessary before the renunciation of first-use options or the redesign of second-use systems becomes politically feasible; this debate will itself have great educational value because it will create direct controversy between those loyal to the state system and those who ad-vocate drastic world-order reform.[38] Thus, such a discourse could help shape a con-sensus on whether or not S_1 was durable enough to deal with mounting pressures against it. Because arms policy is so central to the functioning of the state system, efforts to replace the logic of laissez-faire rivalry by a more cooperative policy could become central dramas of immense historical significance. The outcome cannot be confidently predicted at this time, but the early enactment of such a drama within the United States would undoubtedly raise the question for other societies as well. In t_1, the immediate period ahead, two elements of global reform should be understood:

—the world-order learning process will be primarily internal, especially for prin-cipal states, although directions of response in one domestic arena will generate trans-national effects in the others.

—such a segmented learning process, adapted to the immense diversities of national and group situations, could have a number of results. It might produce convergent attitudes, although not yet a global consensus, regarding both the inevitability of a transition from S_1 to S_2 and the desirability of creating S_2 by voluntary (contractual) means as soon as possible. On the other hand, the learning process could lead to a generally approved and well-substantiated dismissal of the ecological challenge as an issue in international affairs on the grounds that its significance has been exaggerated.[39]

V. Three Possible Objections

I should now like briefly to consider three of the most important lines of objection to this approach to arms control. First of all, it may be argued that the gap between academic problem-solvers and governmental problem-staters has been broadened to unmanageable proportions. Arms-control negotiations inch forward, based on a painful process of intra-governmental and intra-societal consensus that is, at best, rather delicate. To encumber this process with an array of concerns arising from the credibility of the ecological challenge is not desirable. My response is simple: A scholar-citizen working in this subject needs to depict the situation objectively. He may sacrifice some short-term influence on the policy-makers, but, to the extent that his statements of the problems adhere to the facts, the evidence will eventually bear out his appraisals and ultimately come to influence policy. A time of transitional crisis may be identified, in part, by the size of the gap between problem-solvers and problem-staters, but only thought-control advocates or extreme cynics would want to narrow that gap out of deference to the meager capabilities of governmental problem-solvers. For the moment, the immediate objective is to reform *behavior* in the realm of foreign policy (i.e., national strategies of participation), but only *attitude* or orientation with regard to the broader issues of world order.

A second objection would contend that an analysis of this sort tends to overstate the role of reason and reasonableness in governmental and human behavior. In essence, no appeal to evidence is likely to be influential in the realms of power, where bureaucratic factors of habit, interest, and pressure prevail. I would agree that the reasonableness of an argument does not very frequently account for basic behavior. However, a persuasive argument based on evidence may strengthen the position of members of the elite already amenable to change, or the tactics and strategies of counter-elites.[40] In any event, analysis and evidence are fundamental to education, and education in global reform should be given high priority in the present period of turmoil and confusion.

A third objection might maintain that, if a nation such as the United States prematurely accepts the case for drastic world-order reform, it may become particularly vulnerable to the rapacity of some less enlightened states. It, along with other more enlightened states, would then be risking exposure to a known evil for the sake of pursuing an uncertain good. Again, this anxiety seems at least premature. A learning process that would include acute sensitivity to the behavior of possible rivals should provide sufficient reassurance. Loyalists to the state system—a commanding majority for the foreseeable future—would also lose no opportunity to publicize any evidence of attempts by other powers to take unfair advantage of shifts in foreign-policy position and world-order perspective.[41] Especially in the area of arms control, the huge overkill arsenal of weaponry provides an enormous safety factor that insures a long period of virtually risk-free experimentation with global-reform postures.

In short, each of these objections contains some partial truths, but neither separately nor cumulatively do they convincingly refute the case for drastic global reform. It still seems essential to advance the case for foreign-policy and world-order reform in emphatic terms and to clarify the link between the two in the setting of arms-control policy.

VI. Conclusion

This essay has made two main points: First, the present foreign policy of the United States is sustaining old patterns of behavior at a time when fundamental changes are both possible and necessary. The possibility has been provided by the ending of American combat in the Indochina War and the muting of the Cold War. The necessity has been created by the damaging domestic and global consequences of sustaining a counter-revolutionary mission in many parts of the Third World and by the continuing large investment in military capabilities during a period of national peace and relative international stability.

Second, foreign-policy reforms of the sort specified above need to be supplemented by a serious consideration of the pressures building up against the existing world-order system dominated by interacting states. These pressures are inducing a variety of globalizing tendencies, especially manifest in new patterns of great-power geopolitics and in the extraordinary surge of multinational corporate activity. These tendencies fall short of an adequate response to the pressures on the state system, because they neither deal directly with the ecological challenge (pollution and shortage of resources), nor do they provide a response to the great blights of poverty, war, oppression, and waste.

These two dimensions of appraisal influence our assessment of arms-control policy. In the first instance, arms-control policy is, and should be, an integral part of a rational foreign policy for the nation; it should not be considered autonomous (except for bureaucratic reforms) or be subject to inviolable domestic political constraints. Therefore, it is important that the United States take both the unilateral and the cooperative (i.e., negotiated) actions necessary to implement the possibilities for arms control that would be implicit in a renunciation of counter-insurgency military options and in other concrete steps to move beyond the hostile confrontations associated with Cold War tensions. These arms-control steps involve the relationship of the United States to Third World conflict, as well as our strategic arms competition with the Soviet Union. Arms sales, military and policy training and aid programs, foreign bases and deployments, and defense spending levels are among the areas appropriate for creative, bold, arms-control activity. More ambitiously, perhaps, this may now be the time to revive the consideration of "deep disarmament" and even "general and complete disarmament." The war system is more dangerous than ever, but rarely succeeds in translating battlefield victories into political settlements; the dangers of the future are bound to become greater as the technology of mass destruction is dispersed around the globe to governing elites and even to desperate counter-elites. In addition, arms spending squanders resources at a time of growing resource depletion and

deepening poverty. The failure to consider drastic disarmament may become one
more depressing confirmation of an unsuspected kinship between the human species
and the lemming.

With respect to reforming the world-order system, our immediate emphasis must
be upon education; several key tenets should be central to this educational campaign:
1) the state system is not able to deal with the agenda of human concerns very
   successfully;
2) a large number of attractive alternatives to the state system exist, some of
   which do not involve concentrating power and authority in a governmental
   center;
3) the process of transforming the state system should proceed by nonviolent and
   voluntary means;
4) global reform needs to be conceived as a continuous learning process;
5) a consensus favorable to drastic global reform must initially be shaped
   simultaneously in various national arenas throughout the world; and
6) while the war system is the Achilles heel of the state system, the new awareness
   may become more closely associated with insights into the ecological unity
   of the planet.

From an arms-control perspective, global reform is, for the moment, in an
educational rather than a structured phase. Renunciation of specific military
options—first-use of nuclear weapons, counter-insurgency roles, excessively cruel
weaponry—would revitalize the vague renunciations of aggressive force contained in
the United Nations Charter. In essence, arms-control thinking needs to subvert the
role of force in the pursuit of national goals. It should emphasize the degree to which
the war system drains national treasuries while providing only the most fragile sort of
security shield, a shield which, if punctured, threatens those that it protects as well as
those it is designed to menace with virtual extinction.

High priority, then, belongs to the conceptualization and study of alternative
systems of world order in which the war system is eliminated or drastically curtailed.
No longer is such a futurist inquiry a utopian exercise for a questing imagination. It
should be of relevance to the practitioners of power who govern our destiny as a nation and as a species. If arms-control thinking breaks this new ground in the decade
ahead, then it will have fulfilled a basic function in history.

REFERENCES

[1] The author wishes to thank the following readers of earlier drafts for their suggestions: Robert Art,
Harvey Brooks, Abram Chayes, George Rathjens, Leonard Rodberg, and Janet Lowenthal for her editorial
suggestions.

[2] The persisting Soviet role in the Middle East has certainly dampened American enthusiasm for
detente and discouraged the widely held sentiment in this country that the improvement in Soviet-
American relations was so fundamental as to be virtually irreversible. Mr. Nixon's political collapse, Soviet
repression of prominent dissenters and anti-Israel posture, renewed turbulence in China, the election of a
pro-American government in France, and, perhaps most of all, Soviet resentments over Congressional attempts to condition economic relations on Jewish emigration rights are among the developments in Nixon's
second presidential term that made the future of Soviet-American relations much more problematic than it
had been at the end of his first. Such a pessimistic assessment of trends is to a degree offset by Secretary Kissinger's bipartisan status as a peace-maker and the architect of United States foreign policy.

[3] The tentative Soviet-American understanding reached at Vladivostok in 1974 to put "a cap" on the offensive arms race illustrates the problem of perception. Is this agreement to be considered a breakthrough, as officials of the negotiating governments maintain, or is it better understood as a mystifying gesture made in the name of arms control, but with no dampening effects on war risks or defense costs? A positive claimant can point to the historic establishment of upper limits. On the skeptical side, it can be pointed out that the agreed limits place almost no constraints, as the ceilings are higher than existing arsenals and, in any event, the limits simply legitimize a shift from quantitative arms buildups to qualitative competition. On balance, it would seem that the cynic's view of arms control has by far the better side in the argument, at least vis-à-vis the Vladivostok outcome.

[4] Addressing the conference Pacem in Terris III in October, 1973, even Henry Kissinger called for a national debate on America's world role as a necessary prelude to crystallizing a new domestic consensus for foreign-policy purposes. Because domestic factors so often predominate, it is clear that no given course for United States foreign policy is likely to succeed over time unless it has a domestic mandate. Obviously non-democratic societies can conduct a foreign policy without such a mandate, although analogous requirements for agreement probably exist. It is quite probable that no such consensus on American foreign-policy goals will be achieved in the years just ahead, because isolationist-versus-interventionist issues will not be resolved for some time. But I think it safe to conclude that the appropriate role of direct and indirect military activity by the United States in foreign conflicts is likely to remain both controversial and central to the American foreign-policy process.

[5] See Henry A. Kissinger, "Making Foreign Policy," The Center Magazine, 7 (1974), 34-39, esp. p. 39.

[6] Henry A. Kissinger, American Foreign Policy (New York, 1969), p. 89; for a fuller discussion along the same lines, see Kissinger, The Necessity for Choice: Prospects of American Foreign Policy (New York, 1961), esp. pp. 169-339.

[7] U. S. Foreign Policy for the 1970's—Shaping a Durable Peace, A Report to the Congress by Richard Nixon, May 3, 1973 (Washington, D. C., Government Printing Office, 1973), p. 202.

[8] Ibid., p. 204.

[9] Note that this Nixonian formulation of balance does not allow for equivalence in capabilities achieved by different weapons systems, but seems to depend instead on equivalence of the weapons systems themselves. Such a definition of 'balance' results in great inflexibility, complicating and constraining arms-control prospects still further.

[10] The purpose of this fifth requirement is undoubtedly also to reassure China that bipolar arms-control agreements are not being concluded at her expense.

[11] Nixon to Congress (cf. note 6), p. 18.

[12] Ibid., p. 180.

[13] Ibid., p. 187.

[14] Michael M. May, Wall Street Journal, May 24, 1974, p. 10.

[15] It is admittedly not easy to alter abruptly the drift of American foreign policy in a responsible fashion. Alliances may remain constructive in some regions of the world. In any event, the withdrawal of superpower involvement should be undertaken with care and in an even-handed fashion. There are two distinct concerns: first, asymmetrical withdrawal might expose allies to pressures or even to attack, inducing adversaries to make miscalculations, and conceivably leading to warfare, thereby generating more dangerous and costly forms of reinvolvement; secondly, it might have destabilizing consequences on the internal public-order systems of those states previously dependent for their security on American credibility, as manifested through forward deployment. At the same time, there is no plausible argument for sustaining the American posture of support for counter-revolutionary regimes nor for the American role in planning, training, and executing counter-insurgency missions. This Third World role has been thoroughly discredited by the Indochina involvement. In an atmosphere of detente the Cold War arguments for Third World involvement

are no longer valid, and it is almost impossible to furnish an acceptable security rationale for our past and continuing embrace of reactionary regimes. The only convincing rationale remaining would have to involve the protection of American world economic interests, a rationale our leadership has so far refused to provide.

[16] The issue here, too, is whether there are reasonable policies leading to global unity that responsible national leaders can support. Such support could be manifested in official attitudes toward the United Nations and other international cooperative endeavors. Our leaders could begin to create a political conscience based on human solidarity and upon the need for global planning and sharing as the sole viable basis for upholding the security of Americans. See Lester R. Brown, *World Without Borders* (New York, 1972); Barry Commoner, *The Closing Circle* (New York, 1971); Barbara Ward and René Dubos, *Only One Earth* (New York, 1972); Louis René Beres and Harry Targ, *Reordering the Planet* (Boston, 1973); Edward Goldsmith and others, *Blueprint for Survival* (Boston, 1972); Richard A. Falk, *This Endangered Planet: The Prospects and Proposals for Human Survival* (New York, 1971); Richard A. Falk, *A Study of Future Worlds* (New York, 1975).

[17] There is an ambiguity surrounding the conception of "direct attack." The core idea is clear—a major military attack against the United States needs to be deterred by all possible means. But what of attacks against close allies? Can the United States abandon these allies in the event that they are the victim of such an attack? If not, is it not preferable to be clear about the intent to respond in order to deter direct attacks on American allies? And if this is the case, then cannot one defend the logic, although perhaps not the extent, of forward deployment? And, finally, is there any prospect of inducing the Soviet Union to cease to include within its definition of national security the defense of its close allies against direct attack? In effect, it becomes difficult for the United States to opt out of the mainstream of geopolitics in any dramatic way without incurring greater costs than it now incurs. Therefore a rational foreign policy for the United States seems to require a combination of marginal adjustments to cut the risks and costs of geopolitical patterns and a major effort to transform mainstream geopolitics from a statist to a globalist mold (i.e., world-order perspective).

[18] The United States has never considered itself responsible for guaranteeing the status quo everywhere. Indeed, it has welcomed shifts to the right brought about by coups and illegal violence, although in larger Third World countries it has generally limited itself to exerting marginal influence through diplomatic and economic levers.

[19] The nuclear dimension, indeed, makes a more serious case for the earlier claim that national military capabilities are primarily concerned with keeping the peace among states. The mutuality of deterrence has very likely prevented a third world war from arising, as the prospect of nuclear devastation makes recourse to war a very desperate last resort, rather than the result of a weighing of the probable costs and benefits. The stabilizing effects of nuclear weaponry among the central powers has not prevented either warfare in the periphery of the international system or the military involvement of the central powers in these peripheral wars. Perhaps the most impressive argument along these lines is to be found in Robert E. Osgood and Robert W. Tucker, *Force, Order, and Justice* (Baltimore, 1967).

[20] See McGeorge Bundy, "To Cap the Volcano," *Foreign Affairs*, 48 (1969), 1-20; Fred Charles Iklé, "Can Nuclear Deterrence Last Out the Century?" *Foreign Affairs*, 51 (1973), 267-285; Herbert York, "A Proposal for a Saner Deterrent" (mimeographed); Wolfgang K. H. Panofsky, "The Mutual-Hostage Relationship between America and Russia," *Foreign Affairs*, 52 (1973), 109-118.

[21] It is unclear whether it would be possible, or even desirable, to build a consensus among governments involving the renunciation of war, even in the face of widely endorsed revisionist goals. At present, despite the provisions of the United Nations Charter, no such consensus exists.

[22] One underestimated difficulty with war-prevention schemes is their failure to take account of the traditional role of force in accomplishing social and political change. Without non-violent alternatives to war, it is unrealistic to expect any legalistic framework for prohibition to succeed, nor is it necessarily in the human interest that it should. Obviously, the line between what is tolerable in the name of self-determination and what must be prohibited in the name of world peace is exceedingly difficult to specify in the abstract. In practice, the need to determine on which side of the line a given issue falls should help to sensitize governments to the importance of decoupling local tests of strength from wider global systems of geopolitical equilibrium.

[23] I have attempted a rationale for comprehensive no-first-use pledges as an arms-control measure in "Renunciation of Nuclear Weapons Use," in Bennett Boskey and Mason Willrich, eds., *Nuclear Proliferation: Prospects for Control* (New York, 1970) pp. 133-145.

[24] A substantial ecological challenge can only be met successfully by some reliable mechanism for global administration, which will assure that the planet as a whole is not being imperiled by the behavior of any of its parts. Such managerial globalization need not be hierarchical or governmental in structure, but it must be capable of effective and efficient coordination where standards of behavior or allocations of scarce resources are necessary. Structures of central guidance can be designed with safeguards for diversity in economic, social, and political organization.

[25] Responses 2) and 3) may differ more in tone than in substance. The second response accepts the need to globalize planetary management, whereas the third response is generally confident about the capacities of the state system to endure, provided enlightened leadership emerges to meet the ecological challenge.

[26] I have developed this line of analysis of prospects for global reform in "The Logic of State Sovereignty Versus the Requirements of World Order," *Yearbook of World Affairs*, 1973, pp. 7-23.

[27] World Order Models Project described in Thomas Weiss, "The WOMP of the Institute for World Order," *Peace and Change*, 2 (Spring, 1973), 1-2; Ian Baldwin, Jr., "Thinking About a New World Order for the Decade 1990," *War/Peace Report*, 10 (1970), 3-8. The World Order Models Project is the first comprehensive effort by scholars to design a plausible and desirable future world-order system. Each of the eight groups of scholars arrives at its own independent judgment on world-order problems and solutions, supplying the intellectual diversity that is needed at this stage of international awareness.

[28] It is difficult to evaluate the relative importance to the world order of the rise of the multinational corporation as an important element in world affairs. Does the multinational corporation promise to provide economic prosperity for all peoples living where it operates, or does it offer such a promise mainly to existing enclaves of a small, wealthy upper stratum? Is the multinational corporation generally a substitute for governmental forms of imperialism, or is it a genuine alternative that is increasingly successful in its claim to possess an anational identity? Will multinational corporate growth help sustain the war system by building "military industrial complexes" wherever it operates, or will these multinational corporations come to favor dismantling the war system so as to assure stable operating conditions in a market that embraces as much of the world as possible? Can a profit-seeking corporation contribute effectively to social reform and human well-being in a world beset by mass poverty and extreme inequality?

[29] The proponents of economic growth, larger foreign-aid programs, and an expanded development role for international lending institutions all share a belief in the capacity of the present global system to evolve in a manner ultimately beneficial for mankind, often combined with a profound distrust of, or antipathy to, alternative global designs (regarding them as utopian, in the sense of being unattainable).

[30] As has so often been the case with unpopular methods of control, elaborate efforts to disguise them would be attempted. The imperialism of the duopoly may be hidden beneath attractive labels— "controlling regional arms races," "arms control and disarmament," and "international peacekeeping." The Soviet-American role in the Middle East deserves careful study in this respect. Is this role an experiment in duopolistic management, where arms buildups are encouraged to establish influence and are then followed by the imposition of settlements designed to assure stability of influence? How else, except through Soviet and American guarantees, can a Middle East settlement be reached? How else can guarantees be relied upon except by introducing elements of a military presence? The mystification process reaches its final embodiment when the victim countries of the world call for such solutions.

[31] Other world-order options, whose origins would be neither voluntary nor contractual, should also be studied and understood, especially since their emergence seems more likely at the present time.

[32] Among the requirements for a coherent world-order design are the following: normative goals of universal application; a time horizon that extends for several decades, perhaps even for centuries; a systematic framework of inquiry that embraces all principal elements relevant to the process of change; a conception of transitional tactics and strategies; images of a preferred world.

[33] These minimizing objectives are not always reconcilable in specific contexts of choice; tradeoffs will

have to be made between, say, improving the distribution of wealth and preserving environmental quality. Nevertheless, a program of global reform, if it is to succeed fully, would have to make cumulative progress over time in all four areas. See Garrett Hardin, *Exploring New Ethics for Survival: The Voyage of the Spaceship Beagle* (New York, 1972); Van Rensselaer Potter, *Bioethics: Bridge to the Future* (Englewood Cliffs, New Jersey, 1971).

³⁴ These ideas are set forth in more detail in my essay "Toward a New World Order: Modest Methods and Drastic Visions," in Saul H. Mendlovitz, ed., *On Creating a Just World Order* (New York, 1975).

³⁵ Functional specialization refers to the distribution of tasks in different areas of international life to specialized agencies organized on a regional and global basis (e.g., health, food, environment, ocean resources, space, disarmament). Elaborate checks and balances would be designed to frustrate efforts to concentrate power in the general-purpose institutions needed both to assure some political direction in matters of global policy and to coordinate functional activities. The relationship between efficiency and protection from global tyranny would be the principal constitutional problem for designers of models for drastic global reform.

³⁶ Breakthroughs in information technology have such radical significance because they permit efficient organization without hierarchical structure. These breakthroughs may allow the world-order system to develop mechanisms of coordination and procedures for mutual guidance without building up the sort of institutional "critical mass" that is associated with "world government" conceptions. This administrative possibility would become politically attractive if it were combined with social and technological break-throughs (e.g., greatly reduced energy costs) that would alleviate, if not altogether eliminate, world poverty. For a creative consideration of non-centralized sanctions, see W. Michael Reisman, "Sanctions and Enforcement," in Cyril E. Black and Richard A. Falk, eds., *The Future of the International Legal Order*, III (Princeton, N. J., 1971), 273-335.

³⁷ A 'reverse arms race' refers to the interactive dynamics of reductions in arms spending, military posturing, and the demilitarization of foreign policy. As a government proceeds in this direction, cautiously at first, it reinforces comparable tendencies in adversary societies, or at least it provides such tendencies with an opportunity for further development. This type of arms-control "methodology" lies somewhere between formal arms-control measures negotiated and embodied in treaty form and unilateral initiatives undertaken for purely domestic reasons (e.g., reforms in weapons-procurement practices or constraints on presidential war-making powers).

³⁸ Of course this discourse will also be shaped by differing assessments of the existing inter-governmental setting, especially judgments made about the intentions and capabilities of major rival governments.

³⁹ Note that such a choice does not envision agreement on the character of S_2 at this stage, but only on whether it is necessary, and if it is, on the further necessity to achieve transition by peaceful and voluntary means. The next stage of the discourse would proceed to the shape of a new system of world order that would be both desirable and attainable within a given period.

⁴⁰ Consider, for instance, the role of Marx and Lenin in the world Communist movement. Critics of the state system must develop a persuasive ideology that can effectively convey their fears and preferences to others.

⁴¹ The shift in American geopolitical posture from Cold War to detente provides a constructive analogy. Cold War diehards, such as Senator Henry Jackson, require that advocates of detente vindicate their interpretation of events at every step along the path. The need to sustain a popular and governmental consensus requires advocates of reform—detente, in this instance—to demonstrate continuously that the old assumptions about Soviet behavior are no longer applicable. A policy shift is not an event in time, but a process through time that can be slowed, speeded, and even reversed.

MARSHALL D. SHULMAN

Arms Control in an International Context

THE EFFORT TO REDUCE the danger of war by constraining military competition is not, as Lord Byron said of man's love, "a thing apart." It is rather more like woman's love (on the same authority), an inseparable part of life. Arms control is generally treated as a separable subject for analytical purposes, within the finite boundaries of the military game; but only when it is studied in the context of domestic and international life can we begin to understand why it is that in practice the course of reason does not very often prevail.

By its nature, the study of arms control involves a three-way conversation between scientists, military theoreticians, and students of politics. In the beginning—that is, in the decade starting in the mid-nineteen-fifties—the lead was taken by the technicians. The scientists took to their blackboards to explain the awesome facts of life in the new nuclear age. Soon we were all talking the jargon of "circular error probability," "overpressure," "yield to weight ratio," and "target acquisition." In the truly creative decade of arms control that followed, the basic concepts took shape that we have relied on ever since—the characteristics of a retaliatory second-strike capability as well as all the other elements of the vision of the stable deterrent balance that were to be the most feasible hope of security and survival in the age of intercontinental nuclear-missile weapons.

But, despite this brilliant conceptual effort to stabilize strategic military competition, men and nations went their own refractory way toward still higher levels of destructive capabilities. The baffling contrast between the arms controllers' assumptions of rationality and the behavior of the real world led to a shift of emphasis in the early nineteen-seventies toward the political dimensions of the subject. All who had served in government knew from their experiences that there was little correspondence between the rational models of decision-making and the donneybrook world of service rivalries, bureaucratic jostling, and the clash of parochial interests of pressure groups that determine the way nations behave in practice. While the intellectually more interesting conceptual state of the art moved but slightly from the high plateau it had reached, the facts of life that politicians take for granted became the new preoccupation of the arms-control community. Belatedly and a shade reluctantly, they turned their attention to domestic politics—to the decision-making process and to the bureaucracies and the political and economic constituencies involved in it.

But there is another lesson not yet sufficiently drawn from the study of politics: that the living context in which arms control has to be studied is one of competition and conflict among nation-states, and no amount of technical ingenuity can free us from the necessity of taking into account the competing ambitions of nations for territory, for influence, and for power. Let us go back to first principles. If the essential purpose of arms control is to reduce the danger of a catastrophic war, it has become increasingly clear that the relatively unsuccessful effort to constrain the number of weapons in the overswollen arsenals of the superpowers is only a symptomatic, palliative response to the dominant characteristic of international politics in the present period—that is, the disintegration of the international system as we have known it. Over the three decades that have passed since World War II, international politics has been dominated by the American-Soviet rivalry, partially stabilized by the deterrent balance between the United States and the Soviet Union, and by the restored economic power of Western Europe. Now we are witnessing the emergence of a new group of Middle East oil-producing states to a position of economic, political, and military power, a growing desperation among other developing nations, an economic crisis within and among the Western industrialized states and Japan, and a growing sense of impotence in Western Europe, against the background of continuing military and industrial technological changes that are transforming international life and altering both the configurations of power and the nature of power. The dominant trends in the international system are toward disintegration into violence and anarchy, and any approach to arms control that does not take sufficient account of this central fact is bound to be of limited relevance.

Illustrations of the involvement of international politics in the efforts to negotiate arms-control agreements can be drawn from innumerable familiar examples. There can be no doubt that the United States and the Soviet Union, along with the rest of the world, would be more secure if their arsenals of strategic weapons could be stabilized at half or even a quarter of their present levels. Surely this should be a matter of common interest, and yet the American-Soviet strategic arms limitation talks (SALT) that have taken place over the past five years have so far not been able to keep pace with the continuous accumulation of weapons for mass destruction. It is not only the technical complexity of the respective weapons systems and the internal negotiations within each country that account for the disappointingly slow progress, but also the essential character of the rivalry for power and political influence between these two countries, complicated by their differences in political culture and ideology. Even as it has become clear that the pursuit of strategic superiority cannot yield a significant military advantage to either side, the belief persists that marginal advantages in one weapons system or another may nevertheless have psychological consequences upon the political behavior of adversaries or their allies. The notion of the "credibility" of the deterrent is thought to be measured not by "hardware" alone, but by political will; and indeed the concept of deterrence itself rests upon political perceptions of the intensity of interests, will, and determination of the political leaderships at least as much as it does upon the amount of explosive power at their command. But the psychology of political rivalry has encouraged the persistence of myths regarding the putative political effect of marginal disparities in one category or another of weapons, despite the obvious facts that both countries are well above any reasonable level of deterrence and that only a few weapons would cause unimaginable destruction. In addition to the question of whether the perceptions of the people of other countries are so sensitive to such disparities as politicians and military planners fear, there is the further question of the extent to which their perceptions are shaped by voices of advocacy within the United States and to some extent the Soviet Union crying alarm over perceived or potential gaps in the diverse capabilities of one country or the other.

There are many other examples that could be drawn from SALT to illustrate the involvements of international politics as warp and woof of the problem. The ebb and flow of Sino-Soviet apprehensions is clearly a factor in the negotiations. The announcement by an American President of the arrival of an "era of negotiations" and by the political leader of the Soviet Union of an era of "peaceful coexistence" created the political climate needed for the onset of negotiations, although the reiteration of ideological commitments, however ritualistic, serves as a reminder of incompatible if not hostile ultimate political purposes and is chilling to the growth of confidence necessary to substantial progress in arms limitation. The politics of alliance relationships has been reflected in such issues as forward-based systems, the non-transfer of weapons, and the proposed inclusion of British and French nuclear weapons in the calculation of numbers in the American-Soviet balance.

Developments in Europe offer many other examples of the linkage between arms control and international politics. Negotiations nominally addressed to "European security" and "European force reduction" have in fact become arenas in which the contestants seek political advantages in the process and symbolism of negotiations, rather than in hope of substantive security arrangements. In Western Europe, domestic and international politics have combined to produce a defense strategy that is difficult to justify on any rational military grounds. The political unacceptability of a level of military conscription sufficient to provide a defense of Western Europe by conventionally armed forces has obliged NATO to accept a reliance upon tactical nuclear weapons that conjure up the possibility of a total devastation of the areas to be defended, as well as a widespread dispersion of nuclear weapons difficult to justify from an arms-control point of view. On the other side, the Soviet Union, in the name of "equal security," shows reluctance to diminish a preponderance on the ground, which protects its perceived political interests in Eastern Europe and is thought to have a salutary effect upon Western European political behavior, while neutralist trends are encouraged with talk of an unspecified "Pan-European" security system.

The urgent problem of nuclear proliferation offers another example of an aspect of arms control which cannot be addressed without reference to its political dimensions, including the reluctance of great powers to jeopardize their relations with potential nuclear nations, and even more, the persistent belief on the part of many nations that even a symbolic test explosion can yield political advantages as well as emotional satisfaction.

The examples cited have illustrated the point that many problems on the arms-control agenda today are so intertwined with political complications that technical approaches alone cannot be sufficient to resolve them. Beyond this argument for the integration of arms-control considerations into the broader aspects of foreign policy, there is a more far-reaching question whether the present direction of arms-control efforts is sufficiently responsive to the fundamental transformations in international politics now in process.

There has been at least a partial recognition that the relation between politics and war cannot remain unchanged in the face of the scale of destructiveness made possible by the radical leaps in military technology during the past three decades. What is only beginning to impinge on our consciousness is the realization that a chain of revolutionary transformations in international life is beginning to make its appearance as a result of changes in non-military technology as well. The accelerated introduction of new industrial technology in the advanced industrial states, the development of new sources of energy, the linkage of formerly remote parts of the world by instantaneous communication and jet transportation, the development of space technology—these are among the changes that affect both the process and the substance of international relations.

Partly as a consequence of these technological developments, the political economy of the international system—using "system" broadly to mean the patterns of prevailing relationships among nations—is undergoing radical transformation. Developments such as the oil embargo of 1973, which may have appeared to be transient perturbations at their outset, have clearly dispelled any comforting hope of returning to an earlier "normalcy." The intricate interdependency of the industrialized states, the spread of multinational corporations, the profound social and political consequences within the industrial states of the inflationary explosion, and the threatened breakdown of international monetary arrangements—exacerbated by sharp changes in the oil price structure, which has in turn created a new category of wealthy non-industrialized states—are among the manifestations of these transformations. So, too, is the emergence of the Soviet Union from its years of autarky, in search of capital and technology from abroad to enable it to keep abreast of the technological revolution. As a consequence, the Soviet-American relationship, once the polarizing determinant of post-war international politics, has become more mixed in character and less central to the international system than forces outside the control of these rival states, however great their destructive capabilities. The place of Western Europe, China, Japan, and the Middle Eastern oil-producing states in new balances of power is in flux, illustrating the widening variegation in the nature of politically effective power. The southern arc of Europe, from Portugal to Greece, has become an uncertain element in the strategic balance. The prospect of greater tensions in the relations between the industrial and the developing states grows more imminent as the gap between their capabilities widens and the strains on available sources of food and natural resources increase. Almost daily, the headlines speak of unemployment and famine, of guerrilla actions and terrorism, of the angry and expectant voices of the new majority in the United Nations—all testimony to the passing of the old order and its replacement by something still inchoate.

To identify the changing sources of conflict among these transformations in international politics as a step toward a reorientation of arms-control efforts would be a daunting task, given the complexity of the forces in motion, but some of the following elements come to mind as illustrative of the range of problems requiring study.

One of the most interesting structural features of the changing international scene has been the introduction of a new element of power into the international situation by the growing activities of business organizations across national boundaries. In the process of this expansion, businesses are creating new sources of tension and potential conflict; the result is a paradoxical heightening of both the delicacy and the possibilities for stability that can come with greater economic interdependence. Just as the technical base for international economic integration has been strengthened by the development of industrial technology, so too has the force of national resistance to this tendency been exacerbated within the industrialized countries. It is apparent that the marked heightening of tendencies toward nationalism is a major source of international conflict in the Western world, in the Soviet area, and in what has come to be called the "Third World."

A related concern is the growth of domestic social and political instabilities within the industrialized countries, reflecting the difficulty of adjustment to the rapidly changing conditions of life. Of particular relevance to the problems of arms control are the effects of diminished support for foreign policy in the face of increasing domestic preoccupations and the reduced political support for responsible leadership in articulating a national interest against the pressures of more parochial interests. The weakening of the domestic political base for support of responsible actions in the international realm has greatly complicated the search for concerted international solutions both to economic problems and to international conflicts generally. Further, the prospect that domestic instabilities within the countries of the Western alliance may result in the participation by Communist parties in their governments raises serious questions concerning the continued integrity of that alliance, with unsettling consequences for the power balance in Europe.

For those who are concerned with the moderation of conflict in the world, there are both hope and apprehension to be found in the effect of advancing industrialization upon the environment and the earth's natural resources—hope at the prospect that these issues will in time evoke a constructive response and strengthen international mechanisms at the expense of national sovereignty; but apprehension over the more immediate conflicts of interest between the advanced industrial countries, whose demands for raw materials are straining available supplies, and the acute desperation of developing countries, unable to maintain progress toward even minimum standards of food and living conditions for their growing populations. Along with these sources of conflict, technology has provided new methods for the expression of violence through terrorism, to which the urban societies are at the same time becoming increasingly vulnerable.

Many aspects of the Soviet-American relationship are influenced by transformations in international politics in ways that may have some bearing upon arms control. One possibly hopeful observation is that the domestic institutions of both the United States and the Soviet Union are clearly evolving in response to the imperatives of advancing industrialization, perhaps more than the political leadership of either country may intend or acknowledge. This does not mean that they will become alike—indeed the differences in their respective political cultures and historical experience suggest that they will not converge in essential respects—but it is likely to mean that the systems today called "Communist" and "capitalist" may be quite unrecognizable a few decades from now, and that consequently the ideological component of their rivalry may be attenuated. Even today, it may be observed that the insistent asseveration of the "ideological struggle" as an accompaniment to the policy of peaceful coexistence is powered less by fervor of conviction than by organizational interests.

A related point is the effect on the United States and the Soviet Union that advances in the technologies of communication and transportation are having, as they change the degree of interpenetration of each society with information and ideas from the other. It is becoming technically more and more difficult to maintain a closed society, particularly in a period of broadening economic, scientific, and cultural contacts. Although fundamentalists on both sides may see this interpenetration as subversion, it also presents an opportunity to dispel, through greater knowledge, the dark suspicions that feed "worst case" projections. Jet transportation has also made technically feasible frequent summit meetings between heads of state and foreign ministers, with consequences that remain to be fully evaluated. Such meetings can lead to public confusion over the separation of symbol and substance, and can have the effect, for good or ill, of by-passing traditional forms of diplomatic communication and bureaucratic channels. But it is also true that they can energize action by the bureaucracies to meet summit deadlines, and further that they directly involve political leaderships in detailed negotiations on arms control and related security problems and thereby accelerate the movement of leaders and publics along the learning curve toward a more enlightened security policy. To this extent, they widen the circle of those who are informed and involved in security policy beyond the small group of professional soldiers who tend to regard such matters as their exclusive domain and tend to see them within a purely technical framework.

The technical feasibility of a larger international flow of information also tends to increase accurate perceptions of the internal political processes of other countries, and this in turn encourages the negotiators to take into account the interplay of pressures and concerns that affect decision-making on the other side of the table. Signaling and "back-channel" communication to determine intent or to make exploratory inquiries have been greatly expanded as a consequence. It may also be argued that a symbiotic relationship is developing between cognate groups in adversary societies, in the form of implicit alliances or accelerated processes of interaction between them, as a result of the readier flow of information.

Another illustrative example of the influence of the new technologies of communication and transportation upon Soviet-American relations is one with negative consequences: the cushion of time and distance, which formerly delayed reactions to local conflicts in remote parts of the world, has given way to instantaneous reactions, with a resulting increase in the responsiveness of the international system. In searching for positive advantages in this development, one might have been tempted to claim a reduction in the opportunity for such excesses in remote areas as were once committed by the East India Tea Company, were it not for the—at best—mixed evidence of the Vietnam experience.

Although the net effect of these transforming factors has been to subordinate Soviet-American relations to other sources of international unrest, they also raise disquieting questions about the longer-term prospects for the present stabilization of this relationship at moderate, if fluctuating, levels of tension. The rise of the Soviet Union to the status of a great power in the world has been achieved less by the virtue of the performance of the Soviet system in meeting the needs of its people or the attraction of its particular form of socialism than by the awesome power of its large military establishment and its arsenal of destructive weapons. Will this reliance upon military power as a source of influence and status be argued successfully against the now dominant view that the future position of the Soviet Union as a great power depends upon the repair of deficiencies in its economy and the development of its advanced technological sector? The transformations in international politics tend to strengthen the argument that the technological base is the key to future power. At the same time, however, the instabilities in Western societies and economic relationships resulting from these transformations call into question the fundamental assumption of the at least temporary stabilization of capitalism on which the Soviet strategy of peaceful coexistence is based. The developing situation presents the Soviet leadership with new possibilities for gains, derived from exploiting opportunities for advancing Soviet influence, that must be balanced against the effect of this exploitation upon the flow of goods, capital, and technology from the West. Whether the temptation to take advantage of the disruptions in Western economic relations will weaken and perhaps reverse the present Soviet perception that its interests lie in maintaining stability and continuing involvement in the world economy may depend upon the depth and duration of the Western economic crisis, upon the form in which concrete issues arise and require decisions on marginal risk-taking, and upon what happens to the uncertain balance of forces within the Soviet political system. The equilibrium among these factors will also be affected by the degree of progress in the SALT negotiations. In the absence of substantial progress, it seems probable that the consequent development and deployment of new strategic nuclear-weapons systems will be attended by a rise in international tensions, a spill-over inhibiting effect upon economic progress in the Soviet-American relationship, and a strengthening of pro-military groups in both political systems.

This brings us to some conceptual implications for arms control which require further examination as a result of the present and anticipated transformations in international politics. Perhaps the fundamental concept embodied in the word "security" is the one most in need of reflective examination. The traditional view of security as the defense of the nation-state through maintaining a preponderance in military capacity remains powerful despite the inescapable vulnerability of even the strongest states to destruction and the manifest infeasibility of a successful first-strike attack.

If the concept of security is understood to include the protection of the values of our societies, as well as the territorial integrity of our states, it follows that:

1) the military component of security should be directed at achieving stability and moderation in the central strategic balance;
2) non-military forms of power—primarily economic and political—should be recognized as having increasing importance as elements of security; and
3) a central aspect of security policy should be the development and strengthening of the capabilities of the international system to accommodate processes of political change without violence.

This suggests that, despite the discouragement and perhaps boredom that presently afflict the arms-control community, some of the central objectives of arms control are in need of reinvigorated attention: progress in SALT toward a stable and moderate-level central strategic balance, a more effective inhibition on the further proliferation of nuclear weapons, and limitations on the development and deployment of conventional weapons. But it also suggests that the scope of arms control requires broader horizons to take account of the sources of insecurity and conflict in economic and political relationships, in the evident incapacity of the present international system to deal with turbulent political changes, and indeed in the threat that the present international order may dissolve into anarchy and widespread violence.

From this perspective, the first requirement is the development of more enlightened and rational security policies in both the United States and the Soviet Union. It has become evident that progress in negotiations between the Big Two is constrained, and is bound to be constrained, by the absence of a clear national understanding in both countries that self-interest dictates a stable and moderate deterrent balance. So long as this continues to be the case, domestic pressures will continue to force the pace of military technological development to higher, more complex, and less stable levels, and the process will be exacerbated by the pursuit of bargaining advantages in the SALT negotiations.

Moreover, the complex problem of working out a moderate balance, given the asymmetries of the weapons systems of the two countries and their different defense requirements, is made more difficult by the difference in the perception of the central strategic balance between Washington and Moscow. What has been lacking in these rationalizations for continued military expansion has been a sense of proportion in contemplating a series of imagined scenarios expressed in the subjunctive mood (what the adversary *could* or *might* do)—what Justice Holmes once called "the parade of imaginary horribles"—on which the case for new systems or new doctrines rests. What is also lacking is adequate political leadership in both countries to impose a political sense of proportion upon the understandable tendency of military planners to provide for all conceivable contingencies—the net effect of which is to increase insecurity.

On the border between the military and the political aspects of security is the interesting conceptual and operational problem of the extent to which the stabilization of the military competition can be at least partially compartmentalized from the effects of the political and economic competition. In logic, the limited political utility of nuclear weapons and the common interest of the Soviet Union and the United States in the avoidance of general war should argue for the continuation of efforts to stabilize the strategic military competition independently of the level of tension in other aspects of their relationship. Of course, as a practical political matter, it is difficult to carry forward SALT negotiations when, for example, the political climate is disturbed by a high level of tension and competition in the Middle East; as we have observed earlier, political rivalry is an ever-present factor in the background. Nevertheless, there is an objective basis for the parallelism of interest on either side in operating the strategic competition at moderate rather than at runaway levels. As this interest comes to be better understood, more widely recognized, and supported by public opinion, perhaps the SALT negotiations can be more effectively insulated from the vicissitudes of political competition. A partial insulation may be more feasible as the ideological conflict becomes more attenuated and expresses itself in the competition between the two systems in performance rather than in sterile rhetoric.

More fundamental, however, is the broadened perspective for arms-control efforts that should result from recognizing the implications of these transformations in international politics. It is becoming more evident that some traditional concepts of international politics, such as the reliance upon security through military balances of power, buffer zones, the hegemonical control of territory, spheres of influence, and imperialist relationships, will soon be anachronistic as a result of the technological revolutions now in process.

In the present international environment, which is characterized by powerful and rapidly developing impulses toward change in the political and physical conditions of life, an essential requirement for security is to develop, strengthen, and support the international system, not with the intention of maintaining the status quo, which would be a vain endeavor, but to assist in the development of institutions, practices, and mechanisms that are capable of accommodating processes of change with a minimum of violence. This has long been a part of our declaratory policy, but in practice it has been vitiated by the apparent greater immediacy of strategic considerations. This perspective has led us into the paradoxical situation of having an unprecedented power of destruction while our security and our influence diminish. To work our way out of this dangerous dilemma, we have to begin with the recognition that the central and indispensable condition of our future security will be the emergence of an effective and durable international system. To develop the implications of that recognition should be a high priority in the agenda of future arms-control efforts.

PAUL DOTY

Strategic Arms Limitation After SALT I

IF THE VLADIVOSTOK AGREEMENT of November, 1974, is transformed into a treaty, we will have reached a turning point in the long, tortuous, frustrating effort to bring strategic nuclear weapons under control. This turning point will not necessarily be a breakthrough, however; no substantial controls on existing or planned strategic-weapons systems will have been accomplished. Still, some essential steps have been taken: The issues of forward-based systems, of asymmetries in the throw-weights of missile forces on either side, of strategic compensation for the British and French nuclear-armed submarines, and for the alleged geographical disadvantages of the Soviet Union have been resolved in the process of arriving at agreements on equal ceilings for the number of strategic delivery systems and the number of missiles that can be MIRVed (i.e., fitted with multiple independently targeted re-entry vehicles). The large numbers proposed for these ceilings allow the continuing development and deployment of most of the weapons systems now being planned by the two sides; only after these ceilings are reached will the limits begin to be felt, unless the present agreement is modified. Consequently, the agreement does not in itself constitute timely and visible progress in arms limitation. Clearly it was a disappointment for those who thought or hoped that the time had come for such an achievement. But it does provide for the elimination of several persistent obstacles to significant limitations and for a framework within which these limitations can be negotiated.

In addition, about a dozen other treaties negotiated over the last twelve years limit the nuclear-arms competition in various ways. The 1963 treaty, banning all but underground nuclear-weapons testing, and the 1972 ABM treaty were particularly important for introducing the two leading nuclear powers to the practice of verified restraint and the benefits to be derived from it.

In a sense, more has been accomplished than this assessment implies. In 1963 the concerns expressed in many public opinion polls in this country centered on the likelihood of nuclear war[1] and these concerns were echoed throughout the rest of the world. By contrast, a recent survey of six hundred corporate executives found only two or three who considered a strategic nuclear exchange likely in the next decade.[2] This evidence of diminished anxiety over the possibility of nuclear war is almost surely linked to the improvement in understanding between the two leading nuclear powers—and demonstrations of more rational behavior within them—which has been exemplified by the succession of nuclear treaties. On the other hand, these developments seem also to have produced an air of self-satisfaction and complacency. It is now argued, for example, that there is no urgent reason for dealing with the very difficult problem of curbing nuclear-arms competition to the extent of actually reducing the number of nuclear armaments on each side; the next decade should instead be spent in adjusting our strategic inventory to the Vladivostok ceilings, under the assumption that the present relative calm will continue.

But another side to United States policy is revealed by scrutinizing the three stated objectives set for the Strategic Arms Limitation Talks (SALT).[3] The first objective was to achieve essential equivalence in the strategic forces permitted to each side; the second was to find limitations that would improve the stability of these forces in times of crisis and, in this and other ways, reduce the risk of nuclear war; the third was to reduce arms competition and, in time, military expenditures. When the SALT II Treaty, based on the Vladivostok Agreement, is concluded, these three objectives will have remained largely unfulfilled. At first glance, essential equivalence may seem to have been established by the equal ceilings. But these in fact represent only very vague limitations in the simplest categories of judging strategic force. Moreover, they appear to have been made possible by settling on numbers sufficiently high to allow deferment of many problems that would have had to be solved had the numbers been lower. Thus the commitment to equivalence has so far been one that has functioned only at high levels, where a variety of asymmetries and uncertainties can be accommodated.

Progress toward the second objective has been even more limited. The principal achievement has been the limitation of anti-ballistic missiles to negligible numbers. This was supposed to allow both sides to forego multiplying their strategic forces to compensate for those that might fail to penetrate the defenses of the other side. However, this opportunity has not been grasped: the multiplication of warheads through MIRVing has instead become the major occupation of both strategic establishments. With the number of warheads growing toward a figure that is more than tenfold greater than that originally thought adequate for deterrence, with continued improvements in yield and accuracy, and with a growing effort on both sides to find ways to reduce the invulnerability of the sea-based deterrent of the other, we certainly do not seem to be moving toward a strategic environment that is more stable in times of crisis. That the third objective—the reduction of the arms competition and military budgets in the strategic area—has receded rather than come closer is evident in the budgets and planned strategic programs on both sides.

Thus the objectives that the United States government had set for SALT remain unrealized. Nevertheless, it is now at least possible to move into the area of significant limitations on strategic offensive arms for the first time since the arms competition began three decades ago. The will to do so is the first requirement; it will be absent in those military planners on both sides who seek military superiority rather than mutual benefit through mutual restraint. It will be absent in government leaders who subordinate the slow, demanding quest for the control of nuclear arms to attempts to gain diplomatic advantage from an alleged nuclear superiority in terms of one index or another. And it will be ineffective in those who underestimate the difficulty of reorienting the two largest institutions in the world, the American and the Soviet military establishments. But, for those who have the will, a new effort is clearly required.

The military environment which would be altered by the arms-control agreements that are now possible is itself undergoing rapid change. The complexity of the problems and the potential for further change in the present strategic arsenals were not foreseen in the fifties and sixties, when many of the ideas for arms control took shape. Thus, a new effort is now needed to join these rather naïve and often elementary ideas to the complexity of the present situation. Such an effort will not recapture the expansive period of new conceptions that animated the fifties. The revolutionary phase of nuclear weaponry is over: the present task is the less heady one of finding ways to accept self- and mutual restraint in order to consolidate forces at lower levels more obviously related to justified needs. It is in this context that the role of balanced reductions of strategic forces will be discussed. However, it is necessary first to examine the alternatives that exist.

How many routes to the limitation of strategic arms should be considered? Although a large number can be identified, almost all of them fall into two main categories: 1) control over the numbers of weapons, and 2) control over the improvement of weapons. In other words, limitations can be applied by controlling either quantity or quality.

Numerical limits were placed on anti-ballistic missiles in the 1972 treaty, and on the number of launchers in submarines (SLBMs), as well as the number of SLBM-carrying submarines, in the Interim Agreement of that year. Agreements to slow down schedules for the deployment of new systems represent another form of numerical limit. Outright bans on certain types of weapons (such as space-based ABM systems) can also be considered a numerical limitation (by limiting the number to zero). To complete the set, the banning of weapons from certain locations, as in the Seabed Arms Control Treaty of 1971 and in nuclear-free zones, can also be classed as a numerical limitation (by limiting the number to zero in specific locations).

Qualitative limits, that is, limits on improvement, were placed on ABM radars and ICBM silos in SALT I. However, the greatest effort has been directed toward attempts to limit the quality (as well as the number) of MIRVed missiles. Restricting MIRVing to missiles below a certain size, limiting the number of re-entry vehicles per missile, and placing a ceiling on the total MIRVed throw weight (i.e., on the total throw weight of missiles allowed to be MIRVed) are illustrations of proposals that have failed to attract support from either side. Qualitative restraints on bombers, to limit their weight, range, and the numbers and types of missiles they may carry, are likely to be examined in the negotiations of a SALT II Treaty.

The foregoing illustrations show the basic distinction between the two types of limitation. The problems in numerical limits lie in deciding precisely what categories of weapons are to be subject to numerical control and how maintaining the numbers agreed upon is to be verified. Qualitative restraints usually enter the picture only after numerical controls are considered enforceable, for then it becomes evident that, if numbers are to be controlled, improvements in the quality of the weapons must also be limited by collateral restraints if the limitation of numbers is to retain its usefulness. Without qualitative restraints, agreements on number could simply shift the objective of an arms race from numerical to qualitative superiority.

The recognition that an arms race can easily shift from a quantitative to a qualitative one under the influence of numerical restriction is absent from earlier arms-control literature. Before the mid-sixties, it was commonly assumed that a numerical limit would provide a freeze, in which weapons, if they were replaced at all, would be duplicates of the ones that had been eliminated, and that inspection would reveal the violation.

But this assumption regarding replacements became untenable as the speed with which technological improvements could be introduced was demonstrated and as satellite systems for verifying compliance were developed. In its place, three new categories of modification were recognized: 1) detectably different and allowed; 2) detectably different and not allowed; 3) undetectably different or the same, hence allowed. In almost every case, improvements can be gradually introduced into a fixed number of weapons using 1) and 3), although some specific major improvements can be prevented by enforcing 2) to control the rate of possible improvement for a fixed number of weapons. Not unexpectedly, the discussion of, and eventually the agreements regarding, qualitative restraints—and their operational counterpart, verifiability—became central issues in SALT I, in both the internal and external negotiations, and will continue to be central features of arms-control treaties.

The complexity of the issues arising from qualitative restraints is the result of the many features of a weapons system that significantly affect its military utility. For example, when considering an ICBM we are concerned with its size, payload for a given range, number of warheads, megatonnage of the warheads, guidance of the warheads (MIRV or not), accuracy, reliability, readiness, and silo hardness. Yet verification measures generally provide only for the counting of silos and approximate estimates of their size. Observations of flight tests can provide additional information if they can be reliably tied to missiles known to be in particular silos. However, it is obvious that limitations in the possibilities of verification severely restrict the extent to which qualitative limits can be agreed upon.

A potential solution to this problem arises from the fact that most substantial qualitative improvements of missiles require a development and testing stage that is also observable by the other side. Consequently, most substantial qualitative improvements can be controlled by severely limiting the annual number of flight tests. This kind of control could greatly retard the development of new or improved missile systems designed to replace existing ones. Moreover, such a restriction could also reduce the number of confidence firings of deployed missiles to the extent that a "first strike" would be even less conceivable than at present. Despite these desirable consequences, limitations on flight tests are very unpopular with the military, and the possibility of their being proposed at SALT is, at best, uncertain.

The usefulness of qualitative restraints in limiting improvements in a fixed number of weapons systems is also subject to the shortcomings of human foresight—it is impossible for all future developments to be discerned in advance and forestalled by negotiating qualitative restraints. Were one to try to do so, the number of necessary prohibitions that the imagination might suggest becomes too great and therefore too cumbersome to negotiate.

A further difficulty with qualitative restraints is that, to be effective, they must be introduced prior to large-scale deployment. The current attempt to negotiate a partial MIRV limit in SALT bears testimony to this. The appropriate time to have negotiated a MIRV ban or limit would have been in 1969 or 1970, before American deployment began. But the prudence of that course is only now becoming apparent to government leaders. At that time, the pressures on them to exploit the American advantage were too strong and their perceptions of the complications it would introduce were too dim

1) All those to be controlled can be put into a single class, usually designated as an aggregate. This may, in the view of one or both parties, involve only a part of the strategic force.

2) Sublimits may be imposed on the aggregate number, that is, there may be separate limits for broad categories of weapons (for example, ICBMs, SLBMs, and heavy bombers).

3) Size, or other characteristics, may be used to define other categories with specific limits. Thus, MIRVed missiles may be treated as a separate category, as in the Vladivostok Agreement, or ICBMs may be divided into two classes according to size, as in the Interim Agreement of 1972.

4) Classes may be defined in terms of existing weapons types; they will, in this case, differ for each side. If the classification is done comprehensively, it would represent an inventory for each side according to categories (for example, Minuteman II, Minuteman III, B-52 bombers, Poseidon, etc).

5) Within any category or class the number allowed might be determined by a separate criterion rather than by specific number. Thus the number of MIRVed missiles might be determined by the combined throw weight of the class, thereby allowing different combinations of different numbers.

The choice of the level of aggregation for an arms-control agreement is intimately related to what the two sides wish to accomplish, and it will probably be agreed upon prior to consideration of the manner in which reductions might subsequently be carried out. Reduction programs would then have to be fitted into an already existing agreement, and care would have to be taken to insure that a given reduction program preserves the aims inherent in the prior agreement that imposed the various ceilings and restraints. However, before pursuing this, a few more general observations may be useful.

The level denoted by 1) represents the simplest way of dealing with major systems, because a total aggregate number would be selected. It does, however, require that all major delivery systems (ICBMs of all sizes, SLBMs, and heavy bombers) are assumed to be equivalent, a very distant approximation to the truth. Nevertheless, if the preservation of the freedom to mix, that is, to change the composition of the strategic forces in the future within an agreed aggregate number, is an important condition for an arms-control agreement, this approximation will still be tolerable.

Reduction schedules would obviously lead to different consequences when applied to different levels of aggregation. If applied to the first level, that of a total aggregate number, it is likely that each side would tend to eliminate its older, less versatile weapons and preserve the most modern and effective ones. Under 2) or 3) the bias would be against the oldest or smallest weapons in each category. Since the freedom to mix would not be allowed outside of broad categories, each side could predict with some confidence the manner in which the other side's force structure would change over time. The results may not be equally agreeable to both parties. Consequently, the negotiation might again return to definitions of equivalency or relative value, so that asymmetries would not develop or increase as reductions proceed. This situation is avoided in schedules of the type indicated under 4), which represents the most controlled mode of reduction. Here all asymmetries are taken care of in the original assumption of parity, and each side's inventory is reduced on the same schedule, for example, by five per cent per year. Consequently, problems of equivalency do not arise. Totally new weapons systems would not be allowed. However, it seems likely that each side would prefer to concentrate its reductions in categories that it wished to phase out. This could then be the subject of separate negotiations between military staffs.

The expectation that each side would insist on deciding for itself which weapons are to be retired, subject to the agreed reduction schedule, is so readily taken for granted that the consideration of any alternative seems academic. Nevertheless, one can imagine situations in which both sides would prefer random rather than self-selected eliminations of weapons. For example, if the land-based ICBMs of both sides were partially MIRVed, but both sides were uncertain of the extent, then it might be to the advantage of both not to risk passing through a potentially unstable period in which the missiles of one side were almost completely MIRVed and those of the other were not. Such a situation could be avoided if the missiles to be inactivated were chosen at random: this would then insure that the MIRVed-single-warhead mix was approximately preserved through the reduction stage. This unusual procedure would have the further effect of discouraging any attempt to improve the weapons systems being reduced, for a fraction of the newly improved weapons would also be picked for destruction. It is, in effect, an alternative way to avoid the development of asymmetries as reduction proceeds.

The final distinction lies in how weapons designated for elimination are dealt with. Their destruction under the supervision of inspectors would be unambiguous and decisive: it would convey dramatically the intention of the superpowers to curb the arms race. Insofar as the weapons involved would be those nearing obsolescence, this procedure would present little difficulty. But when more recent weapons in substantial numbers are designated, many objections can be expected. The anticipation of this opposition will surely affect the negotiation of the rate at which reductions proceed, although it is difficult to estimate the extent of its influence. Therefore, it is useful to consider the alternative of putting at least some weapons designated for elimination into an inactive state. Their availability in the event of abrogation of the treaty or other emergency would itself be the subject of negotiation. Another alternative would be to store them in groups, which would make them easy targets in the event of a nuclear exchange. In any event, conditions can be found that would diminish the anxieties of the negotiating parties, and, by adopting them, higher rates of reductions might be negotiable. Whether designated weapons are destroyed or inactivated, it would be useful if their identification were subject to inspection by the other side. This is contrary to a long-standing Soviet position, but it would greatly improve verification.

Still another option for weapons removed from national inventories lies in their being assigned to some future international force. Most versions of this option seem patently unacceptable, but one can envision some possibly acceptable versions, such as one in which the contributing nuclear powers could exercise some joint control and even have power of gradual withdrawal of weapons in crisis periods.

Although the foregoing considerations may appear somewhat theoretical, they do permit some practical observations on the course that might be followed if reductions were to be pursued in the framework expected from the Vladivostok Agreement. That Agreement proposed a ceiling (2,400) on the total aggregate of strategic delivery vehicles subject to two sublimits: one set a ceiling of 1,320 on the numbers of MIRVed missiles for each side and the other limited overall missile sizes to approximately the sizes of those now deployed. The latter limit has the effect of allowing the Soviet Union about three hundred quite large ICBMs (of the SS-9 and SS-18 class) while denying comparably large missiles to the United States. Presumably this apparent asymmetry was equalized by such unspecified considerations as the decision not to provide numerical compensation in the aggregate for British and French submarines, and other similar requirements that the Soviets have now abandoned. Whatever the rationale, the critics are correct in pointing out the missile throw-weight gap in the present agreement, but it should also be noted that there is at present a bomber gap in the opposite direction.

The reason for emphasizing these two asymmetries lies in the importance that they would assume if reductions were undertaken. Reduction schedules that preserve the high degree of freedom to mix in the Vladivostok formula would allow the Soviets to carry their heavy-missile advantage and the Americans their bomber advantage into the smaller force structures prescribed by a reduction agreement. Asymmetries that were acceptable at high ceilings may become unacceptable to one or both parties when these ceilings are lowered.

This example illustrates a more general observation that is becoming increasingly apparent: In order to preserve a rough balance, or essential equivalency, a reduction program must diminish asymmetries as it progresses. To do so, it will be necessary to introduce new sublimits along the way in order to insure that the asymmetries are diminishing at least in proportion to the reductions. In this particular instance, specific sublimits may have to be established for heavy missiles and heavy bombers, and their numbers may have to be decreased on a separate schedule.

In retrospect, it seems likely that the very high ceilings of the Vladivostok Agreement were deemed desirable at the time because they permitted the agreement on an overall aggregate number and the ignoring of asymmetries within the respective strategic forces. If this is true, it follows that it would be unrealistic to assume that the ceilings could be greatly reduced without reopening and solving the problem of these asymmetries. Substantial reductions that allow each side to select what is to be removed from its strategic inventory will almost certainly increase the asymmetries in both force structures. Moreover, a preference to retain MIRVed missiles over un-MIRVed missiles, large missiles over small missiles, and quick-reacting weapons over slow-reacting weapons will probably produce a less balanced and less stable strategic situation. The principal task in negotiating a reduction program will be to avoid this and to promote more symmetric, more obviously equivalent strategic forces that are also more stable in crisis situations.

In order to keep the foregoing discussion general, we have employed the concept of a schedule of reductions proceeding over a period of years that would be widely applicable. This should not obscure the virtues of the simpler procedure of a single-step reduction where it is appropriate. At present, it would be appropriate in working out the Vladivostok Agreement. The number of MIRVed missiles allowed is now unnecessarily high. Despite the excursions into fantasy that are required to visualize either side mounting a first strike on the other, the degree to which this scenario has become a test of arms-control options is very great. By this test, the stability of the strategic situation would be vastly improved if the ceiling for MIRVed missiles were cut in half, either in the SALT II Treaty or by a subsequent treaty negotiated in 1975-76. With this lower number of MIRVed missiles, a first-strike scenario would be assigned to oblivion. More important, such an agreement would in one step confer many of the gains that would take a decade or more to achieve were the MIRVed forces to be built up to 1,320 and then reduced back to the much safer number of, say, 660. Alternatively, both sides could agree to identify a comparable number of its older missiles for future retirement and refrain from upgrading or improving them. In either event, the capital and resources, not to mention the energies of the negotiating diplomats, that could be saved for more useful purposes are prodigious. Subsequent negotiations could then concentrate on the orderly restraining and reduction of already more manageable strategic forces.

This survey of what might be called the tactics of reducing numbers of strategic weapons has attempted to present the versatility and the complexity of this mode of arms control and to demonstrate that reductions would become unavoidable if the containment and the decrease of strategic capability are desired by both sides. Moreover, it has become apparent that numerical reduction programs would introduce a new dynamic into the arms-control situation. As reductions progress, it will become necessary to institute new sublimits, and accompanying reduction schedules, to deal with asymmetries that would otherwise increase. Likewise, verification procedures, which may have been acceptable in the context of high ceilings, will have to be tightened as numbers are lowered. In short, a commitment by the two leading nuclear powers to a treaty calling for substantial reductions will engage them in procedures exceedingly more complex than that process of simply certifying weapons for destruction that is sometimes taken to represent arms control.

Despite all that might be said for the usefulness, and indeed necessity, of reductions, it must be admitted that this mode of arms control is certain to encounter strong resistance. The destruction of expensive weapons has about it a touch of the futile and the tragic. This view is strengthened by the very short life of the SALT I option (Option D) which, according to the Newhouse report,[4] contained a substantial reduction schedule, the removal of one hundred strategic missiles per year for seven years, and had a "half life of one plenary session."

Apocryphal or not, this view was much more prevalent a few years ago than it is at present. Fundamentally, there are only two options in arms control: either control and limit numbers, or control and limit the technology that permits improvement. The armed forces, charged with maintaining the military strength of the nation, naturally find neither of these options congenial. But as the political interest in genuine arms control grows, some accommodation by the military will have to be made. The choice will not be an easy one for either side.

The military position, of course, will be based on what is perceived as constituting an advantage over the adversary. In this respect, the Soviets face a particularly acute problem. Their recollection of American production of planes and tanks—and especially the astronomical production of motor vehicles—in World War II tells them to seek controls on numbers and to reject technological restraints. On the other hand, they can sense the continued superiority of American military technology, reflect that the United States has been the side to introduce almost every new weapons system into the strategic inventory since World War II, and conclude that it would be preferable to seek controls on technology rather than on numbers. But if they acquiesce in this, do they not risk placing themselves permanently in an inferior technological position? This must represent a continuing dilemma for the Soviets, and might explain much of the stalling that characterized the SALT talks.

It should be evident, however, that the current state of affairs is not so sharply drawn. For two decades the United States has been shifting to progressively more sophisticated weapons systems, with a consequently high unit cost that makes the large numbers turned out by endless production lines neither acceptable to us nor within our budgets. The technological "superiority" argument is also now open to question as the Soviet defense industry increases in sophistication and remains the recipient of unrestrained budgetary largess. Moreover, the Soviets could hardly expect the United States to make concessions on the expectation that we would have a permanent technological lead. Although these considerations moderate the dilemma, they do not remove it.

American views on this question display a characteristic diversity. The Soviet reaction to the apparent American technological lead has been to field much larger missiles and to concentrate a greater part of the Soviet strategic force in this visible, and potentially more threatening, component. The American response has not surprisingly involved proposals to limit the size and MIRVing of Soviet missiles. In these efforts both technological and numerical restraints are requested. At a rhetorical level, several branches of the American government have devoted a great deal of attention to the Soviet lead in the throw weight of ICBMs and the number of warheads that could be deployed in them, ignoring the fact that the deliverable megatonnage of the whole strategic force on each side is approximately equal, that the United States has a three-fold lead in warheads, that weapons beyond one or two thousand are of increasingly more marginal utility, and that we prefer our more diversified force in any case. More important, this concern is not, for the most part, matched by enthusiasm for jointly limiting technology so that the larger Soviet missile throw weights cannot be fully exploited. Instead, American interests tend to prefer limiting numbers and sizes of launchers, evidently assuming that, under these restraints, a continuing technological lead can be assured.

Taken together, these observations suggest that the military leadership on both sides would probably much prefer numerical reductions to equally drastic restraints on either technological improvements of existing systems or the development of new ones. Some further evidence for this preference can be found in official pronouncements on both sides. Despite allegations that Soviet representatives have not expressed any great interest in reduction formulas in the SALT discussions, we do have specific endorsement of them from Chairman Brezhnev in statements dating from the past three years.

Evidently it would be a good thing to give some thought to how we could move from the limitation of arms to their gradual reduction, and also to the establishment of some kind of limits on their qualitative improvement.

The successful completion of the new phase of talks between the U.S.S.R. and the U.S.A. on questions of the further limitation and possible reduction of strategic arms can play a considerable role.

In short, if the government of the United States adheres to the principles of equal security and renunciation of attempts to gain unilateral advantages as set down in our agreements, it will find the Soviet Union to be a conscientious and active partner in such an important undertaking as the limitation and reduction of strategic arms.[5]

On the American side, we find that reduction proposals have also been made by several Senators.[6] And, although Secretary Kissinger insisted in the early days of SALT that reductions could not be negotiated, he has more recently modified his opinion, as the talks enter a new phase. The following statement was made in defense of the Vladivostok Agreement in a *Newsweek* interview:

Now, what in fact is the significance of this agreement? The nightmare of the nuclear age is the fear of strategic arms based on the expectation of what the other side is doing. One has to get one's priorities right. The first objective must be to get that cycle of self-fulfilling prophecies interrupted. That has now been substantially achieved. Once that is built into the planning of both sides, I think the negotiations on reductions will be easier.

A number of people gained the impression that the reductions were to start only after 1985. The Vladivostok announcement in fact said that negotiations would start no later than 1980 for reductions to take place after 1985. That has now been eliminated from the aide memoire because it was never intended to preclude an agreement on reductions to take place well before 1985. So it is clear that negotiations can start as soon as possible and take effect as soon as there is an agreement.[7]

Finally, in his 1975 budget statement, Secretary of Defense Schlesinger states that:

. . . we would welcome reductions in these [strategic] forces provided that the Soviet Union were willing to reciprocate in an equitable fashion.[8]

It would seem, therefore, that a negotiated, balanced reduction in numbers of strategic weapons has at least become an acceptable item on the agenda for the next steps to be taken in arms control.

REFERENCES

[1] Gallup poll in *New York Herald Tribune*, July 5, 1963.

[2] B. M. Russett and B. C. Hanson, "How Corporate Executives See America's Role in the World," *Fortune*, May, 1974.

[3] P. H. Nitze, "The Strategic Balance Between Hope and Skepticism," *Foreign Policy*, 17 (Winter, 1974-75), 136.

[4] J. Newhouse, *Cold Dawn: The Story of Salt* (New York, 1973).

[5] L. I. Brezhnev, *Pravda*, December 22, 1972, p. 1; October 27, 1973, p. 1; June 15, 1974, p. 1.

[6] E. g., Senator H. Jackson, *Congressional Record*, December 4, 1973; Senator W. Proxmire, *Congressional Record*, February 5, 1974.

[7] Henry A. Kissinger in an interview published in *Newsweek*, December 30, 1974.

[8] "Statement of Secretary of Defense James R. Schlesinger to the Congress on the FY 1976 and Transition Budgets, FY 1977 Authorization Request, and FY 1976-1980 Defense Programs" (mimeographed), February 5, 1975, p. 27.

HARVEY BROOKS

The Military Innovation System and the Qualitative Arms Race

FOLLOWING THE CONCLUSION of the first round of SALT negotiations in June of 1972, a limitation on the rate of technological progress in weapons systems is emerging as a central problem for the future of arms control. In SALT I, technological progress threatened to overtake the slow pace of the negotiations. At the start of the negotiations, for example, the multiple independently targetable warhead (MIRV) was in its later development stages, but by the time the agreement had been concluded, it was a fairly well-tested weapon, ready for full-scale deployment in the Minuteman system and in the Poseidon missile for the Polaris submarines. MIRV potentially multiplied the destructiveness carried in a single missile to the point where any agreement to limit the deployment of offensive strategic missiles was made much more difficult. Fortunately, technological progress in ballistic-missile defense did not make obsolete an agreement on ABM limitation, but even here the emergence of possible exotic ballistic-missile defenses (such as high power lasers) almost threatened agreement and did complicate the negotiations. Since SALT, a whole panoply of new weapons possibilities has emerged into public view and is being vigorously pursued in the United States: the Trident submarine, the B-1 bomber, the long-range cruise missile, the maneuverable re-entry vehicle (MaRV), a program for increased missile accuracy. Meanwhile the Soviet missile program has also made great progress, with MIRV being tested, apparently successfully, on three different new missile systems.

After the partial test ban treaty, and again after SALT I, it was necessary to assuage domestic critics of these treaty agreements by promising a vigorous research and development program. Indeed, the partial test ban apparently resulted in very little limitation on weapons progress, as both the United States and the Soviet Union pursued increasingly elaborate and sophisticated underground testing. The SALT agreement was used in part to justify new weapons programs in this country, while the vigor of the Soviet missile test program suggests that this may have been the price paid for the agreements by the Soviet leadership to its military critics within the Soviet Union. There are indications that both sides intended to utilize some of the resources that would be saved by the agreements not to deploy ABM in order to accelerate research on new offensive systems. These could then be substituted for existing systems within the quantitative limits set by SALT. In fact SALT, by permitting the substitution of qualitatively improved weapons for older ones, provided a powerful incentive for weapons-system innovations on both sides.

The testing or demonstration of new technological weapons can be politically as destabilizing as their actual deployment, especially in the absence of reliable intelligence. Thus the projected bomber gap of the mid-nineteen-fifties and the alleged missile gap of the early sixties were inferred from Soviet capabilities that had only been demonstrated on the level of research and development or prototype testing. The inferences proved unfounded, since there was no major deployment of either bombers or ICBMs. But the United States had in the meanwhile launched a major build-up of bombers and ICBMs, which gradually acquired a justification of its own, independent of the hypothesized but non-existent threat that had originally inspired it. Similarly the mere possibility that the Soviets were about to demonstrate an ABM capability around Moscow was used to justify the vigorous pursuit of a MIRV program in the United States and ultimately the deployment of MIRVs on both the sea-based and the land-based forces.

Until recently, official scientific advisers and some of the scientific community interested in such matters have advocated research and development to improve certain weapons technologies, even when they have strongly opposed the deployment of the corresponding specific weapons, whether because they were ineffective or because they would accelerate the arms race. Over a period of nearly fifteen years, independent scientific advice discouraged deployment of successive ABM systems. But each time the independent scientists recommended against deployment, they also advocated more research aimed at the next level of improvement, primarily on the grounds that we could not afford to be taken by surprise over what was technically possible. Thus Nike Zeus was abandoned in favor of the development of Sentinel and, subsequently, of Safeguard. Next, the limited deployment of Safeguard was accompanied by advocacy of a strong research and development program for Hardsite, which turned out to be a system designed to meet the arguments of those who had publicly opposed the deployment of Safeguard. Only the ABM treaty brought about the abandonment of this program.

Since SALT, however, one hears less talk of the pursuit of "R and D" as an alternative to deployment. The possibility of limiting technological progress in weapons *prior* to a deployment decision is beginning to be seriously discussed by those interested in arms control.

This essay will be concerned with the impact of qualitative progress in weapons technology and with some possible means of controlling it. We will first deal with the impact of technology on the stability of the strategic deterrent and with the potential political effects of qualitative progress in conventional weapons. We will then consider several types of proposals that have been made for slowing the rate of technological progress in weapons development, with emphasis on strategic weapons. The final section will discuss the overall system of weapons development and procurement and will analyze those parts of the system that appear to generate pressures and incentives to perpetuate it.

I. Prospects and Impact of the Qualitative Arms Race

How do qualitative changes in weapons affect the world military balance, and what does "stability" mean in the military situation? Clearly any change that increases the advantage of the side attacking first contributes to instability, and any change that reduces this relative advantage is stabilizing. This is true at both the "strategic" and "tactical" levels. Thus the development of invulnerable retaliatory systems, such as Polaris, has contributed to stability because these systems guarantee the destruction of the side that attacks first; the first attack would scarcely attenuate the completeness of the retaliatory strike. An increase in the relative effectiveness of antitank weapons would also tend to reduce the incentives for a first strike in land warfare. Improved strategic intelligence, that is, instant knowledge of the opponent's deployments, is also generally stabilizing, especially if the intelligence capability of each side is fully known to the opponent. The ABM, on the other hand, was considered destabilizing because it presented the possibility of limiting the damage from a retaliatory strike. MIRV was also considered destabilizing because it potentially limited the effectiveness of a land-based ICBM system deployed in a retaliatory mode. Forward-based nuclear weapons in Europe are destabilizing to the extent that they might be immobilized by surprise attack, especially a conventional one. Finally, conventional weapons whose effectiveness in an initial attack can be greatly enhanced by time for mobilization are destabilizing because they provide an incentive for the opponent to counterattack before mobilization can be effected; the classic example of this can be found in the outbreak of World War I.

Stability is a political as well as a military concept. It is in its political aspect that technological innovation is particularly important because of the long time lapse between a demonstrated capability and full deployment of the corresponding weapons system. Thus any technological achievement that becomes known to the other side and that, when fully deployed, would jeopardize the effectiveness of retaliation (whether at the strategic or tactical level) is bound to create apprehension about the future and stimulate counteraction. The result is a spiral of technological innovations. The principle of overreaction or "worst case analysis" generally guarantees that the reaction to a revelation of technological innovation in weapons exceeds what was justified by the actual situation.

Technology and Military Equilibrium

In the past twenty years, technological change has sometimes increased and sometimes decreased the stability of the strategic deterrent. For example, the first liquid-fueled ICBMs contributed to instability because they were not "hardened" and could not be made instantly ready to fire. This would have provided an incentive for the other side to launch its weapons first, in order to destroy the vulnerable weapons before they were functional. On the other hand, the development of solid fueled ICBMs, and especially of submarine-launched ballistic missiles, resulted in a less vulnerable retaliatory capability; this reduced or eliminated the incentive for pre-emptive strike and thus improved strategic stability. Similarly, the development of satellite surveillance decreased the likelihood that either side could deploy strategic weapons secretly. Satellites with infrared detection insured immediate warning of a missile attack launched from anywhere in the world, which reduced the likelihood of successful pre-emptive attack. It also decreased the instability that results from exaggeration of enemy capabilities or a misinterpretation of enemy intentions stemming from unreliable intelligence.

When the ABM emerged as a technical possibility in the nineteen-sixties, its technological threat to strategic stability was immediately recognized because it cast doubt on the effectiveness of a retaliatory strike. In principle, the development of MIRV similarly threatens stability, as the ratio of the number of independently targetable re-entry vehicles to the number of missile launchers increases the likelihood of success of a pre-emptive strike against the enemy's land-based launchers. The prospect of anti-submarine-detection technology, which could make impossible the concealment of sea-based missile forces, would also be a potentially destabilizing development.

If neither the ABM nor MIRV had been developed, the strategic situation at the end of the nineteen-sixties would probably have been at its most stable. Both sides possessed land-based and sea-based missiles, which were virtually certain to survive any initial attack with undiminished effectiveness, while the cities and industrial capacity of each superpower were defenseless against retaliatory strikes. A basic objective of the SALT negotiations would then have been to freeze—or at least prolong—this balance. The ABM treaty contributed greatly toward this end, but the other developments mentioned earlier worked against it. What now are the prospects for the future?

It is first fair to ask whether we can expect the development of a qualitative arms race to be as rapid today as it was from 1955 to 1965. The revolutionary technological situation that existed then may have been unique. Since the perfection of MIRV, most of the military technologies that have been proposed are only evolutionary refinements of basic systems concepts developed and implemented earlier. The Trident submarine and missile system is simply a parameter extension of Polaris. The B-1 bomber is an embodiment of previous developments in supersonic fighter and reconnaissance aircraft. Recently proposed versions of the ABM were extrapolations from the basic elements of the Nike-X system, which were incorporated first in Sentinel and then in Safeguard. Prospective improvements in missile accuracy are logical evolutions of technological trends that have been evident for a long time.

The revolutionary fifties and sixties were made possible by the confluence of several basic technological advances which came to maturity at more or less the same time—solid-fuel rocket propulsion, high yield-to-weight thermonuclear warheads, inertial guidance, compact solid-state electronics and computers, MIRV and re-entry technology. With the possible exception of the application of laser techniques in missile defense and ground warfare, comparable technological developments are not now on the horizon that promise the sort of qualitative leaps we witnessed then. We ought, however, to remind ourselves that the rapid advances from 1950 to 1960 were not anticipated until they were almost upon us, even though they may appear in retrospect to have been foreseeable. Scientists and technologists, in trying to foresee the state of the art more than five years into the future, have been notoriously myopic—conservative as to actual possibilities and inaccurate in their anticipation of the direction of development. Thus, it would be injudicious to hope that the posture of mutual assured destruction is proof against technological change for more than five, or at most ten, years, We cannot reliably see that far into the future, given past rates of technological progress in military weapons systems.

In addition, the cumulative effect of many small evolutionary improvements in the parameters of component technologies can often be as revolutionary as such dramatic, basic developments as the transistor or the hydrogen bomb. There are at the moment several technological areas where such a cumulative evolution might occur. One is in the accuracy, reliability, and compactness of guidance and control, including terminal guidance or "homing" of multiple warheads. One cannot foresee any natural technical limits to improvement, especially as electronic techniques gradually replace mechanical methods.[1] Closely related are prospective gains in the sensitivity and discriminatory power of remote sensing methods, using refined sensors and such information-processing techniques as pattern recognition.

The storage, processing, and manipulation of information are areas still undergoing rapid advance. The cost per logical operation, or per unit of information storage, has not reached any obvious lower limits, and it is likely to continue to decrease by a factor of two or three every five years, at least to the end of the century. The same will apply to the space required for information storage. At the same time, global communications via satellite permit the assembly of many different items of information into a single integrated system.[2]

These developments have only begun to reveal their potential, and they have as yet unclear implications for all kinds of weapons systems, ranging from battlefield weapons to warheads for MIRVed ICBMs, and including automatic map-following cruise missiles and unmanned bombers. In principle, increasing accuracy and discrimination should make it possible to decrease the collateral destructiveness of warfare and to confine damage to military objectives, and this may increase the temptation to initiate military action under less provocative circumstances than at present. Accuracy might also be increased to the point where conventional explosives could be substituted for nuclear weapons, thus making possible military actions which, under present circumstances, would require crossing the nuclear threshold. Increased accuracy might also raise the temptation to deploy very low-yield nuclear weapons, especially in Europe, and might thereby erode the "fire break" between conventional and nuclear tactical warfare. It is, of course, difficult to generalize about the effects of such technological improvements on the likelihood of hostilities or of escalation; it would depend upon a specific situation.

The use of "smart bombs" in Vietnam provides the first case history for this type of development. However, according to R. L. Garwin, the bombs were used in such limited quantities that it is difficult to draw any conclusions regarding their effect on collateral damage. As yet there is no indication of modification in the long-range trend toward increased collateral destruction by high explosives in conventional war. If one plots the rate of delivery of high explosives as a function of time in the wars this country has waged in the twentieth century, one finds that this rate has doubled every eight to ten years. This increase in accuracy and discriminatory power has, however, been more than offset by technological developments that have increased the feasible rate of delivery of high explosives, and, consequently, the amount of non-military damage has continued to escalate, as evidenced by the destruction in Vietnam.

The combat manpower needed to deliver a given amount of destruction within a given time has also constantly declined over the years, although the value of this manpower measured by the time and cost of training has increased. In other words, conventional war has become increasingly capital intensive. In consequence, it has become possible to inflict more and more damage with less and less risk to the lives of combat personnel—and hence minimal political cost at home. It was in this way that improvements in technology made it possible for the United States to escalate the civilian destruction in Indo-China while "de-escalating" the intensity of combat from the perspective of domestic politics. If the laser-guided bomb, or another comparable sophisticated weapon, had been available sooner, it is possible that the war could have been carried on with even less internal political opposition than it finally generated. As technology facilitates ever more sophisticated automated violence, the possibility of clandestine intervention in local conflicts by the superpowers, with minimal internal and external political cost, may increase. This could become a growing source of instability.

It seems only a matter of time before increases in the accuracy with which re-entry vehicles can be aimed or guided will make fixed land-based missiles vulnerable to attack. Whether such attack would actually be a serious threat would depend upon the vulnerability of the other components of the potential retaliatory force, especially the sea-based deterrent discussed below. Even if a first strike against the land-based missile force were not credible, the justification for a fixed land-based force as part of the deterrent would decline. In fact, the mere presence of potentially vulnerable land-based missiles would tend to present "hawks" on each side of the Iron Curtain with arguments for building up the strategic-weapons inventory. The missiles would become a target to be defended just because they were there, even though they made no contribution to overall retaliatory capability. In this sense, they would be an "attractive nuisance," tending to draw enemy attack for precautionary or symbolic reasons. To this degree, improvements in re-entry vehicle accuracy will contribute to strategic instability, psychologically if not in fact.

Another question is whether submarine-based missiles can eventually achieve sufficient aiming precision to pose a credible first-strike threat against the other side's land-based missiles, or against other military targets. There is no fundamental technical obstacle to this, although the military advantage of such a development would be dubious so long as each side retained an invulnerable retaliatory capability.

Invulnerability of the Sea-Based Deterrent

Perhaps the most serious question for the stability of mutual deterrence is whether any technical changes are in prospect that might compromise the invulnerability of the submarine missile forces of either side, and thus undermine the certainty of retaliation. An anti-submarine-warfare (ASW) system that could compromise the deterrent effect of the submarine-based missile force would have to meet very stringent requirements. It would have to be able to make a surprise pre-emptive attack simultaneously on all the enemy's submarine missile forces, including those in port. Such an attack would have to be made with close to one hundred per cent confidence, for if even one submarine escaped destruction it would have the capacity for inflicting serious and probably unacceptable retaliatory damage on cities and population. Furthermore, any action against the submarine force short of pre-emptive attack would provide strategic warning and hence would risk drawing some form of counterattack.

A war of attrition against the sea-based deterrent would be technically somewhat more feasible and could be imagined as a form of political backmail. Unless the nation attacked were in a position to retaliate without at the same time destroying itself, this form of political blackmail is risky, but barely credible. In practice, however, there are too many options for a less drastic response, including a retaliatory campaign of attrition against the enemy's sea-based forces. Nevertheless, belief that an opponent had the capability of conducting such a war of attrition could contribute greatly to tensions and produce political instability. Thus the demonstration of certain qualitative capabilities in ASW, without any evidence of deployment, might provide incentives to accelerate the arms race, much as the mere hint of a possible Soviet ABM system contributed to the deployment of MIRV.

Returning to the question of pre-emptive attack, the difficulties seem almost insurmountable. It would require detection, positive identification, and close and continuous tracking of all missile-firing submarines, plus the ability simultaneously to launch a lethal ASW weapon at each submarine on command from a central point. The requisite assured destruction could probably be achieved only with nuclear underwater weapons fired from vehicles that could carry sonar tracking gear close to the target, while remaining relatively immune to the effects of nearby underwater nuclear explosions. Hydrofoils, hovercraft, helicopters, or similar exotic vehicles might be made to have these characteristics. However, the tactics for such an operation could not be developed without a great deal of rehearsal and training, probably including the fairly routine practice tracking of potential targets. Such exercises could hardly be ignored by an alert opponent.

One could also imagine the disposition of passive and active sonars over the oceans, which could be monitored by satellite and would assist tracking operations, but the necessary dispositions would be very costly and would have to be in place continuously and be highly reliable. As sophisticated signal-processing electronics and information storage become more compact and inexpensive, world-wide monitoring of submarines, closely coordinated with trailing vessels, becomes conceivable, though still very costly. For this reason, there are arms-control incentives for trying to inhibit such developments, whose mere demonstration would stimulate doubts about the future invulnerability of the deterrent. The nation under threat could also develop decoy vehicles to confuse both the trailing vessels and any ocean-wide surveillance system designed to assist them. The same electronic sophistication that facilitated ocean surveillance would make possible relatively inexpensive decoys against tracking techniques that could simulate the characteristics of submarines. Even a small number of sufficiently realistic decoys could confuse the would-be attacker and greatly increase his uncertainty as to whether some part of the retaliatory force might have survived his attack.

A careful consideration of possible technical threats to the sea-based deterrent therefore forces the conclusion that they do not reveal a clear-cut technical advantage either to ASW or to the survival of the deterrent. The launching of a major ASW program would most likely simply trigger a race between measure and countermeasure, ending in an expensive stalemate similar to that which probably would have resulted from an ABM versus land-based missile race.

Conclusion

In the foreseeable future, the qualitative arms race is not likely to lead to major strategic instabilities, provided the ABM treaty remains in force. Nevertheless, continued innovation could lead to wasteful and expensive deployments of weapons, and it could offer many opportunities for internal bureaucratic maneuver aimed at exaggerating technological breakthroughs in order to justify new programs. One counter to this is certainly more open discussion and criticism of weapons proposals in a wider arena of opinion. By carefully considering the reaction to, and possible countermeasures for, the next generation of systems, such discussion would have the effect of deflating the benefits claimed for the development and deployment of proposed new systems.

II. Potentials for Curbing the Qualitative Arms Race

In the past it has often been assumed that limitation of progress in weapons technology was rendered impossible by the difficulties inherent in verifying such limitations, especially in the research and development stage. Thus, arms-control discussions have tended to concentrate on agreements for numerical limitations to the deployment of certain classes of weapons that can be verified with reasonable confidence through unilateral intelligence means. However, even the Partial Test Ban (PTB) was an attempt to limit technological progress in the sense that it was expected, through the prohibition of atmospheric tests, to inhibit the development of high-yield nuclear weapons and to make all weapons testing more costly and thus slow it up. In fact, the PTB did not prove to be as inhibiting as expected. Its main benefit was the reduction of atmospheric contamination. But driving tests underground made them publicly less visible, and thus reduced the pressure of world opinion for further damping the qualitative race in nuclear arms.

The SALT agreements did include a specific prohibition of the testing of certain kinds of ABM components of satellite-based ABM development. Less than complete confidence in verification was accepted in these agreements, which seem to have set a precedent for other possible limitations without insistence on verification. That verification is as much a political as a technical matter, that perfect verification is impossible, and that it is also unnecessary if there is some measure of political trust are also increasingly accepted ideas. The terms of an arms-control agreement are sufficiently interconnected to allow each element to affect the others, and hence not every element has to be verifiable with complete confidence so long as some parts of the agreement can be tested on a sample basis.

Obviously, the closer a weapons system is to deployment the more readily can its progress be verified. The final proof-testing of a weapon, necessary to demonstrate sufficient confidence in its reliability to warrant deployment, is a large, complex process, and it is difficult to conceal. On the other hand, once a weapon has reached that stage, bureaucratic vested interests have usually consolidated to insure its further development, so that ease of verification is offset by greater internal bureaucratic momentum. In what follows, we shall examine a series of proposals, starting with those that aim at inhibiting innovation nearest to the final deployment stage and ending with attempts to limit innovation at earlier stages of the process. The object of all these proposals is to prohibit or retard developments that are politically or militarily destabilizing or that simply add to the costs of maintaining a military posture on both sides without contributing to the security of either.

Comprehensive Nuclear Test Ban (CTB)

The prohibition of all nuclear testing has been an important aim for arms control from the very beginning. Its importance derives from the belief that no nation will place a new type of weapon in inventory if its properties cannot be realistically tested or its reliability verified by proof testing. It is theoretically possible to develop and deploy a nuclear weapon on the basis of scaled laboratory tests alone, but confidence in the reliability and the characteristics of such a weapon would probably be too low for use in a crisis.

The past obstacles to conversion of the limited test ban treaty of 1963 into a permanent comprehensive test ban (CTB) have been American insistence on the need for on-site inspection for suspected underground nuclear tests and the alleged value of underground nuclear explosions for peaceful purposes, such as large earth works or the stimulation of natural gas sources. On the Soviet side, a desire not to subject itself to limitations not enforceable against the Chinese was probably also an important factor. More generally, neither side was prepared to accept constraints that would decisively impair its subsequent freedom of action. The PTB was acceptable precisely because it contained no real constraint on innovation in nuclear weapons or peaceful uses.

Since 1963, the technology of detection and identification of underground tests by unilateral means has advanced rapidly, more rapidly than most scientists then expected it could. It is now doubtful that significant weapons advances can be made using tests that are small enough to escape detection with certainty. Even if progress could be made with such small tests, reliable warheads would probably not be placed in inventory without conducting many proof and training tests, a few of which are likely to be detected and to provoke suspicions. The non-adherence of other powers to a CTB could be handled by an agreement of finite duration, subject to reopening if a universal ban were not achieved within a specified period of time. Such an interim agreement would probably increase the pressure on all nations to adhere formally to the ban. Unlike the situation in the non-proliferation treaty, the superpowers would be taking the lead in foregoing their freedom of action, as opposed to demanding a forebearance from others that they were unwilling to impose upon themselves.

There is, perhaps, a risk that significant new results achieved in the laboratory would become dammed up, as it were, behind the test ban, and that one power might then denounce the ban and launch an accelerated "testing race" to verify its laboratory findings, thus creating political tensions that might not otherwise have occurred. Such a risk seems worth taking in view of the political benefits of a CTB.

New weapons that might be developed clandestinely under a CTB would principally be very small pin-point battlefield nuclear types. Indeed, with sufficient improvement in accuracy, such "mininukes" could be used in conjunction with MIRV to threaten land-based missiles and other military targets, with very little collateral civilian damage. On the battlefield, the use of such weapons would tend to blur the threshold between conventional and nuclear war and thus reduce inhibitions against crossing it; this might tend to make nuclear war more likely. The threat to land-based missiles would be similarly destabilizing. On the other hand, it is doubtful that such weapons could ever be decisive in providing military advantages to the side that developed them. Their destabilizing effects would outweigh any contribution they might make in terms of military advantage. Hence one could argue that, to the extent that a CTB made the development of such weapons more difficult and risky, it would be advantageous to world security, while, to the extent that it did not preclude such development, the security of one side or the other would not be seriously jeopardized. In sum, the possibility of the development of "mininukes" provides an additional argument in favor of a CTB.

Limitation on the Number of Missile Launchings

Experimental launchings are an essential part of missile development and are at the same time readily detectable by unilateral methods, using observation from satellites as well as electronic monitoring of communications and telemetering. In addition, training and confidence missile firings are necessary to keep a weapons inventory in readiness. Therefore, limitation of the number of test firings is a potential means for retarding innovations in missiles that can be verified unilaterally. The limitation that would be most practical to enforce would be one on the total annual number of firings, whether for research and development, proof testing, or training. The difficulty is that the number of launchings permitted would have to be sufficient to allow each side to retain confidence in the readiness of its deterrent, but that this number, if entirely diverted to research purposes, might permit one side to achieve a dangerous technological advantage. Separate limits on confidence firings and on research and development launches would be a preferable alternative, but they would be much harder to enforce because of the difficulties involved in distinguishing experimental from proof launches. For this reason, a limitation on total number of launches, combined either with agreements or with mutual declarations foregoing specific kinds of research, development, testing, and evaluation, would be more practicable.

Restrictions to Permit International Observation on the Location of Target Areas

As pointed out by Herbert York,[3] the SALT agreements included a provision for restricting ABM tests to specified test ranges. This stipulation suggests an excellent precedent for a restriction on all kinds of missile testing to specified ranges and for a restriction on down-range impact areas to locations that can be fairly easily observed by other countries, for example, international waters, or land sites close to international boundaries, or coastlines. Such mutually agreed-upon restrictions would improve ability to distinguish between experimental and proof tests, and they might thus make separate limits on the number of such tests more feasible. Furthermore, the SALT agreements have established a precedent for prohibiting interference with unilateral means of observation, either directly or through attempted concealment of certain classes of activities, such as construction of missile silos. The reaffirmation of this concept in the case of missile testing would clearly be desirable.

Specific Prohibition of Potentially Destabilizing Missile Improvements

When York[4] suggested restricting the location of the target areas, in 1972, he had in mind the testing of such improvements as maneuvering re-entry vehicles, re-entry vehicles with greater "fineness ratio" (i.e., that could be aimed at more widely separated targets), and tests involving complete MIRV systems. Unilateral observation methods, combined with the restrictions outlined above, would have made the probability of detection of tests involving any of these improvements great enough not to warrant the risk of being caught in a violation. Unfortunately, most of the technological deployments these proposals were designed to prevent have now already occurred.

Even at the present stage in the evolution of MIRV, however, the prohibition of testing of complete missile systems could still prevent obtaining confidence in the reliability of MIRV sufficient for use in pre-emptive attack. Indeed the dismal record of the Poseidon missile[5] is illustrative of the pitfalls along the path from the drafting board to a weapons system of fully demonstrated reliability.

Any agreement to forego specific weapons improvements, even if not strictly enforceable or verifiable, would still provide a strong argument for opponents of these developments in the internal bureaucratic debates within a country. It would be difficult to conceal illegal developments that could gradually become known to large numbers of people. Even a simple mutual declaration could strengthen internal opposition. On the other hand, it could equally be argued that illegal weapons developments could be more easily concealed in the compartmentalized research systems of the closed societies, and this would tend to limit the extent to which unverifiable agreements on innovations could safely be undertaken by the United States.

Another danger is that ambiguous results from unilateral observation could be misinterpreted as evidence of prohibited activities when none existed and could create political tensions unnecessarily, or at least put a potent argument in the hands of the internal opponents of agreements. This is an objection that still has to be answered; but the Standing Consultative Commission created by the 1972 SALT agreements might prove a useful mechanism for insuring against such misinterpretations.

Improved missile accuracy is also a potentially destabilizing development which has recently been the subject of a great deal of discussion in the United States. While it would no doubt be desirable to inhibit such improvements, it is very hard to see how this could be done and still maintain confidence on either side that the prohibition is being observed. Improved accuracy is extremely difficult to verify in the observation of proof testing. On the other hand, given the size of present strategic forces, accuracy has no military value so long as the posture on both sides is truly confined to mutual assured destruction. The problem arises when more limited "counterforce" options are included into the overall deterrent posture. The United States is already ahead in this respect, and little would be lost by even an unverifiable agreement to forego further development in such technology.

In principle, mutual recognition of the impact of technological developments on the stability of deterrence might have considerable political value, even in the absence of verifiable restrictions. The major powers could declare their intent not to develop weapons threatening the survivability of the other side's invulnerable retaliatory capability. Such a public declaration by the United States and the Soviet Union could have the salutary effect of forcing communication within each government about every new weapons system and even some of the old ones. It would legitimize, at a very early stage, internal concern about the destabilizing effects of various potential weapons developments. Declarations of this sort would be no different in principle from the declaration of intent in the 1972 Moscow agreements to forego both interference with the unilateral intelligence means of the other side and concealment of strategic weapons. Such a declaration might become the basis, within this country at least, for requiring an "impact statement" for each new major weapons development, analyzing the impact of the proposed system on actual and perceived strategic stability and on international political stability generally.

Restrictions on ASW Research and Development

As we have already seen, strategic stability is especially sensitive to technological developments that tend to compromise the invulnerability of a sea-based deterrent. This suggests that possible limitations on ASW developments are of special importance in any attempt to inhibit the qualitative arms race. Unfortunately, it is very difficult in practice to distinguish between techniques that threaten the submarine deterrent and those directed at protecting sea communications generally from submarine attackers. In this respect there is a geographic imbalance between China and the Soviet Union, on the one hand, and the Western industrialized nations, on the other. The latter, including Japan, are much more dependent on sea communications, both economically and militarily. The maritime nations will, therefore, be unlikely to forego the development of any ASW technique that would offer protection against submarine attack on commercial shipping or naval forces. Even an ocean-wide surveillance system, designed primarily to monitor and track the opponent's deterrent fleet, would offer considerable incidental protection against submarines deployed to raid shipping. Since the main shipping lanes cover only a small fraction of the oceans over which a deterrent fleet might range, we might try confining surveillance to those vital lanes, leaving large areas of the ocean as "sanctuaries" for missile submarines. This would work most effectively if the surveillance systems were of the "distributed" rather than the "searchlight" type. By a distributed system, we mean an interconnected array of passive or active sonic detectors distributed very widely over the oceans, but with each individual sensor capable of detecting a submarine only within a relatively short range. By a "searchlight" system, we mean a much smaller number of highly sophisticated, directional, long-range sensors capable of detecting submarines and locating them over a very extended geographical area—hundreds or even thousands of miles distant from an individual sensor. The distributed system could be deliberately confined to major shipping lanes, or "corridors," and thus would not threaten the opponent's deterrent force, so long as it avoided those corridors. The searchlight system, however, would cover large sweeps of ocean, and it would thus inevitably detect the opponent's deterrent force as well as its attack submarines threatening the shipping lanes. The problem is that future developments in technology may make searchlight systems considerably less expensive than distributed systems for a given degree of coverage. In addition, all kinds of intermediate configurations between "pure" distributed and "pure" searchlight systems are possible. In practice, it may be difficult to make distinctions between the two kinds of sensor deployment sufficiently convincing to assure an opponent that his strategic forces are invulnerable, so long as they avoid well-defined geographical areas.

Techniques for continuous trailing of submarines might also threaten deterrent forces without being especially useful for the protection of naval or commercial shipping. This is because, in a campaign against attack submarines that threaten shipping, the primary objective is to destroy the submarine immediately after it is detected and located. Since hostilities would then already have begun, there would be no reason to withhold attack once the submarine is positively identified as hostile. But continuous trailing of such submarines without attacking does not add much to the protection of sea communications, and it is, therefore, probably not worth the extra cost. The only advantage of trailing might lie in more secure identification of submarines as hostile. But, for this and other reasons, maintaining the distinction between protection of shipping and threatening the opponent's deterrent forces may be harder to maintain in practice than in theory.

Nevertheless, a declaration foregoing the effort to develop a trailing capability may have considerable political value, especially if coupled with an agreement limiting the construction of attack submarines capable of interdicting sea communications. Such a *quid pro quo* would make for greater symmetry between the "heartland" powers and the maritime nations, and it would make limitations on ASW of a more fundamental sort worthy of serious consideration.[6]

Finally, more searching questions must be raised as to how realistic, under modern conditions, concern about sea communications really is. The powerlessness of the non-Communist industrial nations in the face of the Arab oil embargo suggests that, in a world as interdependent industrially as ours, sea communications may no longer be the weakest link in maintaining war-fighting capability in a long-drawn-out conflict. At the very least, the traditional arguments for sea power and sea communications need to be carefully restudied in the light of a world economy now radically different in the extent of its interdependence from that which existed at the outbreak of World War II.

The Limitation of Military Budgets

There are two main arguments for limiting military expenditures. The first is that it is the most direct means for slowing the arms race without having to conduct endless technical bargaining over the equivalence of specific weapons systems. The second is that the resources thus saved could then be devoted to the solution of other basic international problems. Indeed, to the extent that military expenditures divert the world's resources from economic development, they become major contributors to world political instability, quite apart from the more direct effects of the "toys" on which the money is spent.

Two ways of approaching reduction of military budgets are: 1) reduction of the total military budget by mutual agreement of the superpowers (with the intention also of constricting military research and development); or 2) direct reduction of military research and development budgets only. Either of these methods presents problems because a great deal of military-related research is supported from outside the formal military budget. In this country, the AEC and NASA budgets include a large military component, and some military research and development is probably hidden in other appropriations (*vide* recently highly publicized technological expenditures of the C.I.A.). Early exploratory research is especially easy to bootleg under other categories of expenditure. In the Soviet Union a great deal of military research is apparently part of the "science budget," and it is not included in reports of military expenditure.

Another difficulty is that what we call "test and evaluation" and what the Russians call "assimilation into production" are excluded from research and development in the Soviet system, though included as such in American expenditures. On the other hand, a considerable amount of "independent R. and D." by industry in this country is not treated as military, although it is indirectly financed out of military procurement appropriations. There are also important differences in the cost factors for military research and procurement between the United States and the Soviet Union, so that direct comparison of any military budget is exceedingly difficult. Although salaries of technical personnel are lower in the Soviet Union, the rate of "productivity" in technical work is almost certainly much lower as well. For example, the Russians lack a high quality instrument industry, with the result that much experimental equipment is made and maintained by individual scientists.

Nevertheless, even recognizing these difficulties, the possibilities of mutually agreed limitations in military budgets should not be dismissed completely, especially if they could be coupled with agreements to deploy the skilled manpower thus released for some more beneficial purpose, such as the development of new energy resources related to world development.

Demobilization of Manpower and Facilities Devoted to Military Research and Development

York[7] has proposed a plan for the gradual removal of secrecy from research, so that scientific findings may ultimately be redirected to other purposes, and he cites the conversion of the Fort Detrick biological-warfare facility to cancer and related biological research as a precedent for what might be achieved on a larger scale in other areas of military-related technology. He proposes the annual transfer of five to ten per cent of the people now working on secret projects to "non-secret projects conducted in open facilities." Since this would result in a much more rapid increase in non-secret publishable research than could be accomplished through the normal growth of the scientific community, the transfers could be readily monitored, especially if the United States and the Soviet Union would also agree to an exchange of statistics on scientific and technical personnel, including the occupations and organizational affiliations of new university graduates.

There is no question that secrecy in research has contributed greatly to the mutual suspicions and the apprehensions about "technological surprise" that have characterized so much Cold War thinking. The monitoring of the transfer proposed by York would be facilitated by the natural inclination of scientists and engineers to disseminate their work among their peers and thus gain public credit for priority in discovery or invention. It might even be possible to organize official international meetings dealing with military technology, its progress, and the assessment of its broader effects and socio-political implications. Eventually an authoritative public literature on military technology might appear, open to criticism and evaluation by the international technological community.[8]

This greater openness in military technology may not only reduce apprehensions about "technical surprise," but also make it more difficult for the "hawkish" experts in any country to use selective release of information about an opponent's technical capabilities as an argument for large new weapons programs. On the other hand, too much publicity may stimulate irresponsible "gadgeteering" and unreasonable public fears about weapons possibilities that are in fact impractical.

There are also those who would argue that secrecy encourages inefficiency and "boondoggling" with resources that might be used much more effectively if the public were really privy to what was going on. While this is certainly a possibility, we believe that the advantages of publicity and open criticism outweigh the dangers of accelerated progress in politically perilous directions.

Unilateral Action of Scientists as a World-Wide Community to Withhold Their Services from Military Research and Development

It has been argued that, were scientists simply to refuse to participate in military research, the qualitative arms race could be slowed and the "technological imperative," which drives advances in military technology, could be dampened. A frequent proposal has been for a kind of Hippocratic Oath of scientists (and presumably also engineers) not to engage knowingly in research whose purpose is to facilitate the destruction of human life or the injury of fellow human beings.[9] Another similar proposal is for a professional "codes of ethics" among scientists, which would be made prerequisite to membership in a professional society and would necessarily be combined with some licensing system. Sanctions could then be applied, after the manner of disbarment proceedings in medicine or law, which would effectively prevent individuals who violated the code from earning a living in their profession. Still other proposals have included forms of strike or boycott against organizations engaged in military research. These, however, are effective weapons only if the decision of a majority of members of an occupational group can be enforced on the entire membership. They are ineffective unless employment in a profession can be given some attribute that the entire group can benefit from collectively, or not at all.

Perhaps the most obvious point to be made in connection with all these suggestions is that, to be effective, they would have to involve sanctions against individuals that could reach across national lines. A code of ethics enforced effectively in one nation and not in another would not much inhibit military technological progress, and it could well lead to alterations in the military balance that would increase rather than decrease the likelihood of conflict. It would also be enforceable only in a world already largely disarmed, i.e., in which the overwhelming number of technical people were engaged in non-military research. At present, one quarter of all technologists derive some support for their work, if not their livelihood, from military research, and—in the absence of realistic employment alternatives for these people—the code-of-ethics idea does not appear very practical. A partial adoption of such a code would only tend to isolate military scientists from the moral climate of the majority of their fellow professionals, thus making military development less rather than more sensitive to broader human implications.

A second and perhaps more fundamental point is that the distinction between "good" and "bad" research is much more difficult to draw in practice than the simplifications required for collective action can accommodate. Except in the final stages of development, most technical progress has manifold implications. Furthermore, so long as the use of force or the threat of force is an accepted instrument of international politics or domestic security, the line between "good" and "bad" research will remain obscure. Is it evil to work on temporarily disabling chemicals when the alternative may be thoroughly lethal bullets? By what logic is tear gas a legitimate police weapon in domestic disorders, but an illegal weapon in international conflict?

If the use of conventional air-dropped bombs is a legitimate form of warfare, is research directed toward improving their ability to discriminate more accurately between military and non-military targets to be regarded as aimed at the destruction of human life or at its protection? Is research directed at improving intelligence gathering about military matters stabilizing or destabilizing? Will research on body armor for infantry and police be condemned or condoned by a "Hippocratic oath"? What is the moral status of research directed at better care of war casualties? These examples just begin to indicate the complexity of the issues. Codes of ethics usually break down when applied to such complex moral questions, as we already know from modern medical practice.

One could, of course, take the position that any research whose results are likely to be used primarily in a military setting is morally suspect because its ultimate purpose is to facilitate the killing or injuring of fellow human beings. One could even argue in favor of allowing military action to become *more* lethal for the sake of making force ultimately less acceptable as a means for settling political conflict. Such subtleties, however, do not lend themselves to the kind universal moral consensus essential to the enforcement of a professional code of ethics.

The final argument is essentially a political one. If the majority in a nation decides that a certain course of action is legitimate and desirable, does some small group have the right or duty to withhold its special skills as a means of enforcing its own political value judgments on the majority? Most of us would agree, I think, that the *individual* has the right and duty to follow the dictates of his own conscience, and that he should be afforded some protection by society in doing so. However, in an organization where the views of a majority are enforced on all members and in a situation where membership is a precondition for practicing one's profession, the problem becomes more complicated. For then one is opening up the possibility that national policy will be determined not by a majority of citizens, but by, for example, a majority of physicists or electrical engineers. Is this compatible with a democratic polity?

So long as war and preparation for the possibility of war are generally regarded as legitimate, if regrettable, national activities, it is difficult to see how collective unilateral action on the part of selected occupational groups can be either effective or politically legitimate. However, an entirely different situation would obtain with respect to activities that had been outlawed by mutual agreement of governments. Once agreements have been reached to prohibit or limit certain kinds of research, collective actions of scientists or engineers can become a legitimate and useful tool in enforcing their observation by organizations. Under such circumstances, it might even be legitimate for the majority in a professional group to enforce its views on a minority, if the action thus enforced prevents, for example, the violation of a treaty.

Reorganizing Research and Development to Minimize the "Technological Imperative"

It is frequently argued that the organization of military research in the United States creates irresistible pressures to get the resulting hardware into production, often without adequate public debate as to its full implications. (There are indications that similar kinds of pressures exist in the Soviet Union.) For one thing, the Congress is often reluctant to appropriate research funds without specific plans for a weapons system, thus precluding research to generate options from which to select. Too often development is treated as part of a rational process in which the final result should be fully defined in advance.[10] Research in industry is also funded with the strong expectation that the results will be converted into an operational weapons system. Furthermore, in a period when force levels are relatively stable, service technical organizations and their industrial clients can guarantee their own survival only by generating a continual stream of qualitative improvements to make existing deployments obsolete. This tends to be the case even though, in fact, the majority of systems undergo some development, but never reach operational deployment. The system also tends to favor "product differentiation" for its own sake, much as in other sectors of the industrial economy. Research and development that do not lead to a deployed system are looked upon as failures and a waste of resources; little value is attached in practice to the knowledge gained in a project, if there are no tangible results.

This process is driven by a "military requirements" system that is partly based on fiction. Experience has taught the military technical community that it is much easier to sell interesting research if it can be pushed as a fully conceptualized weapons system meeting a well-defined military requirement based on a well-established threat from a postulated opponent. In practice, both the threat and the requirement may have been invented to provide a rationale for a development program started for other reasons, such as to perpetuate existing organizations, or to exploit a "sweet" technical concept.

For example, in the successive ABM systems, one is struck by the persistence of the hardware and the rapidity with which the rationale for it has shifted. The purpose was originally city defense against Russian attack, became area defense against Chinese attack or accidental launching, and finally was explained as defense of missile silos and command and control centers. In addition, the members of Congress often concentrated their attention on the technical aspects of the system and on its feasibility and cost—which they were poorly qualified to judge—rather than on its political and diplomatic implications, which they theoretically were well qualified to judge. The opponents of ABM tried to find witnesses willing to testify that it would not work technically, rather than to criticize it from the point of view of national policy. Many of the technical witnesses, on both sides, were really motivated by strategic policy considerations, or their personal evaluations of the international situation, or the supposed intentions of the Soviets, but their political allies found it more politic for them to couch their arguments in narrow technical terms, partly because technical experts are often automatically regarded as having nothing useful to say on policy matters. Furthermore, technical testimony appears more "objective" and politically neutral, and it is thus thought to carry more weight with those politicians who have not yet made up their minds.

A system that has passed successfully through the advanced development stage is seldom canceled, at least overtly, through reconsideration of an established military requirement; it would be too great an admission of failure on the highest policy level. Therefore, the justification for cancellation or redirection of a large weapons system must appear to be made on technical or economic grounds. This does not mean that the history of military development is not strewn with the skeletons of canceled systems—one has only to recall the nuclear-powered aircraft, the Navaho missile,

Skybolt, Dynosoar, the B-70 bomber, the manned orbiting laboratory (MOL), and literally hundreds of other smaller projects. But the tragedy is that they were canceled for reasons that in most instances could have been foreseen when the original requirements were established, although the cancellation may have been publicly justified on other grounds. Still others were carried to the hardware stage, not because they were needed but simply because there was no valid cost overrun or technical justification for canceling them.

These situations obviously constitute at least one point of convergence in interest between the advocates of arms control and the advocates of a more economical and cost-effective defense procurement system. The present system is weak because it is insufficiently responsive to policy and strategic considerations at an early stage of a systems development. Military requirements tend to become after-the-fact rationalizations of technical ideas cooked up at a relatively low level in the military-technical-contractor bureaucracy. Even the closely reasoned annual defense-posture statements may involve more rationalizations of existing development programs than appear from their format and organization. The kinds of arguments made by the President's Blue Ribbon Defense Panel,[11] though developed primarily to favor vigorous new weapons development, can be equally applied to arms control and to constraint in new weapons development. In both cases, the argument is for opening the crucial decisions to a broader range of policy considerations and to criticism by a larger public than is now the case.

Military research also leads to premature and useless development of many components of a system. In the nuclear aircraft program, for example, a great deal of effort went into development and acquisition of non-nuclear and rather conventional hardware before sufficient research had been done to determine the feasibility of making a nuclear fuel element that would meet the original performance specifications. Many of these components had to be scrapped as the system specifications were progressively adjusted downward to meet the reduced capabilities of the feasible fuel element. The histories of TFX, the C-5, and several other celebrated military white elephants provide similar examples. Yet development even of these less critical components created pressure to go forward with the entire system, even in the face of other technical failures or a reconsideration of policy.

In the late fifties, many argued against the wastefulness of the military requirements system. Such scholars as Burton Klein and Fred Scherer proposed that a much larger fraction of research and development should be devoted to improving the quality and performance of such basic items as radars, jet engines, rocket-case materials, and guidance computers,[12] without reference to a particular military requirement or systems goal. After the decision to proceed with full development, one could then choose the best "building blocks" available, without having to develop each under forced draft to meet the specifications of a full weapons system.

Criticism of defense procurement tends to focus on the "military-industrial complex" and its dynamic role in generating "planned obsolescence" in weapons systems. Without question, the symbiosis between the technical bureaucracies in the Pentagon, contractor-technical personnel, and the Armed Services committees of the Congress (usually from districts heavily benefited by defense procurement) has been a factor in the continuing preference for new weapons. However, it is not so clear that the problem could be avoided by returning to the government arsenal system, or to the treatment of the defense industry as a regulated monopoly, as has sometimes been proposed. Recent attempts to shut down obsolete military bases suggest that it is considerably harder to close a purely governmental operation than it is to cancel a large contract with a private firm, even when equally large local labor forces are involved. Ownership or control of the military-industrial complex does not in itself appear to be a crucial factor in making military development more responsive to broader policy guidance or to arms-control considerations.

Conclusion

To summarize, the most promising lines of action for controlling the qualitative arms race probably lie in mutually agreed limitations on testing, including limits on the number of permissible missile launches, and on a comprehensive nuclear-test ban. Agreements to refrain from research are often difficult to monitor, though they may have considerable value if accompanied by well-publicized commitments to refrain from actions that would jeopardize the stability of mutual deterrence. In fact, such general declarations may be more useful than attempts to negotiate highly detailed prohibitions, since they can shift the balance of the internal bureaucratic debate on whether to go forward with a given weapons development. The ban in the ABM treaty on the testing of exotic ABM techniques in space provided a precedent, though it fell short of clearly limiting research and development. Attempts at unilateral action by professional groups, such as "codes of ethics" forbidding participation in research aimed at injury to or destruction of human life, are likely to be ineffective because of the ambiguity and lack of consensus regarding what constitutes "good" and "bad" research. However, professional self-discipline that is legitimized by official mutual weapons-control declarations provides some hope.

Changes in the management of weapons-systems development, with clear stages that allow for careful analysis of technical alternatives and of political and arms-control implications along the line, promise not only greater national security for our investment, but also a less frenetic atmosphere of technological competition between the superpowers. There appears to be a convergence of interests here between the advocates of more efficient military expenditure and advocates of arms control.

III. Cutting Back on Military Research: Opportunities and Problems

In 1970, the total research funds in the world devoted to military efforts were estimated at twenty-five billion dollars, about forty per cent of the world total for research generally. Some twenty-five per cent of the world's scientific and technical manpower was engaged in research which, however general its potential application, had been originally justified primarily on military grounds. This twenty-five per cent probably represents the most sophisticated and highly trained segment of the technical community.[13] The military devotes much more money than other economic enterprises do to research and development: it accounts for one-eighth of all world expenditures for military purposes, whereas in manufacturing industries in the United States, for example, it accounts for only about four per cent of sales. From 1958 to 1965, eighty per cent of the personnel additions to research and development occurred in just two industries, aerospace and electrical equipment, i.e., those most heavily involved in government-financed defense research. In 1968 roughly forty-three per cent of the physicists in this country with doctoral degrees were at least partially dependent on military budgets for support of their scientific effort.[14] Moreover, a significant fraction, perhaps twenty per cent, of the scientific recruitment in the nineteen-sixties was accomplished through a "brain drain" of trained people from the rest of the non-Communist world, including the less industrialized countries. These immigrants were either employed directly in the American military space effort, or, probably more frequently, replaced native Americans in less technically glamorous civilian occupations. During this period, some of the less fashionable fields of engineering attracted up to fifty per cent foreign graduate students, many of whom remained in the United States.

There is now fairly wide agreement among economists that the American concentration on space defense in the early sixties had a depressing effect on innovation in the private economy, as well as on efforts for public improvement in such areas as pollution control, public transportation, and housing. A recent study by Boretsky[15] suggests that in the Netherlands and Japan the number of scientists and engineers per equivalent dollar of GNP in civilian industries is more than two and a half times larger than in the United States. This gives a somewhat exaggerated picture, because there is some civilian "fall-out" from military and space research and development in the United States, but it does suggest one reason for the recent poor performance of this country in international trade, and it is indicative of the possible price paid for preoccupation with military research over the past two decades.

To the extent that science and technology and their wide diffusion are important components of world economic development, the statistics quoted above reveal that the diversion of human resources to military expenditures is much more serious than is the diversion of economic resources. Unfortunately, this does not mean the resources can be redeployed for more constructive purposes very quickly. A recent study by Wassily Leontief and his associates,[16] using the methods of "input-output" analysis, shows that a twenty per cent cut in military expenditures in the United States, even with adjustment of aggregate demand to maintain full employment, would cause a more than thirteen per cent net reduction in research activities. This calculation is based on a 1958 input-output matrix, and there is reason to believe that the effect would be much larger if a more recent measure had been available.

While one would hope that these deficits in utilization of scientists would be transient, they do represent a serious, even if temporary, dislocation of the technical community, and they probably contribute to the political difficulties of controlling the military effort.

If one looks at the technical component of the many complex challenges facing our interdependent world in the remainder of this century, one has a sense that humanity can ill afford the diversion of talent represented by its military effort. These considerations also suggest that efforts to control military research expenditures for arms-control reasons should be accompanied by vigorous efforts to redeploy the resources thus liberated to priority civilian tasks. This may prove difficult to do, but such an effort is needed, not so much to cushion the impact of unemployment as to insure the fullest possible use of resources and capacities. These will be badly needed, especially during the last two decades of this century, when the supply of new graduates in science and engineering will be declining. It would be hoped that a significant part of the technical resources liberated from military technology could be devoted to problems related to economic development in deprived parts of the world, although this is the most difficult kind of reconversion.

The longer the world postpones addressing the problem of technological reconversion, the more difficult and intractable will it become. As military-space technology advances, it tends to become increasingly remote from potential civilian applications. In the nineteen-fifties, military aircraft became prototypes for civilian jets, and military and intelligence computers contributed to the data-processing market. But today the sophisticated equipment required for an ABM system goes far beyond what is needed for anything but the tiny scientific computing market, e.g., in numerical weather modeling. The attempt to transfer the technology of supersonic bombers and fighters to a civilian SST is proving much more expensive and of more dubious benefit than was the case with subsonic aircraft. After some early enthusiasm, it does not appear that space vehicles offer much promise for delivering the mail, or carrying intercontinental passengers, or even disposing of radio-active wastes. The booster technology required for communications satellites or earth resource survey satellites is largely of early-1960 vintage. There are still some generic technologies, such as lasers or large-scale computer memories, which have major civilian applications, but these items are mostly at the research end of the development spectrum; they do not benefit much from the large sums spent on end-item military developments. Such civilian benefit as derives from military research expenditures comes largely from the relatively inexpensive background and exploratory research that precedes systems development.

Thus, even if the American military space effort did result in useful economic "spin-off" in the past—a proposition that is increasingly being called into question— it is less likely to do so in the future. The benefits that derive from military research are greatly attenuated when classified and disseminated only within a restricted community. Studies indicate that the number of patents per dollar of research and development expenditure is much smaller for military and space efforts than for industrially sponsored research.[17] In consequence, space and military research must be justified primarily on its own merits and not on the basis of any benefits alleged for the rest of the economy. If the alternative were not to make use of the resources or skills at all, perhaps there would be some slight justification for the "spin-off" argument, but it certainly has no merit when one takes into consideration all of the other needs of society.

Some of the economic adjustments occasioned by decline in military expenditures might be handled more easily on a multinational basis. Many of the serious problems facing the world in resources, energy, environment, population, food, or economic development lend themselves to cooperative efforts among countries, and the political appeal of such cooperation would help to neutralize the negative economic effects of declining defense expenditures. The incentives for military innovation might decline if the alternative uses of technical manpower could be made more tangible through multinational action.

IV. Conclusion

Our discussion has shown that new technology has helped to fuel the arms race, though not all technological developments are potentially destabilizing to the military balance. Without doubt, a less frenetic research effort in military technology would reduce the pressures for deployment of the resulting, often unnecessary, weapons systems. It would also decrease the likelihood of still more new technological development that would give an important military or political advantage to one side, or create a situation in which safety was perceived to lie in attacking first. Any reduction in the rate of military innovation would be most valuable if it were selective, but selectivity will necessitate a system of assessment that assures consideration in a context broader than immediate political or military advantage. The notion of an "impact statement" to be required before each major decision about new weapons development might be useful, especially if it could be brought within an international or at least a multinational framework.

We have considered a number of proposals for limiting the rate of military technological innovation, with special emphasis on forestalling those that might be threatening to the stability of the military balance. Among the most useful are a comprehensive ban on nuclear testing and a limit on the number of missile tests. The political value should be stressed of mutual declarations of policy, foreswearing either development or deployment actions that would jeopardize confidence in each side's retaliatory capability. Such declarations could help to set in motion internal forces which would insure that proposed military developments are looked at more critically. The case of ASW development poses an especially difficult problem because of the ambiguity between ASW for the protection of sea communications and ASW for compromising the sea-based deterrent. However, the increasing ability of nations to cut off vital natural resources at their source without fear of military reprisal may now be fundamentally changing the role of sea communications and naval power in this equation.

Limitations on military research and development are also increasingly required to conserve technical resources for the urgent problems facing humanity. There is a growing divergence between trends in military technology and the technological needs of the rest of the world's economy. The longer the attempt is delayed to convert some military technical resources to other ends, the more difficult will this conversion become. As time goes on swords will look less and less like ploughshares.

REFERENCES

[1] For an excellent, generally available summary of the technical situation, see D. G. Hoag, "Ballistic Missile Guidance," in Feld, Greenwood, Rathjens, Weinberg, eds., *Impact of New Technologies on the Arms Race* (Cambridge, Mass., 1971), cf. esp. pp. 99-105.

[2] See H. Kahn and A. J. Wiener, *The Year 2000* (London, 1967), pp. 86-98.

[3] H. York, "Some Possible Measures for Slowing the Qualitative Arms Race," *Proceedings of the 22nd Pugwash Conference on Science and World Affairs, Oxford, England, September 7-12, 1972* (Oxford, 1973), pp. 228-235.

[4] *Ibid.*, p. 230.

[5] R. Witkin, *New York Times*, September 11, 1973.

[6] H. Brooks, "The Political Interaction Between Tactical and Strategic ASW," C. Tsipis, A. H. Cahn, B. T. Feld, eds., *The Future of the Sea-Based Deterrent*, (Cambridge, Mass., 1973), pp. 79-86.

[7] York, *op. cit.*, p. 232.

[8] An approach to what we have in mind is exemplified by the publication cited in note 1 which was the product of a privately sponsored international conference held at Wingspread, Wisconsin, on the implications of new technology for the future of the arms race.

[9] *Physics Today,* March, 1970, p. 67.

[10] H. Brooks, "Applied Research: Definitions, Concepts, Themes," in *Applied Science and Technological Progress,* a report to the U.S. House of Representatives by the National Academy of Sciences (USGPO, Washington, D.C., June, 1967), pp. 21-56; also H. Brooks, *The Government of Science* (Cambridge, Mass., 1968), pp. 279-332.

[11] Blue Ribbon Defense Panel, Report to the President and the Secretary of Defense on the Department of Defense (USGPO, Washington, D.C., 1970).

[12] Burton Klein, "What's Wrong with Military R. and D.?", *Rand Corporation Report,* P-1267 (Santa Monica, 1960).

[13] Y. de Hemptinne, "Military Research and Its Impact on World Peace," *Pugwash, op. cit.,* pp. 390-397.

[14] H. Brooks, "The Physical Sciences: Bellwether of Science Policy," in J. Shannon, ed., *Science and the Evolution of Public Policy* (New York, 1973), pp. 105-134.

[15] M. Boretsky, "Trends in U.S. Technology: A Political Economist's View," *American Scientist,* 63 (1974), 70-82, esp. table 7, p. 76.

[16] Leontief, Morgan, Polenske, Simpson, and Turner, "The Economic Impact—Industrial and Regional—of an Arms Cut," *The Review of Economics and Statistics,* 47:3 (August, 1965), 217-241, esp. table 1, p. 22

[17] S. Doctors, *The Role of Federal Agencies in Technology Transfer* (Cambridge, Mass., 1969).

GRAHAM T. ALLISON AND FREDERIC A. MORRIS

Armaments and Arms Control: Exploring the Determinants of Military Weapons

DETENTE BETWEEN the United States and the Soviet Union, transition from an era of confrontation to an era of negotiation, and historic arms-control agreements—all are evidently fully compatible with the expansion of American and Soviet strategic arsenals and with increased expenditures on strategic arms. Consider several vignettes from a long and complicated record.[1]

1) In 1963, the United States and the Soviet Union signed the Nuclear Test Ban Treaty. In the eighteen years preceding the nuclear test ban, the number of nuclear tests by the two countries was 469; in the ten years following the test ban, the number of tests was 424.[2]

2) In 1972, the United States and the Soviet Union signed the Strategic Arms Limitation Agreements—a permanent ABM treaty restricting each nation to two ABM sites, and an Interim Agreement freezing the number of strategic missile launchers for five years. Almost immediately Secretary of Defense Laird announced a speed-up in the deployment of Trident (a new nuclear missile-launching submarine currently scheduled to cost over one billion dollars per boat), faster development of the B-1 (a new strategic bomber), and continued deployment of MIRV (more than doubling the number of nuclear warheads launched by American missiles). Shortly after the agreements, the Soviet Union tested four new strategic missiles—the SS-16, SS-17, SS-18, and SS-19—and redoubled its efforts to develop an effective MIRV. In the three years since the SALT I treaties, the United States has added to its arsenal of independently targetable nuclear weapons almost half again as many as it had at the time the treaty was signed.

3) In 1973 and 1974, Secretary Brezhnev and President Nixon signed a number of new agreements relating to strategic arms, "cementing the era of negotiation" and "making detente irreversible." These included accords on Avoiding Atomic War, Basic Principles of Negotiations on Further Limitations of Strategic Arms, amendment of the ABM treaty to limit each country to only one site, and a Threshold Test Ban on underground tests of nuclear weapons exceeding one hundred and fifty kilotons. The Basic Principles of Negotiations assert that "both sides will be guided by the recognition that efforts to obtain unilateral advantage, directly or indirectly, would be inconsistent with the strengthening of peaceful relations between the USA and USSR." Yet after a decade of steady decline in strategic

99

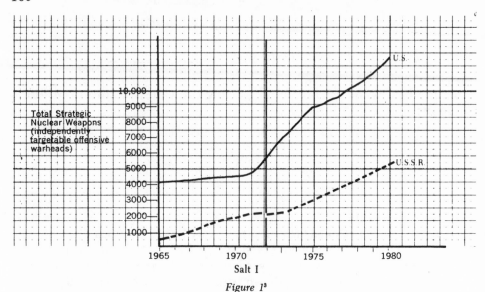

Figure 1[3]

expenditures—in the absence of a SALT Treaty and attendant principles and agreements—defense budgets submitted to Congress in 1973 and 1974 called for a leveling off of that decline and, indeed, for increasing strategic expenditures, including the initiation of programs that will require further increases in strategic spending over the next five years. Estimates indicate continuing increases in Soviet strategic expenditures as well.

It is obvious from these three examples that progress in arms control has been accompanied by advances in armaments. A partial explanation of this anomaly is to be found in an unpleasant fact, which arms-control advocates tend to ignore, namely, that the objectives of arms control are not mutually re-enforcing. These objectives are: 1) to reduce the likelihood of war; 2) to reduce the scope and violence, if war occurs; and 3) to reduce the costs of preparing for war. But not every action that reduces the probability of war also reduces its cost, e.g., hardening missile silos increases cost, while reducing likelihood.

The anomaly also has a more ideological source, namely, the prevailing conception of how to solve the problem of arms control, which tends to focus exclusively on international treaties arrived at by international negotiations. Recent events reflect past arms-control literature almost in caricature. To a much greater extent than has been recognized, the musings of academic scribblers of the late nineteen-fifties have become the "common sense" of statesmen in the nineteen-seventies and have contributed powerfully to the arms-control agreements of recent years. Both the agreements themselves and the process of negotiation by which they were achieved have reduced the probability of war; some have also limited strategic expenditures; some may even have reduced the damage that would result from war. But, as recent events demonstrate dramatically, arms-control agreements are not incompatible with continuing quantitative and qualitative improvements in strategic armaments and continuing high, and even increasing, expenditures on strategic arms. In fact,

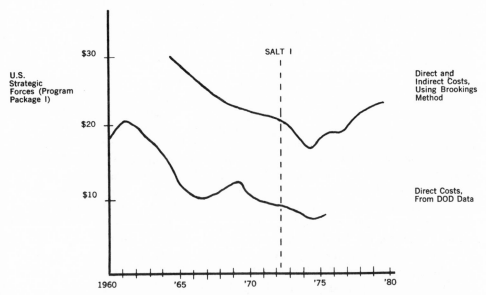

Figure 2⁴ Total Obligational Authority in Billions of FY 1975 Dollars

Sources: Those cited for Table I. Unfortunately, there is no single official source for all important in-dicators of force posture. This chart is based on calculations by Richard Huff from all available sources. While these differ somewhat from other estimates, e.g., IISS, they are, in our judgment, more accurate. Differences among estimates do not affect the basic picture.

arms-control agreements have only *constrained* and *channeled* national weapons-development processes; they have not slowed them down.

How specific arms-control agreements constrain the organizational and political forces in a given nation that produces weapons, and with what effect for arms-control objectives, is a complex empirical question. Some constraints amount to little more than squeezing a balloon, causing it to expand elsewhere, e.g., quantitative limits in-tensify efforts for qualitative improvements. Some constraints eliminate the deploy-ment (and slow down the development) of a specified class of weapons (e.g., ABM) with unpredictable effects on other classes of weapons. The process of negotiating international constraints creates intra-national pressure for progress in an area before further work is proscribed, provides a cover for the development of phony "bargain-ing chips," and leads to domestic bargains for new weapons that would not otherwise have been procured. If statesmen have ignored the impact of arms-control negotia-tions and agreements on the national processes by which weapons are developed and procured, students of arms control must bear much of the responsibility. A careful review of the literature of arms control and strategy finds no important issue less studied than the question of what determines the number and character of the weapons in American and Soviet force postures.

Arms-control analysts have persistently and systematically neglected the processes by which nations develop and procure weapons. Rather than recognizing the weapons-acquisition process as a central piece of the arms-control puzzle, the literature has substituted a simplification of the problem. According to this simplifica-tion, a nation's arsenal of weapons is viewed as the product of governmental choices made on the grounds of calculations about national strategic objectives and doctrines. On this basis, arms-control analysts have proceeded to what they have regarded as the important issues. Let the reader recall (or re-examine) the "bible of arms control," the *Daedalus* issue of 1961, later published as *Arms Control, Disarmament, and National Security.* He will find no discussion of the weapons-acquisition process and no discussion of the impact of the process on arms-control objectives.

Without denying the value of the insights provided by arms-control analysts in the late nineteen-fifties, or denigrating the importance of their contribution to recent arms-control agreements, this essay argues for a significant expansion in the focus of the arms-control problem. National weapons-acquisition processes are, and must be recognized as, a major part of the problem of arms control. Because the problem has been so little studied, the causal factors that shape weapons development are not at all well understood. Yet these factors obviously include many of the same kinds of organizational and political influences that shape other decisions and actions taken by national governments. (In this sense, our insistence on recognizing the importance of national weapons processes in arms control will be resisted by some as adding to the "de-internationalization of international relations"; we prefer to think of it—in an equally infelicitous phrase—as "further politicization of foreign policy.")

The argument presented here has developed from the assignment given the authors by the American Academy of Arts and Sciences Summer Study on "New Directions in Arms Control," which was to make a preliminary review of available weapons case histories in order to discover their implications for arms control. The authors reviewed several dozen such case histories; but here we shall present summaries of only three of them, which will serve as illustrations for the more general argument developed from the larger sample. This essay is essentially exploratory; it attempts to identify important causal factors that shape military weapons developments and to identify issues for further research. Because of the limited information available about the Soviet weapons acquisitions process, we shall concentrate on the American system.

Section I of the essay will identify the simplification relied upon in most discussions of force posture, cite several examples of its use, and note important questions about three of the major strategic weapons systems of the nineteen-sixties. Section II outlines two alternative overviews of the determinants of weapons, and it reconsiders the puzzles about the three weapons systems, summarizing evidence from recent case histories. Section III formulates several tentative hypotheses about the process by which weapons are developed and procured and draws implications of this process for arms control.

I. The Prevailing Simplification and Some Illustrative Puzzles

No public official has been more deeply concerned about the problem of controlling the strategic-arms race than former Secretary of Defense McNamara. In his annual Force Posture Statements and public speeches, he made a sustained effort to educate the public to the dangers of what he labeled the "mad momentum of the arms race." The crux of McNamara's argument can be found in his own words:

What is essential to understand here is that the Soviet Union and the United States mutually influence one another's strategic plans. Whatever be their intentions, whatever be our intentions, *actions*—or even realistically potential actions—on either side relating to the build-up of nuclear forces, be they either offensive or defensive weapons, *necessarily trigger* reactions on the other side [emphasis added]. It is precisely this action-reaction phenomenon that fuels an arms race.[5]

According to McNamara, both the United States and the Soviet Union

. . . have strategic arsenals greatly in excess of a credible assured destruction capability. [They] have reached that point of excess in each case for precisely the same reason: we each have reacted to the other's build-up with very conservative calculations. We have, that is, each built a greater arsenal than either of us needed for a second strike capability, simply because we each wanted to be able to cope with the "worst plausible case."

McNamara illustrated the action-reaction phenomenon with reference to American deployment of an anti-Soviet ABM.

Were we to deploy a heavy system throughout the United States, the Soviets would clearly be strongly motivated to so increase their offensive capability as to cancel out our defensive advantage. It is futile for each of us to spend four billion dollars, forty billion dollars or four hundred billion—and at the end of all the spending, and at the end of all the deployment, and at the end of all the effort, to be relatively at the same point of balance on the security scale that we are now. . . . If we opt for heavy ABM deployment—at whatever price—*we can be certain that the Soviets will react to offset the advantage we would hope to gain* [emphasis added].

The conceptual simplification employed by Secretary McNamara in analyzing changes in American force posture and predicting reactions in Soviet force posture is not difficult to discover. Each nation's force posture is conceived as the product of governmental choice aimed at achieving well-defined strategic objectives that are threatened by specific changes in the other nation's forces.

In "The Dynamics of the Arms Race," George Rathjens "inquires into the nature of the forces that impel an arms race."[6] With a directness and clarity unusual in discussions on this subject, Rathjens lays out the logic of action-reaction analysis. According to Rathjens' summary of his argument, the "Action-Reaction Phenomenon, stimulated in most cases by uncertainty about an adversary's intentions and capabilities, characterizes the dynamics of the arms race." Reviewing American and Soviet strategic forces since 1960, he finds that:

1) American overreaction to uncertainty at the time of the erroneous "missile gap" in 1960 led to the massive growth of the U.S. missile forces during the 1960's.

2) The scale of this deployment may have led in turn to the recent large Russian build-up in strategic offensive forces and also the deployment of a limited ABM system around Moscow.

3) The U.S. response to the possible extension of the Moscow ABM system into a country-wide system (and to the deployment of a Russian anti-aircraft system which until recently was thought to be a country-wide ABM system) was to equip its Minuteman III and Poseidon missiles with MIRV warheads.

4) A likely Russian reaction to the potential counter-force threat posed by the MIRVs is development of land-mobile ICBMs.

The conceptual basis for these explanations and predictions should be obvious. Weapons are the result of national strategic choice; governmental leaders select specific weapons and total force posture on the basis of precise calculations about national objectives, perceived threats, and strategic doctrine within the constraints of technology and budget. This set of assumptions, which we have identified as the prevailing simplification, is really a variant of a basic conceptual model that most people use when thinking about most problems of foreign policy most of the time.[7] That the "government" is in fact a loose collection of organizations and people is readily apparent. That "choices" of weapons by the United States or the Soviet Union are abstractions for the activities of these organizations and people is certainly no revelation. But explanations and predictions in terms of this simplification nevertheless tend to collect the activities of these people and organizations into one box called "the government," and the mechanism which moves potential weapons systems through the box until they emerge as part of the force posture is called a "strategic choice."

That—"other things being equal"—national decision processes choose weapons designed to implement certain objectives or doctrines is probably true, perhaps even tautologous. The proposition, "If the Soviet Union knows that weapons system X will be less effective in achieving a desired objective than weapons system Y, it will be less likely to purchase weapons system X," is no doubt correct. What is less clear, however, is:

a) At what level do summary concepts like "the Soviet government," "strategic objectives," and "doctrines" stop being meaningful?

b) What are the rules of evidence for making summary statements about national goals and intentions?

c) How can one give an empirical interpretation to such statements by reference, on the one hand, to pressures in the international environment and, on the other, to shared national values and assumptions?

d) How much of the variance in outcomes can be explained by factors emphasized by the prevailing simplification, e.g., whether strategic forces are determined to the third decimal place, or ten per cent, or one hundred per cent?

These general questions can be applied in specific terms to three major American strategic-weapons systems of the nineteen-sixties. In each case, a juxtaposition of the characteristics of the weapon deployed with the official objectives and doctrines they were said to serve produces a puzzle.

1) *American strategic forces in the nineteen-sixties:* Defense Secretary Mc-Namara's final Force Posture Statement (February, 1968) provided a detailed review of American nuclear strategy. McNamara insisted that the main objective of our strategic forces was "assured destruction," that is, "an ability to inflict at all times and under all foreseeable conditions an unacceptable degree of damage upon any aggressor . . . even after absorbing a surprise attack."[8] When he introduced this concept in 1965, McNamara set the necessary level of damage at one quarter to one third of the Soviet population and about two thirds of Soviet industrial capacity. In his valedictory statement, the Secretary judged that "a capacity on our part to destroy, say, one-fifth to one-fourth of her population and one-half her industrial capacity would serve as an effective deterrent."[9]

Now, compare these requirements with the capabilities actually acquired under McNamara's stewardship. According to McNamara's final force-posture statement, two hundred "equivalent megatons delivered" (EMTs) would meet the assured-destruction objective against the Soviet population projected for 1972.[10] As McNamara spoke, American strategic forces included over 4,000 EMTs on bombers; 1,000 EMTs on ICBMs; 600 EMTs on SLBMs.[11] Factors such as survivability, reliability, and accuracy affect how many of these EMTs would actually destroy their targets under second-strike conditions. But even under very pessimistic assumptions, that figure grossly exceeds the necessary two hundred. This presents our first puzzle: Why did actual strategic forces exceed capabilities required by the doctrine of assured destruction by such a vast amount?

2) *Hardsite defense and ABM:* In September, 1967, Secretary of Defense McNamara announced the Johnson Administration's decision to deploy a light ABM system to defend population areas against the potential Chinese nuclear threat. In March, 1969, President Nixon announced a "substantial modification" of this Sentinel ABM. While using Sentinel components, Nixon proposed a new system (soon designated Safeguard) which revised priorities, the first among them being the "protection of our land-based retaliatory forces against a direct attack by the Soviet Union."[12] A hybrid that combined area-defense and terminal-defense components, Safeguard had quite limited hardsite capability (i.e., ability to defend hardened ICBM silos against attacks). This provides our second puzzle: Given Nixon's decision to defend ICBMs, why did the government choose a system that would defend them so poorly?

3) *MIRV as a response to Soviet ABM:* According to McNamara's analysis of the arms race quoted above, "actions relating to the build-up of nuclear forces, be they either offensive or defensive weapons . . . necessarily trigger reactions on the other side." Rathjens' analysis identified just such a relationship between the Soviet ABM and the American MIRV, asserting that "the U.S. response to the possible extension of the Moscow ABM system to a country-wide system . . . was to equip its Minuteman III and Poseidon missiles with MIRV warheads." Senator Jacob Javits emphasized this point in Senate Foreign Relations subcommittee hearings on ABM: "Is it or is it not a fact," Javits rhetorically asked Deputy Secretary of Defense Packard, "that the MIRV system began to be developed as soon as we had reliable information that the Russians were deploying an anti-ballistic missile system around at least one of their cities?"[13] In 1971, Defense Research and Engineering Director John Foster confirmed the link between Soviet ABM and the need for American MIRV by arguing the converse: "If a ban were placed on the ABM, in the sense of banning a capability to intercept a ballistic missile attack, then as I see it at the moment, there would be no need for the United States to deploy MIRV."[14] The SALT agreement of 1972 banned equipment capable of intercepting a ballistic missile attack. The United States nonetheless continued deploying MIRV. In this case, the puzzle is twofold: If the American MIRV was a *response* to Soviet ABM, why did American research and development on MIRV *precede* Soviet ABM, *and* why did American deployment of MIRV continue *after* Soviet ABMs were effectively banned?

A review of other weapons (including Trident and the F-111, which are discussed elsewhere in this issue) uncovers similar paradoxes. When examined carefully, weapons systems are found to be "underdetermined" by the prevailing simplification,[15] that is, the factors emphasized by the simplification are not sufficient to explain why one weapon emerged rather than another.

II. Alternative Overviews and Explanations

The most casual observation shows that the actual weapons process differs rather substantially from the prevailing simplification. Review of the record of predictions and explanations based on the simplification indicates that the latter simply has not adequately summarized the causal impact of relevant factors in the process. What we need is a well-defined, tested causal model of the multiple determinants of military force posture. No such model exists; nor can one emerge without a very substantial research effort. In the meantime, analysts and officials will continue discussing force posture, making judgments and inferences in which force posture plays an important secondary role, and taking action on the basis of such inferences and predictions. These activities could be usefully informed by alternative simplifications that capture other important causal factors in the weapons process. Our aim here is to state two alternative simplifications that, while obviously inadequate and crude, may serve as a stark reminder of the limits to our understanding of the actual determinants of military force posture. The alternative simplifications should make persuasive the importance of causal factors now overlooked or underemphasized. Since both the prevailing simplification and the alternative overviews stress somewhat different causal factors, taken together they may serve as a point of departure for research aimed at an adequate causal map of the process.

These alternative overviews can be developed at considerable length, but will only be summarized briefly here in the form of two series of assertions and questions.[16]

A. *Force Posture as Political Resultant*

ASSERTIONS:

a) Analytic uncertainty: problems of force posture are so complex that reasonable men can disagree about which weapons system the United States should have (and even about which strategic doctrine, or which objective). In fact, the relevant parties do disagree about weapons systems, as well as about doctrines and objectives.

b) Differences of opinion among individuals and groups are organizationally based. Many of the sharp differences reflect—and are highly predictable in the light of—position and organization. (When has a Chief of Staff of the Air Force or a Strategic Air Command officer advocated an end to advanced manned bombers?)

c) Political resolution: differences of opinion among participants who share power must be resolved by bargaining or politics.

QUESTIONS:

1) Who plays? Who participates in the bargaining? Whose preferences count in shaping the weapons systems that emerge?

2) What determines the participants' preferences?

3) How are preferences combined? Which groups (and interests) are "heavies" and which are "lights" in the process?

4) How stable is the distribution of influence among participants (and what are the sources)?

B. *Force Posture as Organizational Output*

ASSERTIONS:

a) The fact that weapons emerge from a lengthy process of great complexity accents the importance of organizations in determining results.

b) The configuration of organizations that constitute a government changes very slowly.

c) The behavior of organizations at time *t* is primarily determined by goals and procedures of these organizations at time *t*-1.

d) Government leaders can disturb the behavior of these organizations, but their behavior cannot be controlled to any great extent by a central authority.

QUESTIONS:

1) How is the government organized for acquiring weapons, i.e., what organizations and organizational units act on this issue and with what relative influence?

2) How do the goals and procedures of these organizations affect *information* available at various points where decisions are made, choices defined, etc?

3) How do the goals and procedures of these organizations affect the *alternative* courses of action considered at various points where decisions are made, issues defined, etc.?

4) How do the goals and procedures of these organizations affect the *implementation* of government choices?

These two alternative overviews are obviously not mutually exclusive. Both simplifications are at a level of generalization that permits some reconciliation. For example, the relative stability of the influence of interests in the first alternative overview results in part from the role of military organizations in this process. Still, each overview can be used to provide a relatively straightforward answer to why that particular weapons system appeared in the force posture. The preservation of competing simplifications may help broaden our understanding of the process.

It would be possible at the current stage of research to formulate a single overview of the determinants of force posture, incorporating some of the best features of all the simplifications. We have chosen not to do so because we believe that a single overview might create an impression of understanding greater than that which actually exists. In addition, the competing simplifications serve as a useful point of departure for our own research strategy, which is: first, utilizing the concepts of the simplifications, to examine existing case material in order to make a preliminary determination of the major factors that shape force posture; second, to gather data about these major causal factors; and, third, to formulate and test hypotheses and then, through clustering them, to construct partial models of the process.

In the last few years, students of defense policy have produced a number of case histories of American weapons. In contrast to case studies that simply "tell the story" of a particular development, most of these cases were undertaken to provide answers to more general questions (including some raised by the alternative overviews) and to generate hypotheses that went beyond the particular cases. None of the available studies provides a full, satisfactory explanation of the development of a particular weapon, but the researcher usually succeeded in peeling off at least two or three layers of the weapons-development onion—in contrast to the prevailing simplification, which focuses on the onion as a whole. As it happens, most of the cases divide the government into a number of organizations, treat the organizations as individuals, and then explain the weapon development as the result of bargaining among competing organizational interests. Two layers into the onion, one does understand somewhat more; one's predictions improve. But because the innermost layers of the onion remain intact, each case raises as many questions as it answers. Indeed, this initial division reinforces the view asserted at the outset: the determinants of force posture are not understood; analysts do not even have appropriate categories for investigating the causal factors involved.

1. AMERICAN STRATEGIC FORCES IN THE NINETEEN-SIXTIES

By the end of Robert McNamara's tenure as Secretary of Defense, the primacy of "assured destruction" as the central American strategic objective had been established. McNamara's associates had developed a formula for translating that objective into required capabilities. "Indeed," according to Assistant Secretary of Defense Alain Enthoven, "in sharp contrast to most other types of military requirements, those for strategic forces lend themselves to calculation."[17] Yet when one performs the calculation, the answer is unmistakable: American forces have consistently and dramatically exceeded the number of "equivalent megatons delivered" that is required for assured destruction. For example, if one carefully examines McNamara's final Force Posture Statement, one finds that, even if Soviet capabilities surpassed the highest range of national intelligence estimates through 1972 (the standard five-year projection), American strategic missiles alone would be able to deliver six times the number of equivalent megatons (EMTs) required for assured destruction. The question once again is why United States strategic forces exceeded by such a large factor the capabilities required for their strategic objective. Table 1 and figure 3 illustrate some of the history of the build-up in American strategic forces during the nineteen-sixties and offer some perspective on the relation between forces and doctrine. Their evidence raises three important questions:

First, were not the size, mix, and character of American strategic forces chosen *prior* to the doctrine of assured destruction and the associated theory of requirements? In 1960 the number of long-range bombers reached 600 and did not vary by more than 100 for the next eight years. In 1961, the Kennedy Administration settled on Polaris submarines carrying a total of 656 SLBMs. The same year McNamara reduced the planned Titan II deployment to 54 missiles; the following year he scheduled the phasing out of Atlas and Titan I, limiting the number of large-payload ICBMs to 54 Titan IIs. The approved number of Minutemen ranged between 800 and 1,300 during 1961-1963. In 1964, the Secretary of Defense established a ceiling of 1,000 Minutemen. But algorithms for calculating the capabilities that were necessary for meeting the stated requirements were not perfected until 1966.[18]

Second, how did strategic doctrines affect capabilities? Though the McNamara era is remembered primarily for "assured destruction," official strategy shifted a number of times during the nineteen-sixties from deterrence-plus-counterforce (FY 1963), to "city avoidance" (FY 1964), to "damage limitation" (FY 1965), to damage-limitation-plus-assured-destruction (FY 1966), to an increasing emphasis on "assured destruction" alone (FY 1967-FY 1969). Despite this evolution of doctrine, the numbers of launchers programmed in 1961-1962 remained relatively fixed throughout McNamara's tenure, while actual capabilities steadily increased through qualitative improvements.

Third, in what sense were American force levels coupled to Soviet capabilities? The decisions of 1961 and 1962 accelerated our strategic deployments and established target numbers of launchers. But these decisions were taken at the very time that American intelligence had a revelation: the infamous missile gap was a myth, and the Soviet strategic build-up was progressing much more slowly than was previously thought. As early as February, 1961, McNamara made a slip in a background news briefing by discounting the missile gap; and by November, 1961, the government was officially announcing to its allies that the Soviet Union was on the short side of the missile gap. But the dramatic buildup of American strategic forces proceeded apace.

The conclusion that American strategic forces in the nineteen-sixties were being driven by something other than official strategic doctrine and estimates of enemy capabilites seems inescapable. This history even provides some clues as to why our strategic capabilities in 1968 so far exceeded the requirements of assured destruction. The level of American forces was determined in part by choices made prior to the formulation of the assured-destruction doctrine; at the time of the initial decisions, doctrines circulating in the government included some that called for much more than assured destruction. As McNamara has emphasized, the early choices were made when there was considerable uncertainty about Soviet plans and intentions. Thereafter, the number of American launchers was relatively unresponsive to changes either in United States doctrine or in Soviet capabilities.

But why did the United States government initially settle on a missile force of solid-fueled, small payload missiles? Why was the force sized at 1,000 Minutemen and

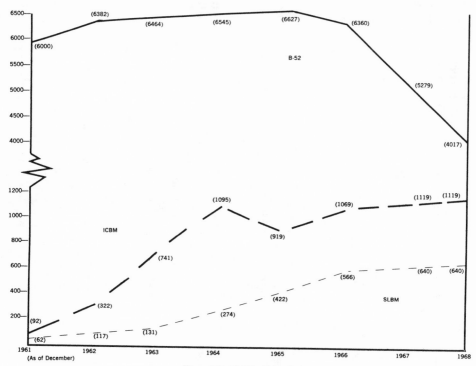

Figure 3: EMTs 1961-68

Table 1
U.S. Strategy and Forces, 1961-1968

Year	McNamara's Announced Strategic Doctrine	Contemporary Estimates of Soviet Forces Deployed; Retrospective Estimates in Brackets [ ]	U.S. Missiles Planned	U.S. Forces Deployed as of December
1961 (FY '62)	Emphasis on survivability and control. No real strategic doctrine yet articulated.	50 + ICBM [10] 190 long-range heavy bombers	126 Atlas 54 Titan I 54 Titan II 800 Minuteman 656 Polaris	54 ICBM 80 SLBM 600 long-range heavy bombers
1962 (FY '63)	Deterrence through the ability to destroy the enemy's "war-making capabilities," even after the US has absorbed the first blow.	75 + ICBM [40] 200 bombers	54 Titan II 800 Minuteman 656 Polaris	180 ICBM 144 SLBM 630 bombers
1963 (FY '64)	"City avoidance" strategy: maintenance of a "second strike force" capable of (1) striking at both military and non-military targets simultaneously, or (2) striking at military targets first, holding the cities hostage as an incentive for the Soviets not to strike at US cities.	100+ ICBM [80] 100 SLBM 200 bombers	54 Titan II 950-1300 Minuteman 656 Polaris	534 ICBM 160 SLBM 630 bombers
1964 (FY '65)	"Damage limiting" strategy: maintenance of forces capable of (1) destroying Soviet society under all conditions of retaliation, and (2) limiting damage to the US by striking not only Soviet cities, but also their unlaunched forces.	200+ ICBM [130] 120+ SLBM 200 bombers	54 Titan II 1000 Minuteman 656 Polaris	907 ICBM 320 SLBM 630 bombers

Table 1—Continued

Year	McNamara's Announced Strategic Doctrine	Contemporary Estimates of Soviet Forces Deployed; Retrospective Estimates in Brackets [ ]	U.S. Missiles Planned	U.S. Forces Deployed as of December
1965 (FY '66)	"Assured destruction + damage limitation" strategy: maintenance of forces capable of (1) destroying 1/4 to 1/3 of the Soviet population and 2/3 of its industrial capacity, and (2) limiting damage to the US.	270 ICBM [200] 120+ SLBM 200 bombers	54 Titan II 1000 Minuteman 656 Polaris	854 ICBM 464 SLBM 630 bombers
1966 (FY '67)	"Assured destruction + damage limitation."	300 ICBM [300] 150 SLBM 200 bombers	54 Titan II 1000 Minuteman 656 Polaris	1004 ICBM 592 SLBM 600 bombers
1967 (FY '68)	"Assured destruction," substantial retreat from damage limitation.	520 ICBM 130 SLBM 150 bombers	54 Titan II 1000 Minuteman 656 Polaris	1054 ICBM 656 SLBM 555 bombers
1968 (FY '69)	"Assured destruction."	900-1000 ICBM 125 SLBM 150 bombers	54 Titan II 1000 Minuteman 656 Polaris	1054 ICBM 656 SLBM 465 bombers

Sources: Strategic doctrine: Secretary of Defense's annual Force Posture Statements
Forces deployed: US—U.S. Air Force, Strategic Air Command, *The Development of Strategic Air Command 1946-1973*; U.S. Navy, Strategic Systems Project Office, *Polaris & Poseidon FBM Facts*
USSR—International Institute of Strategic Studies, *Strategic Survey* (1961-1969)

656 Polaris? And why did the number vary so little during the McNamara era? Desmond V. Ball's study, "The Strategic Missile Programme of the Kennedy Administration, 1961-1963," addresses these questions.[19] It is not possible to do justice to Ball's carefully researched 400-page study here; but the major strands of his argument can be made tolerably clear.

Five major factors seem to have determined the limits within which Kennedy and McNamara could hope to work. First, Kennedy's 1960 campaign pledges to strengthen strategic forces made it politically difficult for him not to enlarge the missile programs in Eisenhower's fiscal 1962 budget. To renege would be to disappoint campaign supporters and to deny expectations generated in Congress, industry, and the military.

Second, in 1960 the political consensus endorsing nuclear "superiority" pervaded all thought about strategic forces among military and civilians, experts and laymen. Having a greater number of missiles than the Soviet Union was a "requirement" that transcended specific strategies. Third, the services had developed their own conclusions as to the level of strategic forces required. Given their allies in Congress and the reluctance of any Administration to argue with the military, their views weighed heavily. These factors seem to have produced defense estimates ranging from about 450 Minutemen and 20 Polaris submarines on the low end (Eisenhower's budget) to 3,000-10,000 Minuteman and 45 Polaris on the high end (the military's "wish list").

In determining the actual ceilings, bargaining with the military figured prominently. As Ball concludes, "The decision by the Kennedy/McNamara Administration to procure 1,000 Minuteman missiles and 41 Polaris submarines was, in essence, the outcome of a 'political process,' involving bargaining, negotiations, and compromise between the various relevant groups and personalities both inside and outside the Administration, each with their own perceptions and interests."[20] The services, and most particularly the Air Force, deliberately inflated their missile "requirements" to gain bargaining leverage. Kennedy and McNamara favored considerably fewer missiles; figures as low as 450 ICBMs were mentioned. But they kept in mind other goals as well, particularly their de-emphasis of manned bombers. Thus they were willing to allow more missiles in exchange for stopping the B-70 and Skybolt, and deferring manned forces.

Recollections of this episode vary. Some Department of Defense civilians recall that McNamara was willing to limit numbers, but that Kennedy was reluctant to alienate Congress (and thus lose support for his other programs) by settling on too low a number. Others recall that Kennedy was willing to agree to a lower number, but that McNamara felt he would "not be able to live with the Pentagon" with the smaller figure. As for the precise number of 1,000, Ball reports that "according to one of the principals involved in setting the programme level, 1,000 was simply the result of a 'visceral feeling' on the part of McNamara and his aides that that figure was a satisfactory and viable compromise."[21]

Third, the shape of the forces—Polaris, small-payload ICBMs and a large bomber force—was not chosen from a blank slate. A number of factors severely constrained the range of possible alternatives. McNamara and his colleagues inherited from the Eisenhower Administration a set of strategic weapons programs at different stages of development and deployment. The decision to deploy had been made on Atlas and Titan I ICBMs, the Polaris SLBM, the Snark air-breathing cruise missile, and B-47, B-52, and B-58 bombers. Weapons at various stages of development included: Minuteman and Mobile Minuteman ICBMs, the Skybolt air-to-surface missile, and the B-70 bomber. Thus the new Administration could not really ask, what strategic forces should we have? Inevitably it asked, what shall we do about strategic programs already in existence?

Fourth, the Kennedy Administration inherited a military establishment of three major services, each with its own role and mission. Choices about the shape of strategic forces would have major consequences for the strength of the Air Force, Navy, and Army, and for the relative positions of subunits within each service. For example, Senator Jackson recalls early Navy resistance to Polaris:

I was interested in this program from the very outset, going back many, many years. I found that in trying to get the Navy to do something about it, I ran headlong into the competition within the Navy for requirements in connection with their day-to-day operational require-ments; whatever it was . . . I was told that this strategic system would just eat away and erode their limited funds. . . . The result was the Polaris was not pushed hard until Sputnik came along.[22]

Obviously, Administration questions about strategic needs could not be considered apart from service questions about organizational needs.

Finally, the decisions were made in a hurry. The emphasis on solid-fueled, small-payload Polaris and Minuteman missiles dated from decisions President Kennedy an-nounced in his special defense message to Congress of March, 1961.

Why these programmed levels were not reduced when their excess capacity became apparent is a further question, and one that Ball does not really answer. One rule of thumb suggests that forces-in-being are replaced or improved, but are never eliminated. In strategic debate, a rachet effect seems to be at work: logically, changes in strategic objectives could require a reduction in forces; rhetorically, such conclu-sions are occasionally drawn; in fact, the reductions never happen. For example, Mc-Namara stated that the forces needed to provide the "no-city option [a 1962 enthusiasm] must be larger than would otherwise be the case" and that, if the option were eliminated, "there would be strong reasons to reduce the forces we are re-questing funds to procure."[23] But shortly thereafter the option was abandoned, and the forces were not reduced. Similarly, McNamara argued in 1965 that offensive forces beyond those required for assured destruction must be justified on the basis of their contribution to the damage-limitation objective. Damage limitation was later de-emphasized, but the forces were not trimmed. The flexibility of strategic doctrine in justifying programmed (or desired) force levels was illustrated dramatically by the elaborate "Kent Study" of 1962-1964: it analyzed alternative strategies and forces, contributed the concept of "damage limitation," and concluded that "the presently planned inventory of strategic missiles is approximately correct in this time period, whether by accident or good intuitive planning."[24]

2. HARDSITE DEFENSE AND ABM

In September of 1967, Secretary of Defense Robert McNamara announced the Johnson Administration's decision to deploy an ABM. Designated "Sentinel," this system was supposed to protect the country's population centers from a primitive

Chinese attack, to catch accidental launches, and to provide some protection for the Minuteman ICBM force against an all-out Soviet attack. In March of 1969, President Nixon announced a "substantial modification" of this Sentinel system. Relegating the mission of population defense to a poor third, Nixon's speech placed primary emphasis on thè protection of Minuteman sites. To achieve this objective, the President proposed replacing Sentinel with "Safeguard." But under the "Safeguard" label, one found the same components that had been developed for Sentinel, only now they had shifted to Minuteman sites.

According to numerous experts, including many who applauded Nixon's intention to defend ICBMs, Safeguard provided poor protection for Minuteman. Its interceptors were too few and too slow to foil a determined Soviet attack. Even more critically, Safeguard's "soft" radar made the entire system vulnerable to a single attacking missile. Technology did not dictate Safeguard's deficiencies. An effective system was feasible. The question is, therefore, why did the Nixon Administration choose a system so ill-suited to the defense of the Minuteman?

The explanation must begin with politics. The new Administration faced growing opposition on Capitol Hill. Having pushed ABM into Lyndon Johnson's lap, Congress now threatened to take it away from Richard Nixon. The new President was determined to deploy ABM—for bargaining leverage in the upcoming SALT negotiations and for other reasons—but he needed to act quickly. As a result, exploration of the possible options suffered. Better analysis alone, however, would not necessarily have improved the outcome. The Administration had to select from the available set of hardware alternatives. In 1969, no ABM well suited to the protection of Minuteman had reached the stage of system development. Having decided to deploy *some* ABM, the Nixon Administration was forced to choose from a list that lacked the appropriate item.

But why was the array of options so restricted? Unfortunately no detailed account maps all the twists and turns in the development of ABM. Several related discussions, however, do shed some light on the issue.[25] Drawing on these accounts, we will attempt to explain why no "hardsite" (Minuteman) ABM had reached advanced development, while ABM components designed for population defense were nearing completion.

From the beginning, ABM belonged to the Army. In 1945, the Army initiated Project NIKE, giving contracts to Bell Telephone Laboratories (BTL) and Western Electric. NIKE's mission called for defense of the United States against air attack by enemy aircraft. The means of achieving the mission was a surface-to-air missile system: networks of radar, interceptors, and computers which would identify an incoming target, track it, and fire an interceptor whose warhead would detonate within a lethal radius. In the decade following the original contract, the Army deployed two such systems, NIKE-AJAX and NIKE-HERCULES. Both defended against attacks by conventional aircraft. In 1953, as the prospect of a Soviet missile force appeared, the Army asked BTL to examine the feasibility of defense against ICBMs. By 1956, BTL concluded that appropriate modifications to NIKE-HERCULES would indeed make ABM feasible. Thus the first ABM was conceived as a follow-on to systems already deployed by the Army.

The Army responded favorably to the BTL report. In 1957, Army headquarters established the NIKE-ZEUS project. Hardware development began. From that time, the Army consistently advocated deployment of a large ABM system to defend the population against a major Soviet attack. The Army's determination seems to have stemmed from several factors. First, ABM was following a major service weapon (NIKE-HERCULES) that performed a major service mission (air defense). Second, the Army had surrendered much of its share of the budget to the Air Force and Navy during the nineteen-fifties. President Eisenhower's "New Look" policy emphasized strategic nuclear war capabilities, and the Air Force and Navy captured the strategic offensive missions. In its Jupiter IRBM, the Army had hoped for a small piece of the action, but operational control of Jupiter was given to the Air Force. ABM seemed to be the Army's last chance for a strategic nuclear role. Finally, many within the Army believed ABM could save American lives in the event of nuclear war and could thus make a major contribution to national security.

The Army's strong advocacy (usually with Congressional concurrence) could not alone have secured deployment. That decision rested with successive Presidents and their Secretaries of Defense, and the Defense agencies on whom they relied for information, alternatives, and advice. In particular, while the Army controlled the advanced development of systems hardware, Robert McNamara and the organizations that advised him decisively influenced the character of the systems themselves. Their power to approve or reject deployment, to set standards of acceptability, and to supervise exploratory research and development insured them a major voice. The systems that emerged were the products of Army reactions to these initiatives.

The Directorate of Defense Research and Engineering (DDR&E) and its semiautonomous subunit, the Advanced Research Projects Agency (ARPA), played key roles. ARPA was established in 1958 as a separate agency reporting directly to the Secretary of Defense. Partly a response to Sputnik, ARPA was a low-budget operation charged with performing research that the services handled poorly, especially "quick reaction" and long-range projects. Early assignments included all military and civilian space programs, notably ABM technology beyond the NIKE-ZEUS stage. ARPA conducted research. It did not develop actual hardware. As an ARPA director has explained:

A general principle of ARPA's operation is to work in an area until feasibility has been established. Hardware development for these projects are the responsibility of the services upon assignment by the Secretary of Defense so that those projects can compete against other weapon system elements within the service or services most likely to use them.[26]

Created later in 1958, DDR&E assumed authority over ARPA. DDR&E's mandate called for supervising all Defense Department research and development, including that of the services, and advising the Secretary of Defense on weapons decisions.

From the beginning, the scientists and engineers who manned DDR&E and ARPA questioned the basic feasibility of the Army-development NIKE-ZEUS. Their arguments fueled the skepticism of President Eisenhower. No deployment decision had been made by the time John Kennedy and his Secretary of Defense, Robert McNamara, entered office.

The objections of DDR&E and ARPA, which bridged the two Administrations, centered on the low acceleration of ZEUS's interceptors and the inability of its radars to track a number of incoming warheads at once. ARPA research suggested solutions to these problems in an electronically steered "phased array radar" and an interceptor called Sprint, capable of higher acceleration than ZEUS. At DDR&E's behest, the Army incorporated these advances into its ABM during the period 1961-65. The modified system acquired the name NIKE X.

At the same time, ARPA explored ever more advanced technology, including hardsite defense. As Dr. Jack P. Ruina, ARPA's director, explained in 1963:

The U. S. program in this field has consisted of two parts. The first is the hardware development of complete systems and this is the responsibility of the Army in its NIKE-ZEUS and NIKE X programs. The second is a broad research and exploratory development program, which is ARPA's Project DEFENDER. . . . Project DEFENDER has an active hardpoint defense system program where we study the technology required for the defense of hardened sites such as missile silos and command posts.[27]

The hardpoint program yielded several components that reached the stage of exploratory development. Thus ARPA both improved the Army's ongoing system for population defense and began designing alternative technology for hardsite defense.

The Army accepted the modifications to the system as their price for improving its chances for deployment. The Army was not interested in hardsite ABM, however. Hardsite defense would have competed directly with the Army's chosen mission, which was large-scale defense of population. The Army Project office did not want such competition. Nor were the Navy and Air Force attracted to ABM. The mere availability of its appropriate technology did not make hardsite defense a genuine option. Development of a complete system would have required service sponsorship, and no service was about to undertake the task without McNamara's forceful intervention. For his own reasons, McNamara did not intervene.

For Robert McNamara, the question was never simply, "Does it work?" He also asked, "Do we need it?" At the beginning of his tenure, McNamara opposed NIKE-ZEUS because he believed it would not work and NIKE X because it was not ready. By 1965, he based his opposition on the twin benchmarks of "assured destruction" and "damage limitation": as a full-scale population defense, NIKE X could not significantly limit damage because the Soviets might easily offset its effectiveness, while it would contribute to assured destruction only at a far greater cost than other, simpler measures. In 1966, McNamara became sufficiently concerned with the Soviet strategic build-up to institute a study called STRAT-X, which was to explore alternative means of preserving the deterrent. He did not, however, support the development of a hardsite ABM system. His failure to do so seems to have been compatible with his goals at the time. By 1967, he opposed ABM in general and hoped that an agreement with the Soviet Union would eliminate the need for deployment. When the Glassboro summit dashed hopes for such an agreement, the pressures of the impending Presidential election left McNamara with little choice but to submit to deployment of NIKE X. However, the question was not, what is the best ABM? but, what is the least provocative rationale for a system that has become unavoidable?

McNamara rejected the defense of Minuteman as a suitable rationale, a suggestion of his advisers in Systems Analysis. NIKE X was a "low-confidence" weapon in the hardsite role. Moreover, any system directed against the Soviets might create pressures for a full-scale anti-Soviet population defense. McNamara's immediate concern with the arms race outweighed the consideration of possible Minuteman vulnerability in some future year. A small-scale version of NIKE X directed at the unsophisticated Chinese threat suited his purposes—thus, Sentinel.

This compromise served the succeeding Administration poorly. Sentinel's minimal hardsite capability represented a cheap addition to a modest system for population defense against China. As Air Force Secretary Harold Brown phrases it, "If you are planning to put in an area defense of the population, which would be, say, a $3.5 billion expenditure, then the additional expenditure required to defend the missile complex to a reasonable degree of protection is somewhere between a half billion and a billion dollars. . . ."[28] Obtaining the limited Minuteman defense could be justified by its low marginal cost, given the money already spent on a light population defense. When Minuteman defense became the primary objective of the entire system, the cogency of this rationale diminished.

The implications of this brief sketch seem clear. The Nixon Administration chose an ABM with a relatively poor capability for hardsite defense because the President insisted on immediate deployment, and no other system with a greater capability for this purpose was in a sufficiently advanced stage of development, since it had not previously been required to further the ambitions of any service or strong service subunit. The Army had captured ABM development, and, from the beginning, the Army's ABM Project Office sought only a full-scale population defense. Robert McNamara did not force the issue of hardsite defense, and the Project Office repeatedly rejected suggestions from elsewhere that the Army develop hardsite ABM. Some observers have speculated that the Army's resistance stemmed from apprehension that, should an ABM fit within the fence surrounding a Minuteman squadron, ABM would become the property of the Air Force.

Not only did the Army's control of ABM impede the preparation of hardsite defense, but, equally important, the Army refused to present an alternative—rarely do organizations put forward more than one option. At the outset of the new Administration, presided over by a President who had taken a campaign stand in favor of ABM and a Secretary of Defense who was in favor of giving the Pentagon back to the military, it was not surprising to find the normal short list: one apparently viable option framed by two phony extremes. Since the issue mattered little to the Air Force or the Navy, the Joint Chiefs of Staff were united in support of the Army's position.

3. MIRV as a Response to Soviet ABM

Arms-race analysts always explain MIRV as being the American response to Soviet ABM. Because the Soviet Union was deploying a defensive weapon that threatened the ability of American nuclear warheads to reach their appointed targets, the United States moved to negate the Soviet advantage by deploying a weapon that multiplied the number of independently targeted warheads aimed at the Soviet Union. Without Soviet ABM, so the argument goes, the United States would not have developed or deployed MIRV.

In fact, American research and development on MIRV *preceded* the Soviet ABM, and American deployment persisted after the ban on ABM. How, then, did the United States come to develop and deploy MIRV? The evidence available is insufficient for a complete explanation,[29] but it is sufficient to make plain the limits to our understanding of American weapons development. First, the lengthy periods required for development complicate the task of distinguishing "actions" from "reactions" in cases such as MIRV. For example, one popular explanation emphasizes Soviet deployment of ABM as the inspiration for American MIRV. But this explanation ignores the central fact about strategic forces, namely, that they take a very long time to develop. The normal incubation period for a strategic weapon, that is, the period between initial research and actual deployment, is seven to fifteen years. MIRV deployment took a decade. Furthermore, in a situation where one nation cannot be sure what weapons the other may be researching or even deploying, the long periods needed for development demand that prudent research *anticipate* threats and requirements. Secretary McNamara emphasized this problem in 1965:

The weapons we have in being are the result of research and development programs initiated as long ago as 10-15 years. We believe that the programs we have under way are more than adequate to insure our superiority in the years ahead.[30]

If American research were to await evidence of Soviet research before acting, the United States could not be confident of maintaining superiority. Consequently, research pursues any technological possibilites that seem promising to the research community, within given budget constraints. DDR&E Director John Foster testified to Congress: "Our current effort to get a MIRV capability on our missiles is not reacting to a Soviet capability so much as it is moving ahead again to make sure that whatever they do of the possible things that we can imagine they might do, we will be prepared."[31]

To be fully prepared for all contingencies—McNamara's "worst plausible case"—American procurement and deployment of counter-weapons would have to precede Soviet deployment of weapons that the United States wanted to be certain of offsetting. McNamara justified MIRV deployment in 1968 not in terms of what the Soviets *had* done, but as a precaution against what they *might* do:

Because the Soviet Union *might* [emphasis in original] deploy extensive ABM defenses, we are making some very important changes in our strategic missile forces. Instead of a single large warhead our missiles are now being designed to carry several small warheads. . . . Deployment by the Soviets of a ballistic missile defense of their cities will not improve their situation. We have *already* [emphasis added] taken the necessary steps to guarantee that our strategic offensive forces will be able to overcome such a defense.[32]

But this logic permits "reactions" to precede the action that might provoke them, a possibility that jumbles the action-reaction sequence. Because of such factors as the lengthy period involved in acquisition, uncertainty about the opponent's research, and the consequent necessity for anticipating it, decisions about weapons research, development, and procurement cannot be based on evidence about the opponent's actual weapons programs. Rarely can such evidence be decisive. Thus, the action-reaction hypothesis, which emphasizes tightly coupled, specific, offsetting reactions to particular weapons, seems less important, even logically, than a loosely coupled, general competition in which each nation pursues broad strategic objectives that may be readjusted periodically in light of forces that the other assembles.

When we move from logic to evidence, we observe that each nation pursues its weapons strategy through large organizations for research, development, and use. What drives these institutions are not only estimates of the other side's activity, but also their own internal dynamics. In contrast to the notion of Soviet actions encouraging American research, it appears that, in the case of MIRV, the United States mainly provided its own encouragement. Because research is typically multi-purpose, identifying the moment when research on a particular weapon might be said to have begun poses severe problems. Whatever the date of MIRV's origin, however, the proposition that Soviet ABM provided *the* trigger seems suspect.

In 1957, William Holaday, Director of Guided Missiles for the Department of Defense, established a committee called the Re-entry Body Identification Group and asked it to investigate difficulties for the defense that could be posed by offensive missiles using penetration aides. The immediate spur for this action was the need to elaborate the challenges that American designers of ABM would have to face in meeting an attack that employed penetration aides. He also wanted to identify opportunities for American offensive missiles against a possible future Soviet ABM.

The research agenda established by the committee powerfully influenced American research over the next several years and led directly to MIRV. According to Herbert York, the first Director of DDR&E, the Re-entry Body Identification Group

. . . pointed out the feasibility of greatly complicating the missile defense problem by using decoys, chaff, tank fragments, reduced radar reflectivity, nuclear blackout, and last, but by no means least, multiple warheads. . . . At first, the idea involved a shotgun technique in which a group of warheads plus some lightweight decoys were to be launched along several different paths, all leading to a common target. But shortly after, methods for aiming each of the individual warheads at separate targets were invented.[33]

It is impossible to determine the moment of MIRV's conception. Greenwood identifies at least five independent inventors of the idea. York traces the evolution of technology that built a base for MIRV. By 1962-63, ideas and technology had been combined in research programs for both the Navy and the Air Force aimed explicitly at multiple, independently targeted warheads. It is difficult to escape the conclusion that, at every stage, the reasons for MIRV's development were many. Everyone recognized the possibility that the Soviets had an ABM. Some people worried primarily about that threat; but others had different concerns.

Air Force sponsorship of MIRV research seems to have been motivated largely by the organization's interest in the expanded list of vulnerable targets, which had been acquired by American intelligence in the late nineteen-fifties and reinforced by Mc-Namara's doctrine of counterforce. The Navy's interest in MIRV stemmed in large part from competition with the Air Force for the overall strategic mission, including the expanded target list authorized by McNamara's counterforce doctrine. The technical community seems to have been driven by the "sweetness" of the technology and the researchers' competitive instincts, which were aroused primarily by American ABM research, since so little was known about Soviet ABM activity. This competition, which has characterized much post-war American weapons research, generates what we might call an intra-national action-reaction phenomenon. As York describes it:

It is most important to note that these early developments of MIRV and ABM were not primarily the results of any careful operations analysis or anything that might be called provocation by the other side. Rather, they were largely the result of a continuously reciprocating process consisting of a technological challenge put out by the designers of our defense and accepted by the designers of our offense, then followed by a similar challenge/response sequence in the reverse direction.[34]

The moral of the story seems to be that the origins of MIRV's research and development were inherently untidy, that it came from many sources, and that, at least in the recent past, American research and development of weapons in general has been as much self-generated as Soviet-generated. As John Foster, the Director of DDR&E during MIRV's research and development, candidly put it:

Now most of the action the U. S. takes in the area of research and development has to do with one of two types of activities. Either we see from the fields of science and technology some new possibilities which we think we ought to exploit, or we see threats on the horizon, possible threats, usually not something the enemy has done, but something we have thought of ourselves that he might do, we must therefore be prepared for. These are the two forces that tend to drive our research and development activities.[35]

A third strand in the MIRV story concerns the decision in 1965 to deploy MIRV on Poseidon and Minuteman III. Weapons decisions proceed in stages. The 1965 decision to deploy MIRV on Poseidon and Minuteman III flowed naturally from the 1964 decision for its advanced development and engineering. We noted above the disparate and sometimes conflicting interests that converged in this development. Greenwood's conclusion makes the central point:

MIRV was a program that contributed to the objectives of all organizations and individual decision-makers in the innovation process. . . . These [organizations'] perspectives were quite different and in some cases opposed. But it mattered little whether the different power centers could agree on underlying policy or priorities as long as they were unanimous in support of initiating and continuing research.[36]

The deployment decisions emerged from this same alliance of interests. Air Force officers supported MIRV because it contributed to their central mission, namely fighting strategic wars, and their special interest, namely destruction of "time-urgent" military targets (that is targets such as missiles and bombers that must be destroyed before they can be launched). Naval interest in MIRV stemmed from judgment about its contribution to the Navy's mission, namely, assured destruction of urban-industrial targets, combined with its competition with the Air Force. The technologists wanted to see MIRV deployed because it had been developed and it worked. DDR&E reflected not only technological fundamentalism, but also the strategic and political preferences of the Secretary of Defense. For McNamara, MIRV wrapped up in a single package a cost-effective, high-confidence, assured-destruction capability against almost any conceivable future Soviet threat, including ABM and the growth of strategic offensive forces. It also increased counterforce capability (in which McNamara retained an interest, even after he had reduced its importance) and targeting flexibility. It provided arguments against Air Force demands for more Minutemen and for a new manned bomber, as well as a defense against critics who charged that growing Soviet expansion of strategic forces threatened the United States. Finally, it provided another argument against our ABM deployment (on the grounds that the Soviets could deploy MIRV and thereby easily overwhelm ABM). President Johnson relied on Secretary McNamara in strategic matters and seems only to have used MIRV as an argument against his domestic critics. The Congressional committees tended to support the services and the Secretary of Defense—whenever the two agreed. So the circle making the decision stopped there. Not until September, 1967, did the public hear its first words about MIRV. All previous decisions about development and procurement were made in secret. Details of the bargaining among these interests show some interesting vacillations, including initial Air Force opposition to MIRV, cancellation of the Mark 17, and mild schizophrenia within the Navy.

The central point, however, is Greenwood's: in spite of the disagreements, no one opposed deployment.

A final deployment puzzle stems from the continuation of MIRV installations after the ABM ban. Director of DDR&E Foster testified in 1971 that "if a ban were placed on ABM, in the sense of banning the capability to intercept a ballistic missile attack, then as I see it at the moment, there would be no need for the United States to deploy a MIRV."[37] Shortly after Foster's testimony, a ban of the sort he referred to was established; MIRV deployment continued unabated.

Again, explanation requires more than the official arguments. If full MIRV deployment had been part of the agreement with the Joint Chiefs of Staff for support of SALT, then SALT's ban on ABM would not have affected deployment. The additional capabilities provided by MIRV were seen by some people as a way of offsetting the Soviet advantage in numbers of launchers. But the primary reason MIRV deployment continued was institutional inertia; stopping it simply because its prime rationale had been eliminated would have required strong action by some officials against the interests of others whose commitment to MIRV had always transcended the official arguments. In the absence of a real effort by someone willing to fight, MIRV deployment would continue. None of the people involved was eager for such a battle.

III. Hypotheses About Determinants of Force Posture and Implications for Arms Control

This brief review documents what we knew at the outset: the array of factors that have an important causal impact on force posture is extraordinarily complex. (Indeed, the attractiveness of the prevailing simplification is precisely that it avoids the messiness of the actual process.) This re-examination of anomalies also illustrates an overwhelming need for many more careful, detailed case histories aimed at developing preliminary causal maps of the weapons-development processes. Each of the cases leaves the reader dissatisfied—demanding much finer detail and analysis than the case-writer provides. (Had we not already overworked the metaphor, we might post a warning sign about the perils of starting to peel an onion.)

But even at this preliminary stage, reflection on the case histories should do something toward stimulating formulation of hypotheses about determinants of force posture. Obviously, the initial statement of such hypotheses will require a great deal of refinement, qualification, and testing. Our aim here is simply to suggest several hypotheses about determinants of force posture, some of which have important implications for arms control.

A major difficulty in the formulation of these hypotheses stems from the fact that force posture, the "dependent variable" (to use a social science term), is not a precise or measurable concept. Sometimes force posture refers to the full inventory of forces deployed and their mix, e.g., American strategic force posture includes ICBMs, SLBMs, and strategic bombers; sometimes it refers to a single weapons system, e.g., ABM or Minuteman III; and sometimes it refers to specific characteristics of a particular weapons system, e.g., range, speed, accuracy, or megatonnage. An effort to draw these distinctions more carefully and to find some crude measures for each is in progress. In the hypotheses that follow, the relevant connotation of the term "force posture" should be clear from the context.

A second difficulty in attempting to generalize about determinants of force posture arises from the "hundred factor problem." Evidently, there are at least one hundred important causal factors (and clusters of factors) involved in the process from which weapons emerge. No one, or group, of these factors dominates the outcome in a normal case. But simple analysis, prediction, and discussion require statements about the impact of single factors or clusters on the weapons outcome. Since other factors change significantly from one weapon to the next, specification of relations between a single factor (or group) and the outcome—"other things being equal"—becomes a difficult and perhaps even questionable enterprise.

A third, though far from final, difficulty in formulating hypotheses about force posture concerns the packaging of such hypotheses. Lists are never satisfactory. But a coherent structure for organizing propositions presupposes a conceptual or theoretical understanding that may only emerge at the end of the research path. Lacking a satisfactory model, or even map of the determinants of force posture, we have fallen back on chronology as an organizing device. Figure 4 depicts in a crude, stylized fashion the major stages in a weapon's program from early research, through development, to procurement. Obviously, different weapons have somewhat different histories. The chart presents a "normal" sequence for a generalized weapon.

General Hypotheses and Questions

What follows are some general hypotheses that attempt to identify relationships between factors in the process and force-posture outcomes. The hypotheses are obviously neither exclusive nor exhaustive. Under each hypothesis, we note several examples.

1) The central but persistently neglected fact about force posture is that *weapons are deployed only after a long process* of research, design, and development. Weapons are not selected at a given moment, from off the shelf. As a consequence, the relationship between a weapon and such factors as strategic doctrines, or estimates of enemy capabilities, or central governmental decisions is enormously complicated by assorted lags. This proposition yields a string of related hypotheses.

a) Major decisions about research are made ten to fifteen years before formulation of the strategic doctrine that will be official when the weapon enters the force posture.

b) Major decisions about research are taken ten to fifteen years before the actual Soviet capabilities against which these weapons will operate is known.

c) Major decisions about design and development are made five to ten years before formulation of the strategic doctrine that will be official when the weapon enters the force posture.

d) Major decisions about design and development are taken five to ten years before the opponent's actual capabilities against which these weapons will operate is known.

For example: Decisions about MIRV were made prior to evidence of Soviet ABM capabilities; design and development decisions about ABM were made prior to the choice of hardsite defense as the primary objective; the size of American strategic forces in the nineteen-sixties was chosen before any of the assorted doctrines promulgated to defend it had been invented.

2) The lengthy process from which weapons emerge involves hundreds of important, relatively independent decisions that no one political official can possibly oversee. Given the terms of office of Presidents and Secretaries of Defense, most of the decisions about research, design, and technical specifications of weapons that an Administration might consider procuring will have been made under a previous President and under a Secretary of Defense twice removed from the one occupying the office.

a) The list of advanced development/acquisition choices—i.e., the array of options—from which an Administration can choose is limited by choices settled under previous Administrations.

b) The agenda of weapons choices—i.e., the array of choices that some organization is pushing—that an Administration must face (because programs at an advanced development stage demand decision) is strongly influenced by choices made under previous Administrations. Each item on the agenda has behind it a powerful alliance of advocates.

c) Force posture at any particular time is unlikely to have been substantially shaped by a single specific doctrine, such as assured destruction. It is possible for an Administration's new strategic doctrine to have some immediate effect on use of previously deployed forces and on current research, development, and procurement outcomes. But the array from which it selects will have been created under a previous Administration, espousing different doctrines. And selections from the choices that it develops will be made by a future Administration with yet another policy.

d) The accountability of political officials for weapons choices is reduced both by the length and by the specific character of this process, for example, Nixon's options for hardsite ABM in 1969, and McNamara's options for a multi-service fighter in 1961.

3) Because of the time involved in the weapons-development process and the number and complexity of the choices involved, no single authority can make all of the important decisions. Organizations play a major role in weapons development. In the present weapons-development process, *the services and their subunits are the primary actors in weapons development.* Consequently, force posture is shaped by the goals and procedures and especially the missions and weapons systems to which services (and subunits) are committed. Political officials might disturb this process; only rarely do they control it.

a) Weapons at a given time *t* reflect the structure of service subunits, their relative strengths, and their missions *t* minus five to ten years. For example: the limited numbers of Soviet bombers in the late fifties reflected the weakness of the Soviet Air Force in the early fifties; the limited numbers of Soviet ICBMs in the early sixties reflected the non-existence of Strategic Rocket Forces in the fifties.

b) Weapons systems in the main line of a service's primary mission will be regularly improved by "follow-ons," i.e., successive generations of weapons that make marginal improvements in principal performance parameters. For example: tactical aircraft from the F-86 to F-15; strategic bombers from the B-26 to the B-1; tanks, rifles; submarines from early Polaris to Trident.

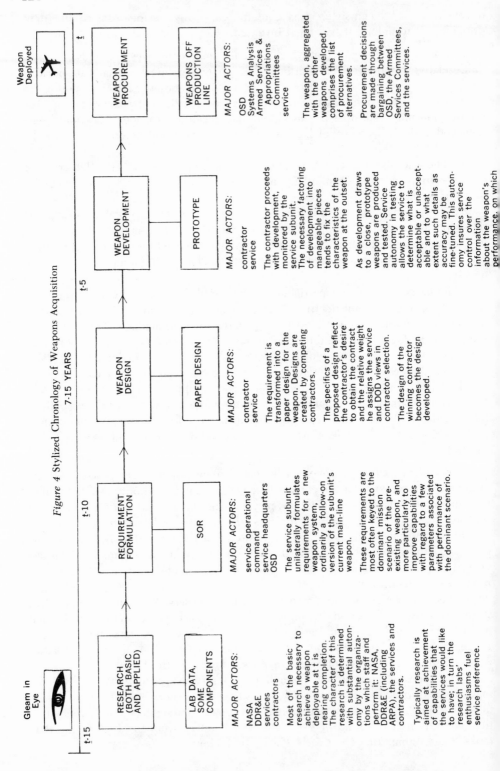

Figure 4 Stylized Chronology of Weapons Acquisition

c) Weapons systems not in the main-line mission of a service or service subunit tend to develop slowly. For example: hardsite ABM; standoff bombers; Navy mines; "smart" bombs.

d) A mission to which a service assigns low priority (or which is not the primary mission of a service subunit) tends to be poorly performed. This is especially true if performance of the mission is essential not to the service performing it but to a sister service. For example: close air support; airlift; sealift.

e) Weapons requiring coordination of existing services and missions will be poor and will develop slowly. For example: multi-service fighters; anti-submarine warfare.

f) Organizational interests and missions are better predictors of weapon characteristics and uses than are appointed officials' pronouncements. For example: McNamara vs. Army on ABM; McNamara vs. Air Force on MIRV.

4) The current weapons-development process consists of a sequence of bargaining games in which service (and service subunit) preferences are weighed more heavily than other interests. Service preferences about weapons reflect service interests, especially the organization's "health." Service organizational health is seen to depend on maintaining the autonomy of the organization and in preserving what its members view to be the "essence" of the organization, sustaining morale, maintaining or expanding roles and missions, and keeping or increasing budgets.

The *structure* of the current weapons-development process emphasizes the power of weapons developers and users as against that of Executive officials and Congress. This structure allows many small choices to accumulate into formal decisions (e.g., specific operational requirements, requests for proposals, and contracts) by minimizing the number of points at which political officials can make clearly identifiable choices among alternatives. This collection of propositions yields an assortment of related hypotheses.

a) The impact of players (and interests) differs markedly among the various bargaining games in the process of weapons development. Most design and development decisions are made primarily by the services or subunits, design labs, DDR&E, the Secretary of Defense (or other units to whom he delegates authority)—but not the President, the Secretary of State, ACDA, Congressmen, or you and me. The participants in major acquisitions decisions comprise a much wider circle.

b) Somewhere in the advanced development stage, a weapons system picks up momentum. While the causes of this momentum are not well understood, they seem to include pressures from weapon contractors and Congressional beneficiaries. For example: MIRV; ABM.

c) The structure of the current weapon-development process blurs the line between development and procurement. An appropriate strategy for coping with uncertainties of technology and enemy weapons development requires wide-ranging research and development. Many of the resulting weapons should not be procured because a threat fails to materialize or a new technology offers greater promise. But a disproportionate number of systems that reach advanced development are procured in any case.

d) Political leaders tend to concentrate on the variables in the weapons process over which they have nearly total control (e.g., pronouncements about doctrine or descriptions of missions), as opposed to variables that can be changed only with nearly endless bargaining and monitoring (e.g., technical performance specifications of an aircraft).

e) "Secretaries of Defense come and go, but the Navy. . . ."

5) Service-budget shares remain relatively stable. Shifts occur slowly and with considerable noise.

6) Because of the complexity of weapons systems, weapon designs must be broken down at an early stage into interdependent components that can be developed simultaneously. As a consequence, the final weapon that emerges diverges only slightly, say twenty-five per cent, from the technical performance requirements set early in the design stage. For example: the F-111.

7) The *details* of weapons systems (e.g., accuracy of warheads) are determined in large part by the interaction between technical feasibility and organizational interests (in the United States, the services and the research community). (This hypothesis is obviously related to two "laws": *Ruina's law,* "On the issue of guidance accuracy, there is no way to get hold of it, it is a laboratory development, and there is no way to stop progress in that field"; *Brooks' law,* "At least ten per cent of an R&D budget is uncontrollable in detail by a central authority.") For example: ABM, MIRV.

Implications for Arms Control

As noted at the outset, the argument developed in this essay implies that national weapons-development processes are an integral part of the problem of arms control and that arms-control analysts must thus expand their traditional definition of the problem. More specific implications can be drawn from each of the hypotheses. But here we simply state some general implications briefly, in the hope of provoking further discussion.

Analysts of arms races and proponents of arms control have tended to emphasize factors *between* nations as the primary determinants behind the arms race and the principal target for proposed cures. While actions of foreign governments and uncertainty about the intentions of other countries are obviously important, the analysis above suggests that the weapons in the American and Soviet force postures are *predominantly* the result of factors *internal* to each nation. Not only are organizational goals and procedures domestically determined, but the resulting satisfactions of political officials are to be found overwhelmingly at home.

Some minimum set of widely shared values (e.g., a secure second-strike capability) combined with enemy actions that may threaten it are then boundaries within which the level of American forces, defense budgets, and specific weapons must fall. But these boundaries seem broad enough to encompass virtually all of the present levels. Therefore, actions by the Soviet Union serve primarily as justification for the American participants in the bureaucratic struggle to advance weapons that they favor for reasons only tangentially related to Soviet behavior. The corollary action in the Soviet Union seems to be even more intense. It is obvious, therefore, that a major concern of arms-control advocates should be to ferret out the factors within the United States and the Soviet Union that influence weapons developments and that increase the probability of war, the probable damage if war occurs, and the waste of our resources in preparation for war.

Many of the prerequisites of arms control appear to be identical with a sensible conception of sound defense management generally: restructure the weapons-development process so as to provide points of clear choice among competing alternatives; increase the responsibility (and influence) of elected officials in these choices, increase official accountability for their results.

In the past several years, the fulcrum of America's widely shared values and beliefs about defense, the size of the defense budget, the mystique of the military, and the threat posed by the Russians has shifted significantly. This shift presents the first real opportunity in the post-war era for a radical restructuring of the basic weapons-development process. Advocates of arms control should join with proponents of sound defense management to take advantage of this opportunity. Before selecting a preferred weapons-development system, we need a much more thorough understanding of the current system and its deficiencies. We need careful analyses in detail of possible alternative systems and their likely products. Such studies should be given highest arms-control priority °

° The initial draft of this essay was distributed to the American Academy's Summer Study, July, 1973. The authors are deeply indebted to the Weapons Project of the Foreign Policy Studies Program in the John F. Kennedy School of Government, Harvard University, for general stimulation, assorted ideas, and specific comments. For helpful comments on drafts of this essay, the authors are grateful to Harvey Brooks, Barry Carter, Robert Coulam, William Fisher, Thomas Garwin, Richard Garwin, Richard Huff, Jerry Kahan, Arnold Kanter, Joseph Kruzel, Franklin Long, Andrew Marshall, George Rathjens, Jack Ruina, Henry Rowen, and John Steinbruner. For general support during revision of the draft, Allison thanks the Center for Advanced Study in the Behavioral Sciences.

REFERENCES

[1] These illustrations do not attempt to present a satisfactory overview of the complex history of the development of American and Soviet strategic arms. Unfortunately, there exist no widely accepted indicators of the critical factors in the history of arms developments..

[2] See *SIPRI Research Reports No. 11* (Stockholm, August, 1974).

[3] Sources; Alton M. Quanbeck and Barry M. Blechman, *Strategic Forces: Issues for the Mid-Seventies* (Washington, D. C.: The Brookings Institution, 1973); Blechman *et al.*, *Setting National Priorities: The 1975 Budget* (Washington, D. C.: The Brookings Institution, 1974); *The Defense Monitor*, Center for Defense Information, Washington, D. C.; Albert Wohlstetter, "Is There a Strategic Arms Race?" and "Rivals but no 'Race,'" *Foreign Policy*, 15, 16 (Summer, Fall, 1974).

[4] Sources: Data for direct costs of strategic forces, annual total obligational authority in constant FY 1975 dollars from Department of Defense, Comptroller, unpublished computer tabulation (1974). Figures for strategic forces, including indirect costs and projected costs of strategic forces, are from Blechman (cited above), pp. 72, 91. The allocation of indirect costs involves a number of necessarily arbitrary assumptions.

[5] Address to the editors and publishers of UPI, San Francisco, September 18, 1967, reprinted in *U.S. Department of State Bulletin* (Ocober 9, 1967), pp. 443-51.

[6] *Scientific American*, 220:4, (April, 1969).

[7] See Allison, *Essence of Decision* (Boston, 1971).

[8] *Statement of Secretary of Defense Robert S. McNamara before the House Armed Service Committee on the Fiscal Year 1969–73 Defense Program and the 1969 Defense Budget* (1968), p. 47.

[9] *Ibid.*, p. 50.

[10] *Ibid.*, p. 57.

[11] See Figure 3.

[12] Statement by President Nixon on Ballistic Missile Defense System, March 14, 1969, *Documents on Disarmament* (Arms Control and Disarmament Agency, 1969), p. 103.

[13] United States Congress, Senate, Committee on Foreign Relations, Subcommittee on International Organization and Disarmament Affairs, *Strategic and Foreign Policy Implications of ABM Systems, Hearings*, 91st Congress, first session (1969), pp. 317-20.

[14] United States Congress, Senate, Committee on Foreign Relations, *Strategic and Foreign Policy Implications of ABM Systems, Hearings*, 92nd Congress, second session (1972), p. 248.

[15] See W. V. Quine, *Word and Object* (Cambridge, Mass., 1960).

[16] These overviews are variants of conceptual frameworks that have been described at greater length as Models II and III in Allison, *Essence of Decision, op. cit.*

[17] Alain C. Enthoven and K. Wayne Smith, *How Much Is Enough? Shaping the Defense Program; 1961-1969* (New York, 1971), p. 176.

[18] *Ibid.*, p. 177.

[19] Desmond V. Ball, "The Strategic Missile Programme of the Kennedy Administration, 1961-63," Ph.D. Dissertation, Australian National University, 1972.

[20] *Ibid.*, p. 334.

[21] *Ibid.*, p. 377.

[22] United States Congress, Senate, Committee on Government Operations, *Organizing for National Security, Hearings*, 87th Congress, first session (1961), Part 1, pp. 1084-95. Quoted in *Armacost, op. cit.*, pp. 66-67.

[23] United States Congress, House, Committee on Armed Services, *Military Authorizations, Fiscal Year 1964, Hearings*, Force Posture Statement of Secretary of Defense Robert McNamara, 88th Congress, first session (1962), p. 332.

[24] Ball, "Strategic Missile Programme...," *op. cit.*, p. 291.

[25] Edward Randolph Jayne, II, "The ABM Debate: Strategic Defense and National Security," Ph.D. Dissertation, Massachusetts Institute of Technology, 1969; John Newhouse, *Cold Dawn: The Story of SALT* (New York, 1973); Thomas Garwin, ABM papers, untitled, undated. On the Johnson Administration's decision to deploy ABM, see Morton H. Halperin, "The Decision to Deploy ABM: Bureaucratic and Domestic Politics in the Johnson Administration," *World Politics*, Oct., 1972.

[26] United States Congress, House, Subcommittee on Department of Defense Appropriations, Committee on Appropriations, *Department of Defense Appropriations for 1963*, 88th Congress, second session (1962), Part 5, p. 155.

[27] United States Congress, House, Subcommittee on Department of Defense Appropriations, Committee on Appropriations, *Department of Defense Appropriations for 1964*, 88th Congress, first session (1963), Part 6, p. 203.

[28] Quoted in Jayne, "The ABM Debate. . . ," *op. cit.*, p. 359.

[29] Our principal secondary sources are David Koplow, "Modeling the Arms Race: The Case of MIRV," honors thesis, Harvard University, April, 1973; Ted Greenwood, "Qualitative Improvements of Offensive Strategic Arms: The Case of MIRV," Ph.D. Dissertation, Department of Political Science, Massachusetts Institute of Technology; and Allison, "Questions About the Arms Race: Who's Racing Whom?" in Robert C. Pfaltzgraff, ed,. *Contrasting Approaches to Strategic Arms Control* (Lexington, Mass., 1974), pp. 31-72.

[30] "Is Russia Slowing Down the Arms Race?" Interview, *U. S. News and World Report*, April 12, 1965, pp. 52-53.

[31] United States Congress, Senate, Committee on Armed Services, Preparedness Investigating Subcommittee, *Status of U. S. Strategic Power, Hearings*, 90th Congress, second session (1968), p. 12.

[32] *Statement by Secretary of Defense McNamara on the Fiscal Year 1969-73 Defense Program and the 1969 Defense Budget*, pp. 52-53.

[33] United States Congress, Senate, Committee on Foreign Relations, Subcommittee on Arms Control,

International Law, and Organization, *ABM, MIRV, SALT, and the Nuclear Arms Race,* 91st Congress, second session (1970), p. 59.

[34] *Ibid,* p. 59.

[35] *Status of U. S. Strategic Power, op. cit.,* p. 12.

[36] Greenwood, *op. cit.,* pp. 80-81.

[37] United States Congress, Senate, Committee on Foreign Relations, *Strategic and Foreign Policy . . ., Hearings,* 92nd Congress, second session (1972), p. 248.

JOHN STEINBRUNER AND BARRY CARTER

Organizational and Political Dimensions of the Strategic Posture: The Problems of Reform

I

FOR AT LEAST THREE DECADES, the defense policy of the United States has focused intellectually, politically, technically, and economically on the problems of responding to the arms deployments—real or threatened—of hostile powers. During that time the nation has undergone successive experiences that have set intellectual and political assumptions about the requirements of strategic defense—assumptions that established massive aggression by the Soviet Union as the central problem. We have also produced remarkable and dangerous additions to our weapons technology, along with large organizations to produce and to operate them. In this long process we have clearly added a major component to the problems of national defense: we have generated momentum in the defense sector of our society that is burdening our capacity for intelligent management. As a result, the central problems of defense policy now include not only the international balance of strategic forces, but also the internal dynamics of defense institutions.

In our intensely introspective society, the internal issues of defense policy have of course been noticed, but the cries of alarm have not been accompanied by penetrating analyses. President Eisenhower's farewell warning of an undue concentration of power in the "military-industrial complex" is still remembered and frequently cited. The warning, however, has not developed into much more than a rhetorical phrase, and it surely must count as one of the great underachievers in the American political lexicon. There are numerous books and articles about the enormous costs and discouraging results of weapons-procurement programs, as well as some very serious work documenting major anomalies in the procurement process and in overall force posture. These studies, however, merely describe the symptoms. Deeper, causal analysis of the workings of the defense machinery remains to be developed.

A major consequence of this situation is a serious imbalance in the analysis of defense issues. Theories of deterrence, developed to understand strategic interactions between hostile powers, dominate both theoretical and practical thinking, including the rationalization of weapons-development and acquisition decisions, whatever the real motives might be. These theories, however, discuss only at the margins the problems of giving coherent direction to the large-scale scientific and industrial processes and the complex military operations that now characterize the national defense effort. While these problems are deeply affected by the Soviet threat and the problems of strategic balance, they cannot be explicated entirely in that framework.

Their internal driving forces are essentially beyond the bounds of governing theories, and yet their impact on the actual course of events appears, intuitively, to be enormous.

The internal dimensions of defense policy ought to be studied as a matter of genuine urgency. International agreements have now officially proclaimed parity and stability rather than dominance as the guiding principles of the superpowers and have thereby introduced what we might reasonably hope will be an era of arms control. If the spirit of arms limitations is to be carried through into reality and if we are to avoid the perverse effects that can derive from partial controls, then we must begin to understand and to adjust the domestic institutional dimensions of weapons acquisition.

Unfortunately, it is likely to require extensive, costly, organized effort to develop an adequate analysis of the defense institutions that have been created, and in the meantime the promise of this approach is likely to outrun its actual performance. This sobering realization need not be incapacitating, however. There is available a great deal of raw information and partially developed case histories of weapons developments. Though these data are far from definitive, they are sufficient to sustain a serious general discussion.

II

Among the most compelling indications of serious organizational problems in our defense institutions are the anomalies that have appeared in the force posture. For these purposes, an anomaly is an inconsistency between military needs derived from objective analysis and the actual military capabilities that the United States has procured and deployed. Two kinds of errors are being made: on the one hand, the United States has bought military capacity that is not needed and, on the other, it has neglected what would appear to be genuine requirements.

Because it has obvious significance for arms control, let us focus for the moment on the first type of error and consider especially two recent cases for illustrative purposes—the F-111 tactical aircraft and the Trident ballistic-missile submarine. In both cases the United States has pursued highly questionable weapons systems.

The F-111 is the principal weapon involved in the "forward-based systems" issue, which promises to be a major problem in arms-control discussions over the next several years.[1] It is a tactical aircraft designed to be able to fly without refueling across the Atlantic, to be able to operate from semi-prepared air fields (or aircraft carriers), and to penetrate deeply into hostile territory while carrying nuclear weapons. Its development program, which began in the late nineteen-fifties, was intended to achieve efficiencies in weapons acquisition by unifying Air Force and Navy tactical air requirements in a single aircraft and a single production line. In order to penetrate Soviet-controlled airspace, the plane was required to fly at very low altitudes (thus reducing radar detection to very short range), and the Air Force insisted this had to be accomplished at supersonic speeds.

The conjunction of the supersonic dash, transoceanic flight, and short takeoff distance requirements involved some very severe technical trade-offs. This fact preordained very high unit cost and, it turns out, rather poor military capability. The F-111 can perform a low altitude supersonic dash in its original mission profile over such a short distance (approximately thirty miles on a deep interdiction mission) that this

construction program. If, despite everything, it were judged imperative to retire the Polaris boats at twenty years of service, then a much more reasonable boat could have been designed as the replacement. A preferable submarine carrying from sixteen to twenty-four of the Trident II missiles and capable of speeds similar to Poseidon boats (twenty knots) might have been designed with less than 14,000 tons displacement and a natural circulation reactor with 20,000 shaft horsepower (shp).[7] This would have cost at least one hundred and fifty million dollars less per boat than the Trident design, thus saving at least one billion dollars over the currently planned program. That possibility was belatedly proposed by Secretary of Defense Schlesinger in February, 1974.

For reasons given earlier, all of the above options were preferable in terms of strategic analysis to the initially planned Trident program, and the original program was itself preferable to the decisions made to *accelerate* it. The accelerated schedule burdens ship-building capacity, doubtless increases cost, runs the dangers that result from concurrent development and procurement, and locks up the ship design at a time when the United States is ignorant of the technical characteristics of the threat that the Trident is supposedly designed to offset.

Finally, as the capstone to a series of logical puzzles on Trident, the Defense Department announced in February, 1973, that the first Trident submarines would be based near Bangor, Washington, and would operate in the Pacific Ocean. Though labeled a "victory for the strategists," the decision was quite the reverse, since the submarines would be more vulnerable there than they would have been in the Atlantic. Access to the port requires transit through a narrow strait in international waters—one place where anti-submarine warfare operations could be effective. Moreover, the Pacific coastline of the Soviet Union provides Russian ASW forces easy and direct access to the ocean and also allows deployment of an underwater acoustic system. Finally, the Pacific offers a smaller operating area with the Trident I missile if industrial targets in the western part of the Soviet Union are to be kept in range.[8]

In sum, factors other than reasoned policy are exercising strong influence over the design, development, and deployment of nuclear weapons. The Trident anomaly can be traced in large part to the workings of politics within the defense bureaucracy; the F-111, to the inertia of its organizational procedures. These are separate though highly interconnected dimensions of the overall problem.

III

Some of the anomalies of weapons acquisition derive, of course, from the workings of domestic politics, though the basic problem derives not so much from the mere existence of weapons-system politics as from a misunderstanding of how the political process is working in each particular case. Though infrequently acknowledged in official discourse, weapons systems obviously have constituencies in the armed services, in Congress, and in the electorate, whose interests are not confined to national security. Weapons deployments that appear nonsensical in terms of national defense can be quite profitable to narrower interests with leverage over the critical decisions—a simple fact that, we can be sure, is inevitable. The problem arises when these ever-present political forces are misread by policy officials charged with pursuit of national interest. As discussed elsewhere in this volume in more detail, the ABM deployment decision in 1967 provides a ready illustration.[9]

In 1967 the Johnson Administration recognized that the Sentinel system for defense against ballistic missiles could not technically achieve the purposes for which it had been designed—defense of the American population against missile attack. The Secretary of Defense at the time, Robert McNamara, further concluded that Sentinel deployment was likely to cause a corresponding increase in Soviet offensive forces. Nonetheless, the President and his chief advisers were facing impending election, a unanimous recommendation for deployment from the Joint Chiefs of Staff, and great pressure from the Armed Services Committees in Congress. McNamara tried to achieve an arms-limitation agreement with the Soviets that would stand up against these pressures. When the Soviets failed to respond within a few months, however, deployment was ordered.

Hindsight suggests that the political judgments of the President and his advisers were not very penetrating. The ABM proposal encountered such virulent opposition in Congress and in the electorate that heavy lobbying by the succeeding Administration was required to rescue it. Rather than a solid front, the unanimity of the Joint Chiefs was merely a fragile coalition, with only certain groups in the Army strongly supporting deployment. With better timing and better analysis, the politics behind the decision to deploy a population-defending ABM would have been more manageable. This observation applies to the Trident program as well.

Trident originated in the Strat-X planning exercise, a paper competition conducted in 1966-67 by civilian defense officials to stimulate cost-effective designs of advanced strategic weapons.[10] Then unglamorously labeled the "Underwater Long-Range Missile System" (ULMS), Trident was the major naval strategic weapon considered in Strat-X. It was advanced as a successor to the Polaris/Poseidon force, which was still in the initial processes of deployment. The nearest competitor was a very large land-based ICBM envisaged by the Air Force as a successor to Minuteman.

Navy planning for missile submarines was done at that time by the renowned Special Projects Office (SPO). That office had been created in the nineteen-fifties to conduct the Polaris development program, and the success of Polaris had given SPO and Rear Admiral Levering Smith, the next director after Vice Admiral William F. Raborn, a reputation for competence difficult to match in the government.[11]

Although the Navy (and SPO) did not make an official submission to the Strat-X study, Smith's thinking was clearly influential. Reflecting Smith's predilections and the Strat-X emphasis on minimum cost per surviving warhead, the Strat-X Trident was to carry a large but technically undemanding missile that could hold a sizeable number of warheads. The boat would necessarily be larger than the Polaris boats, but would use similarly sized reactors. This reduced slightly the expected top speed of the boat compared to Polaris, but speed was considered to be a result of other design goals and not an objective essential to the mission of a strategic missile submarine.

At the conclusion of Strat-X, Smith was named the Project Manager for Trident, the role that SPO had played in the development of Polaris and Poseidon. With that mandate, the office pursued various technical designs on a low-priority basis in 1967-69, gradually evolving its preferred design along the line of the Strat-X conception—i.e., a big boat that carried large missiles and was relatively slow (see Table). However, the speed of the boat—about nineteen to twenty knots versus Poseidon's twenty to twenty-two knots—would still have been ample to cover actual operational procedures.

During this period of evolution, however, the Trident program attracted the attention of Vice Admiral Hyman G. Rickover, who challenged Smith's conception of Trident. Rickover, then approaching seventy years of age, was another of the Navy's remarkable, even legendary figures—perhaps the only one who could match Admiral Smith's technical reputation. If Smith had helped develop Polaris, Rickover had developed the more fundamental technology of nuclear propulsion. The nuclear submarine constituted a revolution of sorts within the traditional Navy that had come only with the exercise of great technical, managerial, and political skill—and with the display of enormous will. Smith's great achievement depended on Rickover's before him. Thus when the two admirals locked horns, it was a major event for the Navy.

The issue between Rickover and Smith was joined in technical terms over the size of the reactors. During the late nineteen-sixties Rickover had successfully developed the natural circulation reactor (NCR) which, by operating without the use of noisy pumps at low speeds and by requiring less use of pumps at higher speeds, provided a significant improvement in quietness. Rickover had even deployed one on the experimental attack submarine *Narwahl*, which was commissioned in 1969. Recognizing the importance of quietness, Smith wanted access to data on the NCR as a candidate for Trident and thought that the 17,000-shp *Narwahl* design provided adequate power. Rickover, however, proposed to develop a far larger natural circulation reactor that would offer not only the increased quietness, but also greater top speed. The analytic trade-off was that a boat using Rickover's reactor would have to be far larger—and more expensive—than the SPO design. It is always better to go faster, Rickover argued, even if the systems analysts could not imagine why. The commanders of operational submarines, always reliable advocates of speed, agreed. Behind the argument, however, lay a critical fact: if the new reactor were used, Rickover would have substantial authority in the Trident program. On the other hand, if an existing reactor design such as the *Narwahl*'s were used, SPO would have maximum control over the entire boat, including the engine room, as it had in the Polaris program.

With the great authority and prestige of the Special Projects Office already being sapped by struggles with Congress over the Poseidon program,[12] Smith could not afford a major fight with a coalition of Rickover and the submarine commanders. By 1970 he compromised with Rickover; the result was a Trident submarine design of massive proportions. The projected boat would have a 30,000-ton displacement and would be powered by two 30,000-shp reactors, which would be over three times the size of the Poseidon boat, with four times the power and a top speed of about twenty-five to twenty-seven knots (still slower than modern attack submarines) (see Table).

This resolution of the Smith-Rickover confrontation presented a clear problem to the highest levels of the Navy. Even informal discussion of the behemoth design was sufficient to inspire outrage in Deputy Secretary of Defense David Packard in late 1970. Perceiving such signals of trouble, the then Undersecretary of the Navy John Warner and Chief of Naval Operations Admiral Elmo Zumwalt knew that they would have to force a redesign, and they began to probe for options.

The result of Warner's and Zumwalt's intervention was a classic compromise rather than a range of options. Some Navy analysts recognized that, given the absence of a known threat to Poseidon survivability, the construction of a new submarine could be delayed and that procurement of a longer-range missile for the

Poseidon boats would provide an ample margin of safety.[13] This option (labeled the EXPO option, for "expanded Poseidon") would restore sole control to Smith, however, and would suspend missile submarine construction indefinitely. In other words, it did not solve the *Navy*'s problems, and thus its appeal in terms of strategic logic only served to make it dangerous. Many efforts were made subsequently to constrain the fortunes of the EXPO option.

When the top admirals held a critical meeting in January of 1971, the unacceptability of EXPO was the only major point of agreement. Needing some constructive solution, Admiral Zumwalt settled on a compromise position that Rickover's office had prepared, a submarine design of 14,000-ton displacement with a single 30,000-shp reactor. The missiles with this design were smaller but, through the use of technical advances, still would have extended range (see Table). Zumwalt did not set a precise initial operational date for the new submarine, but it was generally thought to be 1980 or soon thereafter. In order to consolidate this compromise, Zumwalt named Admiral H. E. Lyon as Project Manager 2 of the Trident program and gave him overall management responsibility—i.e., he was to mediate between Smith and Rickover.

Wanting to strengthen their hands in the continuing bureaucratic infighting, the Trident supporters would not let the Zumwalt compromise hold fast. Under the supervision of Admiral Lyon, at least loosely a Rickover protegé,[14] both the submarine and the missile grew incrementally in size to their current dimensions—the missile by six inches in diameter and four to five feet in length, the submarine by 5,000 shp in reactor output and over 4,000 tons in displacement. Because the growth occurred without any change in the perceived threat or in the goals of the system, its significance is very clear. Whereas the missile design in the Zumwalt compromise was very close to the EXPO missile in size and was therefore vulnerable to suggestions that it be deployed in the Poseidon submarine, the most recent version (now called the Trident II) is decisively larger and unequivocally requires a larger submarine. The larger reactor likewise stilled suggestions that the Trident use the existing 30,000-shp reactor then being deployed on the latest nuclear attack submarines. The schedule of development was also accelerated. The date for initial deployment was advanced to 1979, and funding for the first reactor was included in the 1973 budget (at least a year or two in advance of need). In short, enlargement and acceleration were used as bureaucratic defenses against alternative technical designs.

Having consolidated the Navy position, the Trident program was launched on the broader seas of American politics, and, though there have been some close battles, the compromise technology (with some fortuitous help) has prevailed. David Packard conducted the first attack. In September of 1971, he issued an official Development Concept Paper on the Trident program in which he substituted the EXPO option for the Navy program, deftly renaming the missile the ULMS I (later to become the Trident I) to take some of the sting out of his decision. Packard's plan was to put the Trident I missile on Poseidon boats and defer new submarine construction until "the early 1980's." It looked like a brilliant finesse. It exposed the option that the Navy had labored to suppress and that Packard could expect an increasingly skeptical, economy-minded Congress to find attractive. Congressmen would be loath to resist a program involving the primary component of the strategic arsenal, but they would presumably welcome a version of that program that was cheaper and at least as effective.

The Sequence of Submarine Designs

	Poseidon	Trident Proposals			
		1967–1969	1970	"Super 640" Jan. 1971	Sept. 1971 and present
Time Period	Presently deployed	1967–1969	1970	"Super 640" Jan. 1971	Sept. 1971 and present
Submerged Displacement of Boat	8,250 tons for largest	Approx. 18,000 tons	Approx. 30,000 tons	Approx. 14,000 tons	Approx. 18,700 tons
Propulsion Plant	15,000 shaft horsepower (shp)	Existing design—about 15,000 shp	New natural circulating reactors (NCR). Two reactors of 30,000 shp each	NCR of 30,000 shp	NCR of 35,000 shp
Approximate Speed	20–23 knots	19–20 knots	25–27 knots	25 knots	25 knots
Size of Missiles	34' long, 74" diameter	About twice volume of Trident II	About twice volume of Trident II	37' long, 74" diameter	41-42' long, 79-80" diameter (Trident II)
Comments		Preliminary design. Very little emphasis on new technology. Missile design tentative—Poseidon payload with longer range, or bigger payload with shorter range.	Compromise between Rickover and Smith	Size reduced. New technology missiles. Result of Packard's concern over size.	Boat and missile allowed to grow.

The Navy program survived that assault, however, with the aid of a timely intervention from the White House. In October of 1971, President Nixon wanted Defense Secretary Melvin Laird substantially to increase strategic spending during the next fiscal year (1973), especially in the strategic missile submarine program. The President was not reflecting a special concern for Trident. Rather, the Moscow summit had been announced by this time, and the President intended, if possible, to sign the SALT agreements there. He wanted to make sizeable, "visible" increases in expenditures on strategic forces to minimize any concern that some of our Allies or conservative voters might have over the effect of the SALT agreements on the strategic balance.

The President was also concerned over the status of the negotiations on offensive weapons. It was already certain that the offensive agreement would allow the Soviets four to five hundred more ICBMs than the United States, but it was most uncertain whether the Soviets would agree to limits on missile submarines, which they were building at the rapid rate of seven or eight per year and which we were not building at all. If the missile submarines were not included, the Soviets would be given a large numerical edge in ICBMs, and no controls would be placed on their active SSBN construction program. Threatening to accelerate the American submarine missile programs might encourage the Soviets to agree to limits on future construction. If the threat failed, the accelerated program would help mollify the Allies and the conservatives. Even if the Soviets did agree to include the submarines, it was certain then that the offensive agreement would have a duration of no more than five years. Hence, given the President's commitment to "bargaining chips," he wanted a construction program underway to help him in the subsequent negotiations.

The President's initiative overwhelmed the Packard finesse. It brought Defense Secretary Melvin Laird into the issue and set the decision in an immediate political context favorable to the program. Recognizing the risks and tremendous resources required to accelerate the Trident program, the Navy did not recommend acceleration. However, the Navy (with Rickover pushing the hardest) made it clear to Laird that, if there had to be an accelerated program, the Navy preferred the Trident acceleration and not the EXPO option (regardless of its name) or any other option.[15] To allow any interim program, the Navy reasoned, would push Trident even further into the future and might threaten it altogether. Laird decided, in December of 1971, to accelerate the Trident program. Neither mollifying conservative voters nor pressuring Soviet negotiators would be helped by Navy opposition.

Laird's logic, moreover, was confirmed by the results of the SALT talks. In the interim agreement of May, 1972, the United States accepted an unfavorable numerical disparity in strategic submarines and missiles, and defended this both to the Joint Chiefs of Staff (JCS) and to the Senate as being the natural result of the United States' not having an active construction program in this area. Taking his cue, JCS Chairman Admiral Thomas H. Moorer made approval of strategic funding requests, including that for the accelerated Trident program, a condition for his support of the SALT agreements.

In Congress, the Trident program encountered skepticism and sharp debate, but in the end reluctant and unenthusiastic approval. Criticism focused in the Senate, where even members of the Armed Services Committee, representing a spectrum of political opinion concentrated toward the conservative, perceived that Trident, for all its enormous cost, did not add much to national defense. The legislators, however, are not organized to design weapons systems or define strategic programs, and they remain reluctant to do anything that might seem to jeopardize strategic security. The issue in the Senate thus focused on the less drastic matter of acceleration. For two years running, 1972 and 1973, amendments to cut the Trident program back to the more leisurely schedule envisaged by David Packard were defeated by very close votes both in the Armed Services Committee and on the Senate floor.[16] Despite the irony of having to pressure conservatives it once thought it was mollifying, the Nixon Administration backed Trident with cloakroom arm-twisting and tireless repetitions of the "bargaining chip" argument. That was barely sufficient to obtain grudging approval, and it also made clear that other options and other technical designs would have been viable on Capitol Hill.

An Administration-backed lower-cost option made its first appearance on the Hill in 1974. Presumably reflecting his unhappiness with the size and cost of Trident, Secretary Schlesinger proposed in January, 1974, that the FY 1975 defense budget include sixteen million dollars to start feasibility and conceptual design work on an Improved SSBN, called the SSBN-X. (Reflecting the source of his idea, Schlesinger occasionally called it the "*Narwahl*-type" SSBN.) Although the design was obviously still tentative, the proposed SSBN was to be available in 1984, would be smaller than the Trident, and would carry sixteen Trident I missiles. While the boat would be slightly larger than the Poseidon, it would be unable to accommodate the larger Trident II.

The Research and Development Subcommittee of the Senate Armed Services Committee, which had opposed the Trident acceleration in 1972 and 1973, surprised some casual observers when it recommended that the funds be denied. This recommendation was upheld by the full Committee, won easily on the Senate floor, and was accepted in conference. The Subcommittee's (and Committee's) denial was specifically predicated on the ground that, "while it fully supports the concept of a lower cost submarine-launched ballistic-missile system than the Trident," the request for funding was "premature."[17] Because the procurement for the Trident program was already underway and it was generally accepted that in these circumstances a "minimum buy" should be ten Trident boats, it appeared unnecessary for the Pentagon to begin planning at this time for the SSBN-X. The only lukewarm support for the SSBN-X came from the Director of Defense Research and Engineering (DDR&E), and opposition from some quarters in the Navy (reacting to this potential threat to purchase a large number of Tridents) also did not help to generate support for the alternative. The Committee's report, the Senate debate, and other indications, however, suggest that Administration sponsorship of an alternative to Trident—either the one presented by Secretary Schlesinger or perhaps a boat that could carry the Trident II missile—will obtain strong Congressional support in future years when it must be decided whether to buy more than ten Tridents or to proceed with the lower-cost option. Secretary Schlesinger apparently decided this year not to push for a new lower-cost alternative in his FY 1976 budget, but only to keep the idea alive by requesting a small, two-million-dollar appropriation for a new program called "SSBN Subsystem Technology."

There was also the decision, coming between the two Senate debates in 1972 and 1973, to base the first fleet of Trident boats near Bangor, Washington, and therefore to operate in the Pacific. Though extremely bizarre in strategic terms, there is a clear logic to the decision if one assumes that again the purpose was to protect the current submarine design against technical alternatives. Most Soviet urban-industrial targets are farther away from Pacific waters, and the Pacific operating area from which the Trident I missile would be in range of those targets is relatively limited. The increment in range offered by the Trident II missile, which requires the larger submarine, is far more meaningful in the Pacific, and deployments there would lend impetus to the program. It is also possible that the Navy considered it an advantage to locate the base in Senator Jackson's home state. The influential Senator, normally a solid supporter of weapons deployments, opposed Trident in the Armed Services Committee in 1972, and this defection from an established champion of stronger defenses was particularly dangerous to the program. With the first base programmed for his home state, it would be more difficult for Jackson to oppose Trident, and, in fact, he not only cast favorable votes in the 1973 roll calls, but also was the Senate's leading proponent of the weapon.[18]

The general theme is sustained in this story. Had policy officials chosen to avail themselves of it, there was sufficient political flexibility available to achieve a more sensible design of the Trident submarine and to set a more reasonable pace for the overall program. The balance of forces within the service bureaucracy and Congress was a subtle thing with many possible points of leverage.

Navy support and approval by the Joint Chiefs of Staff of the Trident design were not certain. The coherence of the Navy, as well as of the other services, depends upon maintaining such things as budgets, mission concepts, and personnel career lines. Weapons programs inevitably serve as guarantors of all three. As a consequence, major weapons-procurement programs are scrutinized by the services not only in terms of standard cost effectiveness, but also in terms of impact on the established pattern of organizational relationships. Major decisions are the subject of intense, often bitter bargaining within and among the services. The end result is a recommendation by the Joint Chiefs of Staff for an overall defense program, usually presented unanimously, which reflects a balance of political forces among the many organizational subdivisions. Higher budgets and more programs make the internal bargains far easier to manage, and hence that is what the Joint Chiefs of Staff prefer—i.e., find necessary for national security. The natural competition between Trident and other service programs could have been emphasized, however, and if done early enough this would have disrupted the momentum that developed behind the particular Trident design.

The Congressional committees, once perceived as insatiable promoters of weapons systems, were no longer so, if they ever were, by the time of the 1972 consideration of Trident. The committees and Congress in general are enormously dependent on Executive initiative and will not comfortably contravene the recommendations of a united Joint Chiefs of Staff or the authority of a civilian Defense Secretary. If a reasonable option (or options) to the Trident acceleration proposal had been presented to them, however, and backed by at least some strong elements in the Executive branch, Congress would likely have exercised some discretion by selecting it. As for the general electorate, public reactions to a weapons program have more to do with symbolism and broad intentions than with the details of design and deployment.

In sum, the politics behind Trident were strong but not inexorable. If the politics of the process had been understood in some detail and if basic political forces had been taken into account before the process had ground out its elaborately bargained position, then sufficiently informed, appropriately timed policy decisions could have elicited more reasonable results. This could also have been the case with the 1967 ABM decision and with other major weapons procurement decisions.

IV

Why, then, is political management of weapons acquisition such a poorly developed art? In part the answer seems to lie in the failure to analyze systematically the profound inertia that arises from the exquisitely complicated organizational procedures of the defense establishment. It is these forces that set powerful constraints on weapons-system politics and that overload the capacities of policy-makers.

At the moment, for example, established procedures generally keep high-level policy officials away from weapons projects until the development cycle is well advanced technically and organizational momentum is well established. Before there is any serious effort to conduct explicit analysis and to make national policy judgments, many technical options have been eliminated and the surviving weapons.design is anchored in a well-developed organizational structure. Even when policy officials succeed in penetrating to the details of this situation—which appears to be a rare occurrence—they discover that they are highly constrained and that it would be extremely difficult to achieve the kind of solution that strategic analysts tell them they ought to achieve. David Packard's intervention in the Trident case, for example, though unusually well-informed, came very late in the process. Moreover, even if he had not been thwarted by the White House, his management approach meant that he would still have been essentially dependent on the Navy to propose any new design and that he would have had little control over that design until it had become well-formulated.

Some of these basic forces operating in the weapons-acquisition process are reflected in sharp relief in the well-documented history of the F-111 program. Specifically, experience with the F-111 illustrates three highly related aspects of current organizational arrangements that have caused trouble in most major weapons programs of the nuclear age. These are the setting of military requirements, the concurrent scheduling of development and production, and the procedures for managerial control.

Setting military requirements. One of the most critical stages of weapons acquisition is the specification of performance parameters and technical characteristics of a weapon that supposedly represent military requirements. These requirements appear to be the results of bargains between aerospace contractors and service subunits in a process that is driven by technical and scientific developments. A major advance in technology in itself provides the impetus for applying it to a weapon; military requirements tend to flow from that, rather than from a prior judgment of actual need. Scientists and engineers control the process with occasional and often politically inspired intervention from the specific military commands that will ultimately deploy the weapons. Business is conducted almost entirely in technical terms, with little or no participation by high-level policy officials. Since many details of the general process are obscure, it may be helpful to discuss it using a specific example.

The F-111 requirements were generated by the Tactical Air Command which was seeking a successor to the F-105, a deep interdiction fighter bomber.[19] The three requirements noted earlier—unrefueled trans-Atlantic flight, operation from semi-prepared fields, and penetration of Soviet airspace at low altitudes—derived from the mission generally associated with the F-105 and from TAC estimates as to what improvements would be required for a tactical manned aircraft to continue to perform that mission. It was axiomatic that, coming later, the F-111 would have to demonstrate improvements over the F-105 in its essential technical parameters.

These three requirements were at first judged to be technically incompatible, because studies had indicated that aircraft with the requisite range and low-altitude-dash capability would be too heavy to land on semi-prepared fields. This problem was overcome, however, when the National Aeronautics and Space Administration (NASA) developed a workable design for variable sweep wings and when turbo-fan engines became available. On the basis of these developments, technical studies ascertained that an aircraft with reasonable weight could have transoceanic range, a top speed in the area of Mach 2.5, and a low-altitude-dash capability at high but *subsonic* speeds. These studies led directly to the official military requirement (the Air Force's Specific Operational Requirement, SOR-183) with one major and extremely important exception: the low-altitude-dash speed was set *beyond* the sound barrier at Mach 1.2.

In retrospect, the issuance of SOR-183 was a critical point in the development of the F-111, far more so than anyone seemed to realize at the time. Once set, the requirements became the basic framework for the process of technical design. In that process the plane's manufacture was quickly broken down into an elaborate hierarchy of components that were separately designed and developed. Once that process was underway, the difficulties of coordination made it impractical to change any of the fundamental elements, such as the specified requirements. The critical factor of low-altitude-dash speed, which drove the designers against aerodynamic limits, could not be, or at any rate was not, adjusted as information accumulated. The design process, in other words, was not organized to allow trade-offs involving the specifications established in SOR-183.

The consequences of this rigidity have been severe. Even though the designers did not achieve a supersonic-dash capability over a meaningful range, they pursued this goal with sufficient determination to impose severe losses in other dimensions. The aircraft turned out to be far heavier than the original technical assessments assumed, and this increase in weight was a major factor in the ultimate cancellation of the F-111B, the Navy version. In attempting to reduce drag for the sake of the supersonic dash, a design was adopted that caused highly dangerous engine stalls under demanding flight conditions. The resulting poor acceleration and poor maneuverability make the plane vulnerable to interceptor attacks in clear weather.[20] Finally, the extraordinarily high unit cost—one of the plane's most remarkable and most unfortunate characteristics—is in part a direct consequence of the extremely demanding technical configuration.

A more thorough analysis is unlikely to achieve beforehand all of the insights that completed history provides. Nonetheless, it certainly would have been possible to challenge SOR-183 from a broad policy perspective. The Air Force technical studies argued the narrower question of feasibility, rather than desirability, of the requirements, and even then the assumptions of the technical assessment were arbitrarily extended to provide the supersonic-dash capability. There was ample warning that the project would be technically demanding, and this might reasonably have been expected to trigger a serious review of the mission's concept. That concept, which should never have been approved, was in fact never seriously contested.

Concurrent Scheduling. The second major organizational problem involves the scheduling of development and production. During the nineteen-fifties, with the Cold War at its height and with the spirit of arms competition widespread in the United States, the so-called "Cook-Craigie" procedures were established to reduce the length of time required for development and testing and thus to accelerate the introduction of new weapons into the active armed forces. Under these procedures, the weapons prototypes were produced in relatively large numbers (fifteen to thirty aircraft) on production tooling to expedite final testing and the beginning of production.[21] It was argued that these procedures would also increase efficiency by allowing advanced production of long-lead-time items.

Institutionally the adoption of these procedures meant that the advanced development process was connected to a production line and that the experimental and production phases of weapons acquisition unequivocally came under the same management. With managers planning for production and actually instituting production early in the development cycle, substantial organizational momentum was quickly generated behind any serious development project. The procedure was perfectly logical so long as there was little or no uncertainty about the need for the weapon being developed or about its technical configuration.

Unfortunately it quickly became apparent, even in the nineteen-fifties, that the certainties upon which the logic of the procedure was based simply were not present. Even in the rare situations where military requirements were not in question, there was considerable technical uncertainty. Since almost every major breakthrough was not reached by the time required, there were continual disruptions of the schedule, with its obvious consequences of inefficiency. If major technical changes had to be made, as a result of testing done at the advanced development stage, then the consequences were even worse—so much so that powerful incentives developed not to make technical changes unless the reasons for doing so were truly overwhelming. The net effect was that weapons systems that were only marginally required and technically deficient tended to get pulled into production.

As early as June, 1954, the Navy attempted to adjust these procedures for concurrent development and production by requiring actual operational testing of a small number of prototypes before scheduling production.[22] This, the Navy argued, would allow for a genuine assessment of need and for the identification of serious technical problems before the technical configuration was locked into a production schedule. The program was summarized by the phrase, "Try before you buy."

The attempt at modification has not been successful. There have been continuous discussions and repeated efforts to reach an adjustment, but the problem persists. Indeed, Secretary of Defense Laird, in July of 1970, announced a new attempt at reform under the slogan "Fly before you buy"—apparently unaware of the ironically parallel language.[23] Development projects have allegedly been undertaken under the revised rules, but with very little effect. With other factors taken into account, weapons produced under either system cost about the same, are available at about the same time, have about the same number of problems, and require about the same amount of time and testing between prototype and production stages.[24]

The development procedures have been so resistant to adjustment because they are anchored in powerful organizational forces. The defense contractors rely on many of the same management personnel for conducting both research and development and actual production operations. Minimizing the time between research and development and production is important to them for keeping their technical teams intact (without interruption in employment) and for avoiding the very high overhead costs that would result from sustaining the teams through an extended period of operational testing. Financial management also benefits from the close connection between development and procurement: financial risks can be taken at the research phase to keep bids low and competitive, with any research and development losses being recovered in production. Concurrency in the development and production phases also allows flexibility in accounting practices, which makes the recovery of such losses much easier. Finally, and most critically, the production phase of any weapons procurement obviously involves operations of far larger scale than does development. Production not only provides greater opportunity for profit, but (probably more important to the contractors) it also guarantees work over a number of years. Concurrency gives a clear competitive advantage to the developing contractor and serves to force production decisions. In all, it is a pattern that the contractors have an incentive to promote, regardless of how the official procedures might be structured.

For their part, the service organizations and particularly the commands that use the weapons find no reason to resist the contractors' enthusiasm for concurrency. Not only do they genuinely want new systems at the earliest possible date, but they recognize that momentum is very helpful and flexibility very dangerous in terms of internal politics. They consequently have encouraged an organizational procedure that does not undertake serious development without at the same time beginning the process of procurement.

The woes of the F-111 are closely related to this dynamic. The inlet for the engine can provide one of several dramatic examples. It was originally designed to minimize drag on the airframe—a central problem, given the supersonic-dash requirement. A standard calculation was used to establish its adequacy for the engine (which was being developed by a separate contractor); but when the prototypes were constructed, it was discovered that the calculation was invalid for turbo-fan engines and that the inlet did not provide the air intake that the engine would require under high-performance conditions. The inlet had to be redesigned, and in the process was so substantially changed that it could not be retrofitted on planes built under the original design. Because production was running concurrently with development, one hundred and forty-one planes were produced with the faulty inlet and thus were subject to very substantial performance deficiencies (particularly in conventional operations.)[25] In all, up to seventy per cent, depending upon the assumptions made, of the F-111 production run can be considered technically deficient.[26]

Managerial control. The consequences of technical determination of military requirements and of the natural pressures for concurrency would presumably not be so damaging were it not for the fact that the mechanisms for exercising managerial control are very poorly developed. Managerial control, in the sense intended here, means the ability to determine the details of weapons design and over-all force posture to implement basic national policy. At the moment, the procedures for making and implementing policy decisions penetrate only very weakly into the process where weapons are designed and produced.

This problem of managerial control has long been recognized. There have been many efforts at reform over a number of years, the Planning-Programming-Budgeting (PPB) system introduced by Defense Secretary McNamara in 1961 being the best known and most widely discussed.[27] It included a budget structured by program categories and tied to five-year force projections with associated cost estimates. It also entailed a highly organized effort to bring systematic analysis to bear on budget decisions for the purpose of assessing military requirements relative to cost and thereby resisting deployment based on organizational inertia alone. There was, in addition, an attempt to replace cost-plus-fixed-fee contracting with various kinds of incentive contracts in an effort to control chronic cost increases in major weapons-procurement programs. Moreover, the very able Secretary of Defense personally intervened in prominent cases, including specifically the F-111, in an attempt to impose high-level policy discipline.

In the succeeding Administration, David Packard carried the cause for reform with different means and emphasis, but with similar motivation. Packard inspired the 1970 announcement that weapons prototypes would be subjected to extensive testing before production decisions would be made—the "Fly before you buy" program. He also introduced "milestone contracting" in an attempt to control the negative effects of concurrency, and he instituted the Defense Systems Acquisition Review Council (DSARC) to monitor military requirements.[28]

These various efforts have not been entirely fruitless, and an incorrigible optimist might argue that we are witnessing a gradual process in which defense managers are slowly but surely learning how to exercise policy control. The record looks a bit more gloomy, however, when we realize that the history of the F-111 coincides with the most aggressive period of reform. Budget controls, for example, have regularly been defeated in the early stages of weapons developments by unrealistic cost estimates, by reprogramming of funds, and by the fact that the program budgeting has not taken firm hold on the process. By the time expenditure levels become sufficiently large to make budget controls meaningful, the issue turns on broader questions of politics and the organizational situation. And close examination of the budget process reveals that major budget allocations (e.g., by program or service) have remained essentially unchanged by the reform effort.[29]

Similarly, contracting arrangements have had relatively modest or at best highly diffuse effects. Production processes regularly begin on the basis of a letter contract, and the process of definitization is virtually coextensive with the work in question, an arrangement which allows for a continuous negotiation between the government and its contractors and which perhaps better reflects their relative leverage. Even in cases where the contract has been well specified in advance, the rate of change in contract specifications remains almost the same (averaging two or three per day over the life of some major programs).[30] These realities render the original schedule, cost, and technical specifications almost useless as control devices. Even glaring violations of contract provisions, which are not covered in the process of contract change, emerge so late and create so many political complications that they are not effectively precluded.

The weak influence exercised by the various mechanisms of control is reflected not only in the F-111 case, but also in such famous contemporaries as the C-5A and the F-14. All three programs are notorious for their cost overruns and, at least in the case of the first two, for performance deficiencies. Far more serious, however, neither the F-111s nor the F-14s have characteristics that fit coherently defined needs for defense.

The Trident program was affected by these problems of organization. The design of the submarine hardened around a single option, albeit with some difficulty, and the essence of that design was again to push technology against natural barriers in pursuit of greater speed. As with the F-111, it does not appear that the increment in speed will provide any important operational benefit. Moreover, the acceleration of the program, pushed by Rickover to protect his bureaucratic victories (and backed by the White House for other reasons), will undoubtedly mean a relatively high degree of concurrency—i.e., overlapping of the advanced development stages with production. This is not likely to be so serious a problem in the Trident case as it was in the F-111, since procurement for the entire program will be stretched over a longer period, leaving flexibility for subsequent adjustments, and since submarine technology, on the basis of the record thus far, appears to have been more thoroughly mastered. Even so, concurrency of development and production provides the potential for serious trouble.

On another level, the budget process significantly weakened competitive pressures over the Trident program. Under the system established by Secretary Laird in 1969 (and essentially still in effect today), the services receive "Fiscal Guidance" early in the annual budget-planning cycle that sets a clearly defined amount for each service. Since these guidelines have been maintained over the planning cycle, the services quickly learn that it is fruitless to compete for greater shares of the total defense budget. This is reinforced by the elaborate force-planning process whereby each service has to show in detail what forces the funds can buy. The detail is sufficiently time-consuming for a service to find it difficult to suggest alternative approaches, including ones that would give it a part of another service's funding.[31] As a result of this system, neither the Air Force nor the Army has commented seriously on the Trident program since the Strat-X study.

Moreover, the budget process, as Laird structured it, has tended to discourage competition within the Navy—for example, between the surface fleet admirals and the submariners. When the process was first initiated, each service apparently tried to cut back on the strategic share of its budget in favor of bolstering non-strategic forces. This reflected a bureaucratic maneuver: the services knew that strategic forces were especially visible politically and that the Administration was most likely to give these programs extra funding at the last minute. To prevent this, Laird and Packard soon began to put a "fence" around strategic forces (and a few other budget categories) to prevent these raids, but it also meant that the non-submariners in the Navy saw little gain in challenging Trident. Secretary Schlesinger removed the "fence" protecting the Fiscal Guidance for strategic forces (but not some other categories) for the FY 1976 defense budget preparations; it is still too early to determine what the actual long-term impact will be.

In general the same organizational problems that have been experienced many times before are at work in the Trident program, now projected to become the most expensive weapons program in the nation's history.

V

The United States has survived nearly three decades of the nuclear age without achieving a fully coherent defense posture, and during that time numerous efforts to solve the underlying organizational problems have been frustrated. Against that background one can hardly advance the foregoing diagnosis of organizational malaise with a breathless sense of discovery, nor can one confidently proceed to detailed prescriptions for reform. These facts, however, do not counsel resignation or neglect. The consequences of mistakes in defense posture remain far too serious, the costs of the effort are far too great to allow us to accept the current level of performance as the highest realistic aspiration.

Better management of weapons acquisition will require major organizational adjustments. The politics of weapons acquisition are very likely to defeat even the most compelling, even the most complete policy analysis, if the fundamental organizational posture is not arranged to provide more policy leverage over weapons development and more penetration into its details. The reform effort to date has not achieved adequate results; stronger measures are required.

Though an attempt to provide a detailed design of a more drastic set of reforms would be premature, the preceding analysis suggests a set of principles useful as guidelines for a general effort and for the specific case of Trident. There are four such principles.

First, *military requirements must be integrated with over-all defense policy and operational needs.* At the moment the process of setting requirements is dominated by relatively narrow questions of technical capability. High-level policy officials do not have adequate influence at that point when requirements are defined and applied to a weapons program. As development proceeds, desirable trade-offs between design parameters are not being made, and initial errors of judgment become irreversibly cemented into advanced technical designs. Military requirements, in other words, must be subjected to broader influence and must be implemented with greater flexibility.

A mechanism such as the Development Concept Paper (DCP) must be made available much earlier in the development process so that officials—for example, the Deputy Secretary of Defense and his civilian staff—are involved in the process and have the power, when necessary, to make modifications. These documents should make explicit the connection between requirements and mission concepts to bring under policy review such troublesome issues as the low-altitude-supersonic-dash capability of the F-111 and the speed of the Trident submarine. The formulation of the requirements demands thought and experimentation—there must be sufficient precision to discipline the development process and thereby prevent subtle sabotage by an unhappy service, but this precision should not be allowed to induce rigidity that would prevent desirable technical trade-offs as difficulties in development are encountered. Except where the additional costs are prohibitive, the often announced but rarely achieved procedure of prototyping should be done on a competitive basis—that is, alternative technical designs should be developed to the point of production. This would be a means of preserving flexibility and competition until production commitments were made.

Second, *research and development should be separated organizationally from production.* Defense contractors should engage in weapons production, while the Director of Defense Research and Engineering should maintain a coordinating role over research and development work prior to the time when initial procurement decisions are made. The office should be relieved of its present responsibilities over subsequent development activities—e.g., undertaking production-line tooling to make a prototype.

The actual work on technical design through the state now known as advanced development[32] should be done by small organizations and small technical teams. These organizations should be supported by general grants not related to specific procurement programs, and they should not be subjected to elaborate reporting procedures and detailed contract supervision. These organizations could produce functional and development prototypes[33] suitable for operational testing, and they could be rewarded for the quality of their technical work and not for their success in getting weapons designs into actual production. Some of the organizations should be linked by contract to the civilian offices of the Secretary of Defense, and not to the services. The organizations should be numerous enough to allow competitive prototyping of major weapons systems or their critical components.

Under such an arrangement actual weapons-system production would require the transfer of technology to a separate production organization. This transfer should occur only after independent operational testing of alternative prototype designs, a stage in the process that would allow serious review by high policy officials and operational commanders.[34] In the case of very large and expensive systems, such as the Trident submarine, prototype testing could occur on critical subsystems (e.g., the reactor) instead of on the full system.

Third, *budget procedures in the Department of Defense should be changed to stimulate competition between the services and possibly within each service.* These procedures should include a ceiling set in advance on over-all defense expenditures (ideally, for each year up to five years into the future). The ceiling, of course, might well become the victim of changed international circumstances, but top civilian officials should make it appear as firm as possible. Unless there is a firm ceiling, the services will find it in their interests to unite and, resisting efforts to encourage competition, to fight for a higher total figure.

Moreover, the Pentagon's present Fiscal Guidance system, which assigns a specified share of the proposed defense budget to each service early in the annual budget process and provides no occasion or incentive for the services to comment directly on one another's share, should be changed. Each service should be directed to accompany any request for more funds with a careful explanation of where these funds can be obtained from the budget of another service *or* from its own programs. In addition, top officials might encourage competition for resources between specific programs— e.g., the Trident program and the B-1 bomber.

With proper guidance from top policy officials, the increased competition among the services and possibly within the services would not result in destructive anarchy, but would, on the contrary, provide the high officials with the additional information and bureaucratic leverage needed to make and to implement better decisions.

Fourth, *the Executive branch should conduct analyses of the domestic political implications of weapons programs.* There is a great imbalance of effort at the moment in that hundreds of people in the Executive branch fine-tune the results of strategic war models and hundreds more engage in elaborate cost calculations, while complicated political judgments are made without serious discussion or analytic staff work.

At the moment the processes of technical design, force planning, and budget preparation are nearly completed before the political staffs who deal with Congress and electoral politics become involved. Even then, these staffs generally are not well enough informed on the substance of defense issues to be able to integrate political factors into policy judgments. This strong separation between politics and substance at the staff level does not reflect the realities of defense issues, and its severely inhibits the exercise of informed political judgment. It also prevents the serious discussion among the Executive branch, Congress, and leaders from outside the government that will be necessary if the major anomalies of the strategic posture are to be resolved. The quality of staff personnel should be improved; they and their superiors should be encouraged to consult systematically with Congress and public figures; and their conclusions should be incorporated early and explicitly into the process of decision.

Given Secretary Schlesinger's SSBN-X proposal, the Trident program might well become a test case for reform. Though procurement of some parts for seven submarines has already been authorized and the development of Trident is well-advanced, the technical requirements might well be reviewed when the question arises whether more than ten Trident submarines should be procured. It is unlikely that the size and speed of the currently planned submarine and the range of the Trident II missile would survive a serious policy review of requirements.

Moreover, with the ten-year program costs for each Trident submarine now estimated to be at least 1.8 billion dollars, it is obvious that a large deployment will burden other strategic programs. If budget procedures are revised to require the services to take into account the inevitable allocation problems that will arise, then military judgments on the desirability of the Trident program are likely to be more circumspect. Finally, if the Navy is having difficulty maintaining discipline among its more prominent admirals, then Administration officials ought to recognize and exercise the political leverage that a skeptical Congress and American public will provide.

Even if Trident deployment proceeds beyond ten boats without further question, the general issues of weapons acquisition, clothed in other projects, will command attention. Maintaining economically feasible and technically competent organizations to carry on weapons production requires a reasonably stable and predictable work load. There are similar problems in maintaining large military organizations when there is no war to conduct. Since World War II the defense establishment has been very much caught up in and sustained by a series of technical revolutions, each accompanied by a large procurement program. Now there appear to be fewer revolutions to conduct, and an international process of imposing constraints on arms deployments appears to be taking hold. We can no longer afford the cost and instability that result from working out the problems of organizational maintenance by resorting to large procurement programs. The issues must be raised explicitly and dealt with directly.

REFERENCES

[1] The account of the F-111 relies substantially on a manuscript by Robert F. Coulam, "Illusions of Choice: Problems in the Development of the Fighter-Bomber," *Teaching and Research Materials in Public Policy,* Harvard University, August 1973, cited by permission.

[2] Information on the Trident program was obtained largely through interviews and under the condition that it not be attributed; thus specific references cannot be supplied. Efforts have been made to verify all assertions of fact with more than one source and, where this procedure leaves residual doubt, that has been indicated in the text. The public sources on the Trident program include the extensive Senate and House hearings, reports, and debates. See also G. W. Rathjens and J. P. Ruina, "Trident," in C. Tsipis, A. H. Cahn, and B. Feld, eds., *The Future of the Sea-Based Deterrent* (Cambridge, Mass., 1974); Herbert Scoville, Jr., "Missile Submarines and National Security," *Scientific American,* June, 1972, p. 15; Members of Congress for Peace Through Law (MCPL), "Report on ULMS," April, 1972; MCPL, "Report on the Trident Submarine Program," September, 1973.

[3] The mileage estimates are from Alton H. Quanbeck and Barry M. Blechman, "Strategic Forces: Issues for the Mid-Seventies" (a staff paper from the Brookings Institution), p. 72. (The ocean areas under the polar icecaps and within the 200-fathom line are excluded.) The specific launch points are derived from the maps in Scoville, pp. 18-19.

[4] United States Senate, Committee on Armed Services, *Report on FY 1974 Military Procurement Bill,* 93rd Congress, first session, September 6, 1973, pp. 40 and 181; MCPL, "Report on the Trident," p. 13.

[5] Trident is being designed to be quieter than the Polaris boats, so it will be less vulnerable to ASW using passive acoustic sonars. (Of course, a "slimmed down" Trident could be made slightly quieter because it would create less "flow noise" of water passing around the hull, one of the components of submarine noise.) However, active sonar depends upon the size of the target, and hence the larger Trident might be more vulnerable. Rathjens and Ruina conclude that, against active sonar, Trident will be at a "small disadvantage" compared to Polaris boats (or smaller Trident design).

[6] Even if detected, the missile submarine's commander can resort to a variety of tactics rather than to shift to high speed. These tactics include evasive maneuvering, launching decoy torpedoes, and calling in other naval craft to act as decoys. A submarine running in the range of 20 to 25 knots creates so much noise that it can be detected from a great distance and hence over a large ocean area, thus allowing attackers to converge upon it. Some in the Navy have argued that a pursuing attack submarine (or possibly a destroyer) goes "blind" when a speed of about 25 knots is reached—i.e., its sonar is so hampered by its own flow noise that it becomes difficult to trail an SSBN. The limit of 25 knots is especially convenient since it justifies the planned Trident reactor. The analysis seems tenuous at best. It is based on some data referring to existing hull designs and existing sonars. Moreover, few in the Navy reportedly gave this argument much weight when the decision was made, and less self-interested observers strongly discount it. Even if this point of view is fully credited, the attacker could use slower-moving vessels for tracking and have them coordinate the attack. In short, speed beyond 20 knots does not appear to be useful for a missile submarine.

[7] The attack submarine *Narwahl* has successfully demonstrated a 17,000-shp natural circulating reactor, and this design could easily be developed to deliver 20,000 shp.

[8] Rathjens and Ruina; MCPL, "Report on the Trident," pp. 20-21. There is even a further argument: if Alaska is excluded, the continental shelf is narrower on the West Coast, and ASW operations are likely to be less difficult in deep water.

[9] The article by Graham Allison and Frederic A. Morris elsewhere in the volume discusses the ABM case. See also Morton H. Halperin, "The Decision to Deploy the ABM: Bureaucratic and Domestic Politics in the Johnson Administration," *World Politics,* 25, (1972), 62-95.

[10] The Pentagon Strat-X study was conducted by the Institute of Defense Analysis for the Director of Defense Research and Engineering. It established as the central criterion of judgment the cost per surviving re-entry vehicle, and the assumption was that the system that promised the least cost per surviving RV would gain impetus for actual deployment.

[11] See the account by Harvey M. Sapolsky, *The Polaris System Development: Bureaucratic and Programmatic Success in Government* (Cambridge Mass., 1972).

[12] For example, in 1969 the Defense Appropriations Subcommittee of the Senate made the first conscious Congressional cut ever in the SSBN programs and thereby disrupted extensive scheduling plans (Sapolsky, pp. 222-226).

[13] The option was bootlegged out of the Navy by low-level personnel and appeared under civilian sponsorship in strategic survivability studies associated with SALT.

[14] Lyon had been a reactor safety officer, a career that rarely leads to an admiral's rank in the Navy. Rickover had been a strong supporter of Lyon and reportedly helped get him his stars.

[15] Some civilians in the Pentagon and on the National Security Council staff suggested alternatives other than EXPO. If time were truly critical, additional SSBNs could be deployed most quickly (by 1975-76) by adding missiles to new attack submarines under construction; alternatively, and probably the wiser course, the Navy could avoid some of the time required for the design and planning of Trident by building more Poseidon boats, possibly with a *Narwahl* type of reactor. Either alternative was much less expensive than Trident and would have allowed the Trident submarine to be delayed until future ASW threats were better understood.

[16] In the Senate Armed Services Committee, the Trident acceleration passed by virtue of an 8-8 vote in 1972 and an 8-7 vote in 1973. (In 1972, Richard Schweiker, a junior Republican Senator, switched his vote at the last minute to support the Administration, and Senator Barry Goldwater did the same in 1973—both reportedly as a result of intensive Administration lobbying.) On the Senate floor, the Administration succeeded by a vote of 47-39 in 1972 and 49-47 in 1973. Note that such Senators as Byrd of Virginia, Cannon, Dominick, Saxbe, Jackson, and Goldwater opposed the Administration at least once in these votes in Committee or on the Senate floor.

[17] The language is from the Committee's report, United States Senate, Committee on Armed Services, *Authorizing Appropriations for Fiscal Year 1975 for Military Procurement, Research and Development, and Active Duty, Selected Reserve and Civilian Personnel Strengths, and for Other Purposes*, Report No. 93-884, 93rd Congress, second session, 1974, p. 105. This report, however, also reflects the subcommittee's rationale.

[18] In 1972, Senator Jackson opposed the acceleration of the Trident program in the tie vote of the Armed Services Committee, but he sided with the Administration on the Senate floor. In 1973, Jackson was an outspoken supporter and a major leader in the fight over speeding up the program.

[19] Details of the F-111 case are documented by Coulam, *op. cit.*

[20] The point here is that the F-111 is not the multipurpose aircraft it was originally designed to be. The Air Force argues that the plane would not be vulnerable on a very specialized interdiction mission involving the low-altitude-dash capability because interceptors with better acceleration would fly at higher altitudes and would have difficulty seeing the plane. Even if the argument were granted, however, it is clear that the plane would be very vulnerable outside of this narrow circumstance. All the money and effort were not intended to produce such a highly specialized weapon.

[21] See Thomas Marschak, Thomas K. Glennan, Jr., and Robert Summers, *Strategy for R&D: Studies in the Microeconomics of Development* (New York, 1967).

[22] United States Senate, Committee on Armed Services, *Final Report on F3H Development and Procurement*, 84th Congress, second session, 1956, p. 8. This report was exhumed from the archives by Robert Coulam, who brought it to our attention.

[23] *New York Times,* July 28, 1970, p. 1.

[24] B. H. Klein, T. K. Glennan, Jr., and G. H. Shubert, "The Role of Prototypes in Development," Rand Memorandum Rm-3467, February, 1963; Ronald Fox, *Arming America* (Cambridge, Mass., 1974).

[25] There is an apparent inconsistency in complaining, on one hand, that outlandish technical specifications are being set and, on the other hand, that the actual product is not meeting the specifications.

Nonetheless, the problems are in fact real. A weapons system that fails to meet overly demanding design targets is not the same as a weapons system whose design was accomplished by a calculated weighing of trade-offs. The latter is far more likely to have coherent capabilities.

[26] There were 141 F-111As with the restrictive inlet; 94 F-111Es with an enlarged inlet, but the same relatively low powered engine; and 76 FB-111As with essentially the same inlet but a slightly more power-ful engine. Together these models comprise seventy per cent of over-all production. All are certainly deficient when compared with the original conceptions of the aircraft.

[27] Alain Enthoven and K. Wayne Smith, *How Much Is Enough? Shaping the Defense Program; 1961-69* (New York, 1971).

[28] The Packard reforms are discussed in more detail by Robert Art, "Why We Overspend and Underac-complish," *Foreign Policy*, 6 (Spring, 1972), 95-118; and Michael Getler, "David Packard: Presiding Over a Revolution," *Armed Forces Management*, 16:6 (1970), 29-34.

[29] John P. Crecine, "Defense Budgeting," in W. W. Cooper *et al.*, eds., *Studies in Budgeting* (Amster-dam, 1971).

[30] The rate of contract-change orders and the consequences for controls are discussed by Ronald Fox, a former participant in the process, in *Arming America, op. cit.*

[31] The Joint Chiefs of Staff do prepare a Joint Forces Memorandum (JFM) that involves some inter-service bargaining, but this document is produced early in the budget process (when total funding is still uncertain) and is not closely tied to the rest of the process.

[32] The Research, Development, Testing, and Engineering (RDT&E) budget appropriation is presently classified by the numbers 6.1, 6.2, 6.3, 6.4, and 6.5, with basic research at the low end of the scale. The first three categories include activities that take place prior to the decision to procure a weapons system and comprise less than twenty per cent of the RDT&E budget. Advanced development corresponds to budget category 6.3.

[33] One must distinguish three types of prototypes: 1) Functional prototype: This is a handmade prototype that simulates the final system, but does not necessarily incorporate the production hardware (for example, transistors rather than integrated circuits are used). This makes it possible to test whether a system, if built, would function according to specifications or contain unforeseen weaknesses. 2) Develop-ment prototype: This is also handmade and hence without production tooling, but it is much closer to the final production item in detail. 3) Production prototype: This designates the first unit(s) off the production line. The independent research and development organization would make functional prototypes and sometimes development prototypes.

[34] Recommendations to this effect were made by the Fitzhugh Commission, *Report to the President and the Secretary of Defense on the Department of Defense by the Blue Ribbon Defense Panel*, Washington, D.C., U.S. Government Printing Office, July 1, 1970.

LES ASPIN

The Defense Budget and Foreign Policy:
The Role of Congress

Introduction

IT IS AN ARTICLE OF FAITH among political observers that Congress possesses ultimate control over executive actions because "it controls the purse strings." This is unquestionably true, but it does not help much. Although, under the Constitution, Congress possesses the power to grant or refuse the money necessary for any and all governmental activities, a survey of recent history shows that Congress is extremely slow to exercise this prerogative. Nowhere is this clearer than in the area of the defense budget. Congress could have ended American participation in the Southeast Asia war at any time in the last decade simply by refusing to appropriate money to fight it. However, in the House of Representatives, this was never done, even during the dying days of the war when public sentiment against it was overwhelming.

The "purse strings" argument, which implies a rational decision made on the merits of a given program, is particularly unsatisfactory when it comes to the yearly appropriations for our defense establishment. It is obvious to anyone who is acquainted with the defense budget that Congress could reduce military spending by making any one of a hundred or so possible cuts in the Pentagon's budget. However, this almost never happens. Every year a dozen or so amendments are offered to cut money for elaborate new weapons; every year they go down to convincing defeats. The Pentagon generally comes away with everything it wants, and sometimes more besides.

Why will Congress not exercise its prerogatives and place controls on military spending? Surely there is ample public sentiment for cutting the defense budget. A recent Gallup Poll showed that more than fifty per cent of the population felt that such cuts should be made. If it is true that Congressmen respond to public pressure, why have we not seen more votes against military spending, more control of the purse strings? The answer, I believe, has to do with some generally unrecognized aspects of the legislative process—particularly how Congressmen make their decisions, how they get their information, how they evaluate it, whom they listen to, and the pressures to which they are subjected.

I. Congress

Congressmen vote the way they do primarily because of their constituents, and this is particularly true when it come to votes pertaining to defense. From the beginning of the Cold War until very recently, constituent pressures on defense matters have encouraged increases in military spending. That prevailing sentiment, whether based on Cold War policies or concern for defense-related jobs, was one of the dominant realities of American politics.

Lately, however, there has been a change. While constituencies directly involved in defense production continue to be as interested as ever in larger defense budgets, the rest of the country has developed a different point of view. For evidence, it is necessary once more to look no further than the Gallup Poll. In 1963, only five per cent of the public listed defense spending as their first priority for cuts in the budget. By 1970, over thirty per cent named defense first, and, as already mentioned, over fifty per cent of those interviewed said they were in favor of some form of defense cutback. Clearly, by the late nineteen-sixties, a number of social, economic, and political factors—the unpopular war in Vietnam, high taxes, inflation, and a shortage of money for domestic programs—had converged to create a new attitude in the country about military spending. As a result, Congressmen hear from their constituents today some fairly distinct rumblings in favor of cutting the defense budget, although mixed with cries not to eliminate defense-related jobs. This sounds like a quandary, but it is not entirely. It simply means that a Congressman is likely to be very selective about the cuts in a defense budget that he will favor.

A Congressman who wants to respond to this new mood—to cut military spending but protect jobs—is likely to focus, for example, on such defense issues as manpower questions, cutting troop strength in Europe, and disbanding divisions; these would reduce the defense budget, but would not directly affect employment at home. (The demilitarized troops, of course, will add to unemployment, but not significantly for any one Congressional district.) An amendment to slow down the production of a given weapons systems will gain more votes than an amendment to eliminate it entirely. Finally, if it comes down to cutting a weapons system, one whose economic benefits are highly localized in a single state, or in one or two Congressional districts, is more likely to be cut than one that, through contracting and subcontracting, has managed to spread its economic largess throughout the country.

After constituent interest, probably the second most powerful factor influencing defense votes on the House floor is the pressure groups. Pressure groups that take an interest in reducing the defense budget can be roughly divided into two camps. First, there is the arms-control community, composed mainly of experts at universities and "think tanks," many of them former Defense Department officials. Second, there are the peace groups, which are citizens' lobbies. The arms-control community is primarily interested in producing a "rational" or efficient defense budget, and the peace groups primarily in cutting the defense budget in any way possible. Although the two do not always agree, they can, and do, cooperate on many issues. A classic example is the ABM controversy of 1969.

Opposing these groups are the military services and their allied lobbies. Although, strictly speaking, it is illegal for the services to lobby on Capitol Hill, they do a great deal of it under the guise of disseminating information. When the services really want something, they usually get it. On the other hand—because such an all-out campaign requires great effort—the services cannot mount one for every issue, so that the imbalance between lobbies in favor and opposed to an issue is generally less pronounced than one might expect. Two things may affect the balance. The first is the extent to which the peace groups and the arms-control community can enlist other pressure groups, such as environmentalists, to their cause. A second factor is the degree to which the Administration—assuming that the Administration is one that has a measure of influence in Congress—chooses to exert its influence.

What all this comes down to is a question of countervailing pressure, i.e., whether or not the services want a budget item more than the arms-control community and peace groups do not want it. The services, of course, have greater resources, and so, all else being equal, they usually prevail. For the arms-control community and the peace groups to have an impact on a Congressman's vote, they not only have to find an issue on which they can agree, they must also be extraordinarily committed. Half-hearted efforts will not produce sufficient votes.

A third factor influencing defense votes on the House floor is the Congressman's expertise or, more frequently, lack of it. If pressures by constituents and lobbyists have not already done the trick, this will be decisive. Almost every Congressman feels that he is an expert in education, or economics, or in any of a number of domestic fields. But when he deals with defense and foreign policy, he lacks confidence and tends to depend upon the "experts." To most Congressmen, defense experts are people in uniform, rather than academics in universities or "think tanks." Uniforms are identified with expertise: the higher the rank, the greater the expertise. Needless to say, experts in uniform tend to advise more spending. In addition, when it comes to national security matters, there is a tendency to "play it safe." Playing it safe usually means buying more.

The effect of a Congressman's lack of expertise on amendments to cut weapons systems is enormous. There is a built-in reluctance for Congressmen to question strategic-weapons systems, and the more complicated the system, the greater the reluctance. This reluctance can be overcome, as it was in part in the ABM debate, but only with an enormous effort by outside experts to educate Congress. Generally, amendments have a better chance of success when they concern issues that Congressmen feel are within their range of experience, such as conventional weapons or, better yet, manpower. But even then the Pentagon "experts" and their supporters have a built-in advantage.

There are ways of offering amendments on the defense budget that do not confront the question of expertise directly. For example, if the vote is perceived to be a procedural one, rather than a vote based on expertise or judgment, it has a better chance of success. Congressmen prefer votes that do not pin them down on the issues. A motion to table, for example, is more "comfortable" than a straight up-or-down vote; a motion that involves the prerogatives and privileges of the House will win more votes than one that involves a stark confrontation with the Pentagon. In addition, it is very helpful for the amendment if there is an alternative. Congressmen are more likely to vote to eliminate a weapon if there is something to fall back on—something that the "experts" feel is almost as good.

On the basis of all these considerations, one can conjure up a hypothetical weapons system that Congressmen could vote against on the floor of the House of Representatives. It would have the following characteristics: first, production would not have begun, so no jobs would be involved, or if jobs were involved, they would be concentrated in one geographic area. Second, it would be highly visible and destabilizing, and would therefore be of immediate concern to the peace groups. Third, it would be especially expensive and of doubtful practicality—to enlist the opposition of the arms-control community. Fourth, for whatever reason, the services would not be strongly in favor of it. Fifth, it would be easily understandable, or at least translatable into a procedural issue. Sixth, there would be a readily available alternative. Seventh, it would have adverse effects upon the environment. In addition, so long as we are describing an ideal situation, it would be located in or near some cities so as to displace many people, the proposed contractor would have a terrible record of labor relations, and the financing of the weapons system would be planned in such a way as to undermine the free-enterprise system.

Looking over this list, it is obvious that it will be very difficult to find items in the defense budget that Congressmen will be willing to cut—an observation that is borne out by bitter experience. In recent years no major weapons system has been cut from the defense budget through votes on the floor of either the House or the Senate. The one that came closest was the ABM debate in 1969, which ended in a tie vote in the Senate. Ultimately, the ABM opponents won that war, although they lost the battle. After the vote, the Administration eventually settled for a much more modest proposal that involved only a defense of Minuteman missile sites. When Congress does defeat a defense issue, that is usually the way they do so. An up-or-down vote in which the Executive branch is defeated, such as the SST case, is extremely rare.

In recalling the great ABM debate, it is easy to forget that it was a unique political event, built on an unrepeatable combination of circumstances. Several factors converged simultaneously: the arms-control community claimed the ABM would not work and was ready to come to Washington to explain to Congressmen why it would not; the peace groups said it was destabilizing, and they were frightened enough to lobby intensely; constituent pressure against the ABM (almost unheard of on a weapons-systems issue) was provided by people living near the proposed ABM sites. And, finally, stopping the ABM involved eliminating very few jobs. Up to that point, no part of the weapon was in production, and most of the research and development was in "software." The ABM controversy brought together a constellation of forces that was not likely to be repeated by chance, and is almost impossible to put together by design.

If it is almost impossible to curtail major weapons systems on the floor of Congress, it is not so impossible to reduce manpower. Manpower reductions have always been politically possible because they do not involve eliminating jobs, do not require Congressmen to risk their slender expertise against the generals, and, in the case of cutting troops in Europe, even offer a villain. Politicians can express indignation over those European countries which, given their GNPs and high populations, ought to be able to provide more for their own defense. The only reason troop cuts in Europe have not been passed long before now is that the arms-control community has been, at best, divided on the issue. (In fact it is safe to say that the great majority of the arms-control community thinks that the unilateral cutting of troops in Europe is not a good idea.)

There are, however, many other manpower issues besides troop cuts in Europe. The over-all size of the Armed Forces is one such issue. The number of troops stationed abroad (and not only in Europe) is another. Amendments concerning both of these could be carried on the floor of the Congress. A number of more minor issues on manpower could be affected by a vote on the floor of Congress—a cut in flight pay for colonels and generals who do not fly (which has already been voted in the House), or fewer enlisted servants for general officers (which has been voted in the Senate).

Another possibility for reducing the defense budget on the floor of Congress is through a ceiling amendment. In the past, ceiling amendments—placing a dollar limit on total defense spending with the decision left up to the Pentagon as to where specific cuts should be made—have not fared any better than weapons amendments, for the very good reason that some Congressmen fear that the Pentagon, if left to its own devices, will keep and cut all the wrong things—leave in all the fancy new weapons, for example, and cut out the necessary support. In the past, ceiling amendments have gained the support of those Congressmen who are generally considered fiscal conservatives (because there is bound to be a certain amount of fat in the budget), but have lost the support of some liberals (on the grounds that it is the job of Congress to determine not only the size, but also the shape of the defense budget).

This objection can be met by a ceiling amendment that makes an over-all reduction but retains for Congress the right to approve the adjusted budget. (If the Armed Services Committee is given the final responsibility for approving all cuts, the ceiling amendment should be all the more acceptable to Congressmen, who, as a rule, are not eager to make such judgments on their own.) In voting for such an amendment, a Congressman can register the desire of his constituents to cut the defense budget generally, without directly confronting the job-protection pressure for specific weapons—and without having to confront military expertise.

Any budget cuts made on the floor of the House of Representatives or the Senate are therefore likely to be very selective. Most members of Congress, of course, serve on Committees other than Defense, and these members think about an issue, such as the B-1, only twice a year—at the time of the Authorization bill and again at the time of the Appropriation bill. Among these Congressmen, constituent interest, pressure groups, and lack of expertise weigh very heavily when they cast their votes, and the odds are very strong that the B-1 will stay. What may not stay are other things—enlisted men serving as aides for generals, an overall amount from the total budget, or the number of troops serving overseas. These are the kinds of cuts that are likely to be made on the floor of Congress. If we want to do something more, we had better look for some device or strategy that does not depend on the votes of individual Congressmen.

II. The Armed Services Committees

If there is any place in Congress where defense issues, other than "manpower" and "ceilings," might be raised to any purpose, it would surely be in the Armed Services Committees. Members of the Armed Services Committees (and the Defense Appropriations Subcommittees) are in a position to spend the time necessary for developing some expertise on weapons systems and other aspects of the defense budget that require detailed knowledge. Moreover, the Committees have leverage—an essential ingredient in Congress for procuring information and developing an independent position on defense issues. Individual Congressmen can write letters and make charges and perhaps the Pentagon will respond, and perhaps not. An individual Congressman has nothing to offer that the Pentagon particularly values, and certainly, as things stand now, the Pentagon does not concern itself over individual votes. The Armed Services and Appropriations Committees, however, have something that the Pentagon does value, namely control over the budget, and they can simply refuse to report the budget out of Committee until responses are provided. It might not even be necessary to hold up the entire budget. During any given session of Congress, there are a number of small pieces of legislation, often related to manpower, that have to be passed. Any one of these can be used as a "bargaining chip" by the Committees.

The House Armed Services Committee, for example, would be an excellent place to generate an alternative national defense budget. Studies could be made, the services could be forced to respond to these studies, outside experts could be hired on a consulting basis, independent positions could be developed. And those independent positions would have a good chance of passing on the floor of the House if for no other reason than that Congress, conscious of its own ignorance, almost always accepts the recommendations of the "experts" on the committees. Major legislation in both the House and Senate gains votes simply because it represents the committee's position. Hardworking, vigilant, and informed committees could actually *force* Congress to enact a rational defense budget. . . . A wonderful idea! Unfortunately, it is not the way things work.

Why the defense committees—that is, the two Armed Services Committees and the two Defense Appropriations Subcommittees—do not fulfill their potential as molders and disposers of the defense budget relates first of all to the issue of who obtains membership on these committees and why. When a person is elected to Congress, one of the first things he starts worrying about is how to be re-elected. For a junior Congressman, with no chance to influence national legislation, one of the best ways to be re-elected is through constituent service—and to do this well, the Congressman should first gain membership on a committee relevant to his constituents' basic economic needs. A Congressman with defense bases, installations, or contractors in his district will obviously want to, and usually does, get himself appointed to a defense committee. The consequent problems are usually not so acute in the Senate, perhaps in part because Senators serve a larger geographic area and are less likely to have the majority of their constituents heavily dependent upon one industry. But they do exist in the House. There are House Armed Services Committee members who do not themselves have heavily defense-dependent districts, but they are often chosen to serve on the Armed Services Committee as their state's representative, and they are there to look after that state's interests.

While the economic interest of constituents is probably the most important reason why the House Armed Services Committee is pro-military, it is not the only one. A pro-military stance is also still "good politics" in many parts of the country, and people who are elected from these areas tend to gravitate to the Armed Services Committee. Once there, the careful attentions of the Pentagon public-relations men are certain to keep them content. Liberals who are interested in national security matters tend to seek assignment to the Foreign Affairs Committees, where the cosmic issues are discussed. Conservatives tend toward the Armed Services Committee, where the money is divided up.

Consequently, not only is the House Armed Services Committee reluctant to make innovations in the control of defense spending, it does not even perform the routine functions very well. While it is not entirely fair to say that the House Armed

Services Committee is completely controlled by the Pentagon (they are at times firm about the costs of particular contracts), it is safe to say that the Committee only interests itself in certain kinds of questions. For example, the Committee members are not very interested in the number of DD-963 destroyers the Navy should buy, but they are very interested in the shipyard that will be given the contract to build them. When the Committee does become concerned about the rising defense budget, it is mainly about whether there will be trouble when it reaches the House floor. The result is that amendments to cut the defense budget that receive twenty-five or thirty per cent of the votes on the House floor have little more than ten per cent of the votes in Committee.

A peculiar set of circumstances that affects the Armed Services Committees tends to exacerbate the problem of faulty controls. Although it is not generally realized by the public, it is the Appropriations Committees, and not the Armed Services Committees, that have jurisdiction over the entire defense budget. The Armed Services Committees authorize only about one third of it, mostly in procurement, research and development, and military construction. In fact, when the Armed Services Committees were formed in 1946, the only part of the defense budget that they specifically authorized was military construction (about three per cent of the total). Since 1959 the Armed Services Committees in both houses have generally extended their authority, first to procurement and then to research and development, and it is likely that the authority of the Armed Services Committees will continue to expand in the years to come.

The effect of this historical development on Armed Services Committee members has been considerable. Committee members tend to look upon their job not as overseeing the whole defense budget, but rather as giving particularly close scrutiny to some parts of it. It never occurs to most members of the Armed Services Committee to consider force-structure alternatives, because they simply do not regard themselves as at all responsible for the budget itself.

One way of improving Congessional management of the defense budget lies in forcing a change in the membership of the House Armed Services Committee, but this would be very difficult to accomplish. As the system functions now, constituent interests are heavily weighed in assigning new Congressmen to committees, and there is virtually no agitation in Congress to change this; it works too well for both those Congressmen doing the assigning and those Congressmen being assigned. Without some agitation for change, there will be none. A lottery system of assigning committee places and a rotating system that would prevent Congressmen from staying on one committee for long periods are interesting ideas but politically unfeasible. Nor is it clear that changing the membership of the Armed Services Committee would necessarily produce positive results. There are many demands on a Congressman's time, and, if he were assigned to a committee in which he had no interest, chances are that he would simply not attend meetings or do the necessary work.

A second approach might be to take the budget decisions away from the Armed Services Committee and put them into the hands of some more objective or more aggressive body. The effect (if not the stated purpose) of the recent reforms in the House of Representatives has been to take power away from committee chairmen and to give it to the Party Caucus (and its new steering committee) and, to a lesser extent, the Speaker. These changes may in time modify the way defense matters are treated

in Congress. The Caucus might, for example, have some influence on defense spending by instructing the committees. In the House, the Democratic Caucus has already
successfully instructed the Foreign Affairs Committee to bring out legislation providing a termination date for American involvement in the Vietnam War, and this seems
to be the likely approach in other cases. The Caucus might, for example, instruct the
House Armed Services Committee to bring out a Defense Authorization Bill with x
billion dollars cut from it. But so far the Caucus has concerned itself mainly with
procedural issues involving the way the House is run, who the leadership will be, and
so on. Things may change, but up to now, when substantive issues are discussed in
the Caucus, it is difficult to obtain a quorum.

A third possibility is the removal of power from the Armed Services Committee by
the newly established Budget Committee. This Committee has been established to
centralize control of total federal spending in a system that has a variety of committees and subcommittees dealing with a variety of areas of appropriation. The
Committee is supposed, by balancing the President's recommended budget against
available economic data, to establish an over-all ceiling for total spending and target
ceilings for subunits of spending. Defense will be one of these subunits. One cannot
predict how successful such a super-budget committee will be, and there is no
guarantee that it will be any more willing to limit military spending than are the committees that currently have this responsibility; however, at least it will not labor under
the Armed Service Committee's parochial interests.

Finally, granting additional powers to the Speaker has also been proposed, but, of
all the possibilities, this one is the least likely to result in a reduction of defense expenditure. This is not meant to imply that the current Speaker, Carl Albert, is opposed to
cutting the defense budget—he is in fact not very favorably inclined to lower defense
expenditures, but that is not the point. The point is that the position of Speaker in
itself guarantees that he will not have much influence on the size of the defense
budget, whatever a particular Speaker's inclinations might be. Being a legislative
leader is very different from being an executive leader. When an executive leader in
the political process wants to influence events he does so publicly. He speaks out on
the issues and tries to influence others in supporting that stand. But a good legislative
leader *never* becomes committed to a position too early. He keeps the lines of communication open to all factions, tries to find out what each party's minimum demands
are, tells one group that another group will not accept this or that, and generally
searches for some common ground that a majority of the legislature will feel able to
support. An effective legislative leader announces his position at the last minute, and
since his position is precisely that common ground that he has discovered, if it is
accepted, he receives the credit for being a powerful figure in Congress.

It is therefore unrealistic to expect the Speaker to have a great deal of influence on
defense policy. To do so would require his acting like an executive leader, and this
would weaken him as a legislator. Senator Mansfield occasionally does take a stand on
defense matters, in the manner of an executive leader, to his great credit, but it works
to his detriment as an effective legislative leader. Wilbur Mills would never have done
it. On the other hand, Lyndon Johnson, one of the most skillful of legislative leaders,
ran into trouble when he tried to act as if he were a legislative leader in his executive
position as President.

There is a second reason why the Speaker will not be an influential force on defense matters, even quietly. His function as Speaker is to guide the legislation through the system. The inertia that has to be overcome in a body of four hundred and thirty-five members is enormous, and yet the Speaker is judged, by the press and the country, on whether or not Congress is acting on a President's program. The question on his mind is whether his legislature will be called a do-nothing Congress. In dealing with that problem, it is not long before he ceases to concern himself with the contents of the bills before Congress and becomes almost solely concerned with whether or not they have been acted upon: When will the Defense Authorization bill be through the Armed Services Committee? when through the Rules Committee? when passed by the House? when passed by the Senate? when acted on in the Conference? and when given final approval? Whether or not Trident, for example, has been taken out of, or put back into, the bill at various stages along the way becomes of minor importance.

In the long run it may be possible, by shifting power from the defense committees to the Caucus or the Budget Committee, to change the way Congress handles defense budgets. But in the short run the only way to deal with the defense committees is to give them incentives for cutting the defense budget. In a sense, they already have one. The new mood in Congress (particularly noticeable in the House) and throughout the country as a whole is something the Committee cannot ignore. Committees do not like to have floor amendments passed over their opposition—it represents loss of face. Fear of defeat, therefore, is one important incentive for the Committee to control defense spending. Passing ceiling amendments to cut the defense budget may not be a very precise way to deal with military overspending, but it has one advantage: next year the Committee whose bill has been rejected will be more wary about bringing out a high defense budget. This procedure also has the advantage that the defense committees are more competent, because of their collective expertise, to make precise cuts than is the average Congressman.

III. The Procedural Approach

It is commonly assumed that, if only Congress were reformed, the legislative branch would reassert itself and take its rightful place in the determination of public policy, presumably a more enlightened policy than the present system allows. But is this true? Historically, of course, the legislative branch exercised its greatest power at times when it was the least reformed (i.e., most authoritarian), as, for example, under Speaker Joe Cannon. While some of the reform proposals, such as transferring power from the Armed Services Committee to the new Budget Committee, may somewhat increase Congressional willingness to control the defense budget, most of them will not. Changing the seniority system, for example, is not likely to affect the number of votes for amendments to cut the defense budget. In truth, the basic problem goes much deeper.

What many advocates of Congressional reform really seem to want is for Congress to become more like the reformers. Judging from some proposals, they would like to turn Congress into a kind of Brookings Institution or Systems Analysis office, studying alternative budgets and making decisions about "how much is enough." They would like to see a Congress gathering and weighing information and making rational decisions on that basis, but they fail to take into account that the Congress is based on politics. Legislative conflicts in Congress are resolved more often than not by political pressure, not by any rational presentation of the issues.

Congress could, for example, acquire much better information about defense budgeting than it now does, but there is very little evidence that it really wants better information. Most Congressional offices are deluged with more information than they can absorb. Relatively few Congressmen use the information that is now available to them from outside sources or, for that matter, from such agencies of their own as the General Accounting Office and the Library of Congress. Robert McNamara provided Congress with much more information in his posture statements than Melvin Laird did, but that did not increase McNamara's popularity with Congress—or diminish Laird's.

One of the problems is time: there is simply not enough of it to utilize the information that is available. The number of votes and the complexity of the issues behind them are increasing every year (in 1961 there were 126 recorded votes in the House of Representatives and the House adjourned for the year in September; by 1973 the number of votes had grown to 541 and the House was meeting year round). The problems created by this increase can be and have in part been overcome by adding staff, but there are limits to the extent to which increasing a staff can help. Some things a Congressman must do for himself: the bells for a vote or quorum call require his response; important constituents and interest groups want to see and talk to him personally; committee meetings demand his presence and assume that he knows enough about the subject at hand to ask pertinent questions about it; his constituency expects him to go home regularly to meet the voters, give speeches, and answer questions; television and radio will not accept a substitute. Other things he can and does delegate to staff (such as case work and answering constituent mail), but he must (for his own re-election depends upon it) maintain the fiction that he also does these things himself, and so he must devote a certain amount of time to them. All in all, Congressmen and, to an even greater extent, Senators find themselves spending the day moving from meetings to the floor to the television gallery to the office and then to a plane for home, without time to study the information made available, or even to be properly briefed by a staff member. No wonder Congressmen constantly feel less informed than they should be and never in control of things; no doubt this is accounting in part for the increased number of House members who are not seeking re-election. "It's no fun anymore," they say.

To attract the attention of Congressmen and Senators in this hectic schedule, one needs to provide more than passive information, one needs to exert political clout (organization, votes, campaign contributions). More and more groups understand this, and more and more groups are organizing—which again is putting more and more pressure on the legislator. The result is that Congressmen are being pressured from all sides, and, being less insulated than the Executive, they feel the cross pressures more acutely. And subject to re-election every few years, they are also more reluctant to offend any pressure group.

Finally, Congressmen are prone to feel themselves at the mercy of events—something might happen that proves them wrong. An adage often quoted among Congressmen says, "No one ever got defeated for something he didn't say." When a President takes a strong stand he has broad access to the public, which can enable him to swing the country to his point of view or at least to defend his position.

A Congressman's access is more limited. Congressmen are aware that, on any particular issue, a strong President can appear on television and can turn a Congressman's constituents against him. Thus, while at any given time some Congressmen may take a strong stand on defense or other issues (environment, health care, etc.), Congress as an institution (meaning more than half of the five hundred and thirty-five people in both houses) will not.

Nothing will be more disappointing for those who would like to see Congress assume greater leadership. But Congress, whatever may be said on that subject by Congressmen, is not about to take the lead in anything. Caution is a prime political virtue because it is expedient. Recognizing this limitation helps to explain why Congress is not going to become a Brookings Institution or a Systems Analysis office. It is not simply that, when rational arguments conflict with political realities, Congress is likely to favor the political realities—that is true of other institutions also. The problem goes much deeper than that. Making decisions on the basis of rational argument requires confronting the issues directly, and Congressmen, who are pressured from all sides, who are continually short of time, and who suffer from lack of expertise, are not likely to do that. They will prefer to deal with issues indirectly and procedurally. To understand the functioning of Congress, it is important to understand its procedural approach and what its procedures mean to its members.

If done directly, a Congressional decision—for example, to disapprove money for a new aircraft carrier—would require that more than half of all Congressmen conclude that the Navy can do with fewer carriers in the nineteen-eighties. This would involve a stark confrontation with expertise that would be very uncomfortable for a Congressman. If a showdown is reached on the carrier issue, the vote is almost certain to be cloaked in procedures (motions to table, etc.) that would allow the Congressman to justify his vote, if he needed to, on a procedural question rather than on the merits of the case. The end-the-war vote in the House in 1972, for example, was in fact a motion to table, a motion to instruct the conferees to insist on the House version of the Defense Authorization bill in the light of the Legislative Reorganization Act of 1970. Nobody's constituents would ever be able to figure that one out.

One of the advantages of procedure, then, is to allow Congressmen to mask the real effects of their votes. Confronted by someone concerned by his vote on carriers (or the war), the Congressman can justify his vote not on the merits of the case (where the other fellow may be the expert) but on procedure (where the Congressman is the expert).

In addition, procedure also allows Congress to achieve an objective without direct confrontation with the Executive branch. In 1972, after the SALT agreement was signed, Secretary Laird presented to the House and Senate Armed Services Committees his recommendations for additions to the Research and Development budget resulting from SALT. One of the items in Laird's budget was more money for the Hard Target Re-entry Vehicle, to which there was opposition in the Senate. The House Armed Services Committee was reconvened, and the SALT additions were approved. The Senate Armed Services Committee, however, which had also finished hearings by the time the request had arrived, decreed that, because the request had arrived too late, they had not had time to have proper hearings on the subject, and so they left the Hard Target Re-entry Vehicle out of the bill. Later, at the Conference

Committee, as it was in the House bill but not the Senate bill, it was dropped on the grounds that the Senate had not considered it. In the end the Hard Target Re-entry Vehicle was not approved, but it was turned down *not* on the merits of the case against it (even though the principal people involved understood what they were), but on procedural grounds—first, in the Senate, on the grounds that the Committee had not held hearings on the subject, and second, in the Conference, on the grounds that only one of the two houses of Congress had considered the matter. This procedural approach to decision-making has two advantages: First, in any legislative body consensus is necessary, and it is often easier to achieve consensus on procedure than on substance. Second, in any disagreement with the Executive branch, Congress, in putting forth the procedural argument, has an argument to which the Executive branch has no retort.

An incident described in David Halberstam's book, *The Best and the Brightest*, can serve to illustrate the Congressional instinct to avoid direct confrontation with the Executive on issues to achieve its objectives through procedure. The incident described concerns the American decision not to intervene in Indochina on behalf of the French in 1954:

> . . . the pressure from the French continued to build. With the garrison at Dienbienphu obviously trapped, there was an emotional quality to the crisis, a desire to save the boys. Admiral Radford was sympathetic. Dulles seemed sympathetic. Vice-President Nixon was said to favor intervention. Eisenhower was reported to be ambivalent, not revealing his own feelings. On April 3, 1954, at Eisenhower's suggestion, Dulles met with the Congressional leadership, a group which included Minority Leader Lyndon B. Johnson and the ranking Democrat on the Armed Services Committee, Richard Russell.

> . . . The purpose of the meeting soon became clear: the Administration wanted a congressional resolution to permit the President to use naval and air power in Indochina, particularly a massive air strike to save the garrison at Dienbienphu. Radford made a strong and forceful presentation: the situation was perilous. If Indochina went, then Southeast Asia would go. We would be moved back to Hawaii. . . .

> The senators began to question Radford. Would this be an act of war? Yes, we would be in the war. What would happen if the first air strike did not succeed in relieving the garrison? We would follow it up. What about ground forces? Radford gave an ambivalent answer. . . .

> At this point Johnson took over. . . . Johnson was disturbed by the implications of the Radford appeal for a variety of reasons. He doubted that the necessary resources existed in a war-weary country which had just come out of Korea, and he did not want the blame for refusing to go to war placed on him and the Democratic leadership in Congress. If Eisenhower went for a congressional resolution, then Johnson would be right smack on the spot, which was exactly where he did not want to be—he was always uneasy about being out front. He certainly did not want the Democrats to be blamed for losing Indochina.

> The Democrats, he told Dulles, had been blamed for the Korean War and for having gone in virtually alone without significant allies. Knowland himself, Johnson pointed out, had criticized the Democrats for supplying 90 percent of the men and money in Korea. The patriotism of Democratic officials had been questioned. He was touched now to be considered so worthy and so good a patriot as to be requested to get on board. But first he had some questions, because he did not want to relive the unhappy recent past. What allies did they have who would put up sizeable amounts of men for Indochina? Had Dulles consulted with any allies? No, said the Secretary, he had not.

> By the time the two-hour meeting was over, Johnson had exposed the frailty of the Administration's position. . . . Dulles was told to sign up allies, though it was known that

Anthony Eden was dubious. Thus the burden, which the Administration had ever so gently been trying to shift to the Congress, had now been ever so gently shifted back, if not to the Administration, at least to the British, who were known to be unenthusiastic.

Procedure, then, can be and is used by Congress to avoid direct responsibility. Besides being used by Congressmen to mask the real effect of their votes and being used to achieve objectives without direct confrontation with the Executive, procedure is used by Congressmen to avoid direct responsibility and to protect themselves politically. Congress as an institution also does not like to be "out front."

But Congress is also aware of and very sensitive about its prerogatives. Congressmen like the idea that Congress is a coequal branch of government. While a Congressman's concern over Executive encroachments on Congressional power is often directly related to whether or not he approves of what the Executive is doing, Congressmen generally are unhappy about having their powers usurped by others. Congressmen do not like to have their explicit instructions ignored.

Again the solution is found in falling back on procedure. The decisive votes on a multibillion-dollar defense budget, which contains money for such diverse items as Safeguard missile sites, a naval base in Diego Garcia, and military support for the government of South Vietnam, will most likely be held on essentially procedural questions such as thresholds, ceilings, and cut-off dates. The best and most able legislators understand this—perhaps instinctively. Congress establishes the thresholds that require, for example, that when x happens, then y must happen—when a certain point is reached, then the President must report to Congress (the War Powers Bill is an example). Congress establishes ceilings that require, for instance, that spending for certain functions cannot exceed a specified amount ($2.5 billion for Military Assistance Service Funds, or $500 million for Transfer Authority). And Congress establishes cut-off dates (e.g., the flight pay for colonels and generals who do not fly stops May 31, or the war ends August 15). Congress is most comfortable dealing procedurally with national security matters; there they are the experts.

IV. Legislating Procedures for the Executive

As we have seen, the procedural approach favored by Congress reveals a good deal about what Congress will not do; it is now time to turn to the question of what it can and will do. As I see it, Congress performs three basic roles fairly well. The first and most obvious of these is as a conduit for constituent views. It is, in fact, the only place where the wishes of the people are fed directly into the system. For example, it is an important sounding-board for how effectively federal programs are functioning or how a proposed governmental course of action will be received. As a sounding-board it is not perfect, to be sure; special interests are over-represented, and its votes are not always indicative of the general will. Still, what is said in debates on the floor of the Congress is important, and the mood of Congress, reflected in these debates, is rarely very far from the mood of the country at large. Congress can also act as a vehicle for informing the people or educating them to a particular problem. Many Congressional hearings (e.g., Fulbright's on Vietnam) have as their primary function this educational role. To see the importance of this conduit function, one might compare it with, for example, a comparable situation under the British Parliamentary system.

When Edward Heath was Prime Minister, he decided that to fight Britain's battle against inflation it was necessary to have a showdown with the trade unions. To win in such a showdown, it was, of course, of vital importance that his policy be widely accepted in the country as a whole. But Parliament, with its strong party discipline, was not a place to find out how the policy would be accepted; dominated by Heath's Tory Party, it strongly supported the Prime Minister. As it turned out, the country did not, and this was the shoal on which the policy eventually foundered.

This could not have happened in the American Congress. The speeches and votes in Congress would have given the Executive a fairly accurate reading on the possible acceptance of such a policy in this country. And if Congress strongly supported the President, this support would have provided him with the necessary political backing to carry it out.

A second role that Congress performs is as general overseer of government policies and resource allocation. In this role it acts not unlike a board of trustees. With very few exceptions, Congress is not the place where policy is initiated. Most Congressional committees or subcommittees have no over-all plan or policy which they would like to see implemented in the area of their concern. The Pay and Allowances Subcommittee of the House Armed Services Committee has, for example, no guiding policy about the structure of pay and allowances in the armed forces. They do not initiate legislation in this area, but simply modify, if necessary, and ultimately give their approval to what the Executive is proposing to do. In performing this role they have certain advantages. They have often had long years of experience, and they know what has been tried before. They have lines of communication open to various branches of the armed forces, which provide them with information that the Executive may not have; and they are very sensitive to the conflicting pressures that build up around any change in policy.

There are, of course, exceptions to the rule. Some committees or subcommittees try to take the lead or initiate new policy. (Senator McIntyre is attempting this with his Senate Armed Services Subcommittee on Research and Development.) But any effort to do so is hampered by divergences in the views of individual committee members and a wariness about taking issues to the floor, where, without Administration support, they are likely to be defeated. Most committees wait for the Administration to send over its proposals, and then they consider them from what might be described as a board-of-trustees perspective; this can be very useful, but it does not constitute leadership. Even this board-of-trustees function could be vastly improved—investigative work and legislative supervision are both activities that Congressional committees could and should do better and more extensively.

Congress's third role is to act as guardian of the processes of government—i.e., to establish and protect procedure. In many ways this is the most intriguing of the three roles. Often by establishing new procedures, which are, of course, ostensibly neutral, Congress is able to effect substantive changes.

A good example is to be found in the National Environment Protection Act (NEPA). Congress required in the NEPA that, on any major federal project which would significantly affect the quality of the environment, an environmental impact statement had to be written by the agency that was to undertake the project. Congress intended by this provision to force federal agencies to consider the environmental impact of what they were planning to do before they began it. What happened, of course, was much more than that. Environmental groups around the country found that they could use NEPA by bringing court action against any federal agency that did not comply with its procedures. Then, once complied with, they used the impact statement itself as a source for environmental objections to the project at issue. The impact-statement requirement forced federal agencies into discussion with environmentalists on what the environmental effect of the project would be, and, where the environmentalists were able to make a convincing case, it became politically very difficult to ignore them.

As a result, NEPA brought a new group—environmentalists—into a decision-making process from which they had previously been excluded. A long series of projects—from nuclear reactors to public works (one of the most famous being the Cross Florida Barge Canal)—regarded as dangerous to the environment were brought to a halt. By establishing this new procedure, Congress wrought changes that can safely be said to have been much more significant than any they might have voted for in dealing with these projects individually.

The way new procedures established by Congress effect substantive changes, then, is by changing the decision-making process or bringing new people into it. But, in doing this, Congress sometimes finds that the direct impact of such legislation is less important than the indirect results. To take one of many possible examples, Congress, in 1961, passed the Symington amendment, which required that, in allotting economic aid, consideration be given to the resources various countries were allocating to defense. If a country was spending too much on defense, the President would withhold aid. The direct impact of that amendment was nil—no country ever had money withdrawn because it was spending too much for military purposes. But the indirect impact was considerable. A committee chaired by AID now had to be included in policy decisions which, up to then, had been managed solely by the Pentagon. They had to be included because Congress might wish to investigate compliance with this amendment, and AID would then be asked if they had been consulted. The indirect impact, then, was that a new group of people with a wholly different outlook was brought into the decision-making apparatus.

Historically there are a vast number of procedural devices that Congress has used to change the decision-making process. Structural change is one of them. Congress has established organizations and abolished them; it has given them more influence, by having them report directly to the President, or less influence, by having them report to someone else. If Congress does not think that arms control is being given sufficient consideration by the Executive branch, it can create an agency with independent access to the White House, as it did with the Arms Control and Disarmament Agency. In the field of foreign policy and military affairs, there are any number of examples of how Congress has changed the structure of government—from the National Security Council to the Central Intelligence Agency to the Department of Defense—all of them having great influence on the decision-making process.

A second procedural device available to Congress is to require certain findings before specific programs may be carried out. An example of this is the Walsh Act of 1935, which required that, before the Administration could transfer destroyers to another country, it first had to have the Navy certify that it did not need them. Senator Walsh, the author of the Act, was fearful that President Roosevelt was about to give destroyers to Britain—an action that he thought would eventually drag the

United States into another European war. While the Senator's purpose was to prevent President Roosevelt from giving any destroyers to Britain, he assumed Congress would be reluctant to give that order directly; he thus decided on a procedural device, which would be acceptable to Congress, of saying, in effect, "before we give them away we better make sure we don't need them." As Senator Walsh no doubt expected, the Navy was not about to declare that it had too many destroyers.

A third procedural device is for Congress to designate a person to make certain types of decisions. Placing the responsibility for a decision with an individual who has predictable political or organizational interests naturally tends to affect the decision in a predictable way. The person designated may be the President or another official. The act that established the Naval Petroleum Reserve, for example, requires that any decision to release the reserves must be approved by the Secretary of the Navy. Any Secretary of the Navy would be reluctant to make such a determination.

Finally, Congress can involve already existing groups in government decisions by making them part of a new procedure. This might be a citizen group—such as the environmentalists in the NEPA case—or it might be an agency of government, or it might even be Congress itself. Sometimes the people brought into a decision might not belong to an identifiable group. For instance, under the provisions of the War Powers Bill, if the President commits American forces to hostilities abroad, he must report to Congress within forty-eight hours his reason for doing so, and at the end of sixty days he must withdraw those forces unless Congress votes to allow him to continue the commitment. By establishing this procedure, Congress has included itself in the decision-making process as the final arbiter on whether troops should be used. But, as we have seen, Congress is never happy in such a role, and it is most unlikely to stand up to a President in foreign-policy matters such as this. Indeed one of the objections to the War Powers Bill made by liberals was that it was too weak—bringing Congress into the decision would not change anything, because Congress would simply rubber-stamp a Presidential decision to commit troops.

But this analysis leaves out the effect of this bill on decision-making in the Executive branch. When the President considers sending troops somewhere, he and his advisers know that, under the War Powers bill, an affirmative decision will provoke an intense debate over a consequent decision that will have to be made by Congress within sixty days. Congressmen will hold hearings, editorial writers will write editorials, columnists will construct columns, *Meet the Press* and *Face the Nation* will cross-examine government spokesmen; there will be network specials, demonstrators will demonstrate, and constituents will write letters. The foreknowledge of all this commotion is bound to strengthen the hand of those in the President's council who oppose the policy—they can now put forward objections, not as their own, but as the kinds of arguments the President will have to face. Congress's ultimate verdict is not the most important factor; what is important is that the President and his advisers know that their policy will soon receive intense public scrutiny. They will be much less inclined to embark upon such an adventure without a very good case to support it.

V. Changing Procedures in Congress

The manner in which changes in procedure have been used by Congress in the past suggests that procedure is the method to be used in approaching some of the problems of today. Specifically, perhaps, there are procedural ways of dealing with some of the factors that increase the size of the Defense Department budget. One of the major problems in controlling defense spending is the "requirements" syndrome. Weapons systems become requirements very early in the process—well before Congress ever sees them as line items in the research and development budget. By the time Congress comes face to face with a new weapons system, service and bureaucratic momentum is already behind it; contractors and unions are already aware of it; and it probably is too late to stop it without considerable struggle. What is needed is a vehicle for bringing other decision-makers into the process sooner, perhaps a procedure requiring the President to make the decision on the more costly of the early stages of development. In addition, he could be required to obtain advice from experts who do not have a parochial interest in a follow-on system for every weapon in the inventory.

The question is who should Congress designate as weapons-systems advisers? To be ideal candidates, these advisers should not only be rivals for the funds, but should possess some professional standing that would make their objections creditable. Perhaps there would even be some profit in having each of the armed services comment on the weapons systems of the others. Certainly, as budget squeezes become more painful, the services will have increasing incentive for making critical evaluations of their sister services' major weapons systems. Having the Army and particularly the Air Force comment on the Navy's request for a billion-dollar nuclear aircraft carrier might well put a new focus on a Presidential decision.

Objectivity is another requirement for a weapons-system adviser. Groups in government likely to be the most objective and impartial are those whose members have professional commitments outside the government. The Council of Economic Advisers, the President's Scientific Advisory Council, and the Antitrust Division of the Department of Justice are examples. The professional standing of people in these groups depends to a large extent on the judgment of their peers outside government. Thus, there is a limit to the politically expedient, but professionally unsound, policies that they will abide, even at the cost of their government positions. They are therefore useful groups to be included into government decisions.

One strategy for dealing with the weapons-requirement syndrome might be the following: The President is required by Congress to give his approval before any research and development money is spent, and again before any production money is spent, for any weapons system costing more than x billion dollars. Before making his decision, the President receives the independent views of the Secretary of Defense, the Secretary of State, each of the service chiefs, the head of the Arms Control and Disarmament Agency, and the President's Science Advisor (if there is one). In the advice submitted, each person is required to: 1) estimate the long-run cost of the weapons system; 2) state, evaluate, and estimate the costs of alternative ways of accomplishing the same mission; and 3) evaluate the impact of the new weapons system on future arms-control agreements. If this procedure, or something like it, were established, it is possible that some of the most expensive and most destabilizing weapons systems in the inventory could be stopped before they have gathered irresistible bureaucratic momentum.

Secrecy and inaccurate information are also problems, though of a very different kind. There is no way that the public, the Congress, or the press can react to or give an opinion on government policies and actions unless they have a relatively accurate reading of what is going on. Is there anything Congress can do to improve the quality of information given out by the Executive?

One possibility is to take greater advantage of the confirmation process (perhaps the only opportunity Congress has) to place conditions on Presidential appointees. Here an official, before he has been confirmed, is attempting to be his most agreeable and conciliatory, and therefore he is as likely as he will ever be to accept conditions laid down by the Senate. While candidates for confirmation have an understandable reluctance to be pinned down on specific issues, they would have less justification for refusing to make pledges on procedures.

Suppose, for example, a newly designated Secretary of Defense is appearing for confirmation before the Senate Armed Services Committee. As a condition of his confirmation, the Secretary-designate would be required to pledge himself to carry out a few basic procedures that are requisite to any open administration. A sample list might be: 1) appear when requested by Congressional committees; 2) respond candidly; 3) volunteer information; and 4) express any differences of opinion with the Administration. The Senate Foreign Relations Committee does ask newly appointed Secretaries of State these kinds of questions, but not enough is made of them. The Secretary should be made to swear that he will comply, and he should be reminded of his oath when he comes later to testify.

Such a procedure obviously would not work in the case of an inveterate liar. But it is bound to have some impact on any honest person, especially if he is reminded of it by a Senator who uses it as a prelude to his questioning. Moreover, it may give such a person an excuse for doing something he may wish to do in any case. He can tell the President that his loyalty is unbounded but that those so-and-so's in the Senate made him take an oath in order to be confirmed. If he now gives answers that the President regards as disloyal, it is only because he has no choice.

In a series of well-known events, Elliot Richardson resigned his position as Attorney General over a difference in policy with the President. He did it, or he said he did it, because in his confirmation hearings he had promised that the Watergate Special Prosecutor, Archibald Cox, would have a free hand, and he could not fire Cox as ordered without violating that pledge. Of course, it is problematical whether this was Richardson's only reason, but this is the reason he used. The pledge he made to the Senate Judiciary Committee provided him with legitimate grounds for standing up to the President. The Richardson case should encourage a broader use of this leverage.

This is not to say that setting up new procedures necessarily guarantees that the correct decision will be made or that the right thing will be done. All anyone can seek to guarantee is that the right kinds of people will have influence and some of the right kinds of incentives will be there. Nor is it impossible for the Executive branch to subvert any of the procedures once they are set up, but they would be effective for a time, at least. Subverting them can be accomplished only with effort and at some political cost. Influencing decision-making through procedural change may seem to be influencing decision-making at the margin; certainly it operates at a degree removed from the actual issues involved. But since Congress works that way, when it works at all, it may be Congress's best hope of changing some of the decisions that are made.

Conclusion

Congress is essentially a political institution and responds primarily to political stimuli. Rational arguments in such an institution carry very little weight unless they are politically organized. Political organization can be accomplished, but only with a great deal of effort. Usually, Congressmen will deal substantively and directly only with those issues that are non-controversial or that they feel comfortable with—issues that are within their expertise or issues that they have dealt with before. If an issue is controversial *and* unfamiliar (as most important issues are), Congress will instinctively begin groping toward a procedural resolution.

Congress as an institution is a conservative organization—cautious and reluctant to initiate change. It responds to old stimuli better than new. When it opposes the Executive, it is usually to protect some interest group or some aspect of the status quo rather than to initiate action. Any new things that are going on in the federal government are not going on in Congress. Sometimes a member of Congress will take the initiative, or a group of members will, but Congress as an institution will not.

In earlier days, when the Executive was smaller and the issues that Congress dealt with were fewer and less technical, there was perhaps a greater balance between the Executive and the legislature. But if the balance ever existed, it exists no more. The Executive has grown and can specialize. Congress must deal with all issues and has remained (in spite of some increase in staff) roughly the same size. Congress is much as Congress was, the Executive is not as the Executive was.

On arms control, as on many other subjects, the direct role that Congress can be expected to play will therefore be limited In the jockeying that goes on within the government over our defense posture, the actions that Congress can take will be either too general or too specific to be very constructive—either cutting five per cent off the top or cutting the number of enlisted men serving as aides to generals. The defense committees in Congress could be more effective, but because of their composition and outlook they will not be. Nor will Congress play a direct role in such traditional areas of arms control as negotiating with the Russians. SALT is too complicated—too much a field for the experts.

This is not to say that Congress can be ignored. Even if the SALT treaties did not have to be ratified by the Senate, Congress would set the mood (reflecting the mood of the country) as to the limits within which an acceptable treaty must fall. But Congressional ideas about future arms-control initiatives will be limited to such conceptually simple things as a Comprehensive Test Ban, and even then only a minority of members will delve into the subject.

The failure of Congress to assume leadership in this and in other areas is in part the source of the great interest—and limited progress—in Congressional reform. But Congressional reform, while a worthy goal, is not likely to result in Congressional leadership. The problem with Congress is the people in Congress—how they regard their job and how they make their decisions. It is, of course, possible that in time new people elected to Congress will bring with them new attitudes and Congress will reassert itself. But it should not be counted on; the new members will find themselves in the same position as the old. They, too, will want to be re-elected. They, too, will be cross-pressured. They, too, will feel a lack of expertise, and they, too, will have no time.

Rather than try to make Congress into something that it is not (that is, an alternative to the Executive branch as an implementer of new ideas), we should look at what Congress is and see if there are not ways to improve it. Congress is a conduit for constituent concern; this function could be improved by weakening the influence of special interests. Congress is a "board of trustees" over government programs and policies; this function, too, could be improved by increasing the emphasis in Congress on oversight and investigation. And Congress is a guardian of the procedures of government, a role which certainly could be improved if more attention were given to it.

This may seem like a very pessimistic view of Congress, and perhaps it is. But the importance of the third role, procedure, in affecting the course of government policy should not be underestimated. As the NEPA case demonstrates, manipulation of procedure can be a very powerful weapon. Right now it is a weapon that is understood by some instinctively and by many not at all.

Those who want to change government policy through Congress must give some thought not only to what they want to do but also to how it can be done. One way is to organize sufficient political muscle to effect the change, but issues on which this can be done are relatively rare. The other way is to figure out some way of accomplishing the change procedurally. Congress feels more comfortable dealing with issues this way, and, what is more important, it is possible in this way to gain enough votes to win.

R. JAMES WOOLSEY

Chipping Away at the Bargains

THE TONE AND SUBSTANCE of five years of debate on strategic weapons and arms control were set in 1969 by the controversy over the Safeguard ABM. Following President Nixon's announcement, on March 14, 1969, of his intent to begin deployment toward a twelve-site nationwide ABM, battle lines were drawn for the bitterest fight over a strategic-weapon system in American history. By the time of the famous 50-50 tie vote in the Senate, resolved in favor of the Administration by the Vice President on August 6 after ten weeks of floor debate, it was almost impossible to find an informed American interested in national-security affairs who did not have a strong opinion on the issue. The scientific and academic communities were drawn up in warring camps of distinctly unequal size. Elected officials spent hours puzzling over detailed charts and the relative merits of "shoot-look-shoot" and "shoot-shoot-look-shoot" as defense tactics.

Numerous elements contributed to the vigor of this debate. Public interest was high in some regions of the country because of what the Department of Defense calls the problem of "public interface," since some of the sites were to be deployed near relatively populous areas. The cost of the system and the ordinary friction of party differences between the President and the Congress no doubt added fuel to the controversy, as did the fear that deployment would stimulate strategic deployments by the Soviet Union.

But a large measure of the steam behind the anti-Safeguard position was the result of the dual purpose of Safeguard as it was originally announced. The first four ABM sites were to be at Minuteman ICBM sites, and thus would serve to protect our own deterrent. But the other eight—like the older Sentinel system—were clearly for another purpose: population defense. Although it was argued that the eventual deployment would be thin and would therefore protect only against a Chinese or an accidental attack, most critics, doing a worst-case analysis, refused to base their estimate of the Administration's probable conduct on its stated intentions. The ambivalent purpose behind the Safeguard system's deployment was reflected in its technical characteristics; many of its components, particularly the long-range Spartan missiles and large radars, one to a site, were optimally designed for population defense. Some feared that a thick anti-Soviet defense would follow.

These factors led a significant number of critics to believe that the Administration's objective was nothing less than a complete shift in national strategy—away from assured destruction, with its emphasis on preventing nuclear war, and toward damage limitation, implying, in their eyes, a foolish and immoral willingness to accept the greater risks of nuclear war in exchange for the empty hope of mitigating the damage to the United States if war should occur.

Some supporters of Safeguard did in fact hope it would lead to more complete population defense, and several argued passionately that this strategy was the only one that would save American lives in all cases—by deterring nuclear war but also by improving any war's possible outcome.

It was this battle of strategies that so fanned the fire of the ABM debate. Although many were able to maintain perspective, for some the debate became a clash of heroic self-images—each side could, in angry moments, see itself as the savior of civilization and its opponents as wrong-headed, even wicked, triflers with human lives. In such an atmosphere, it was not easy for moderation or compromise to take hold. The following year, on June 17, 1970, the Senate Armed Services Committee voted 11-7 to delete those funds in the Administration's request necessary for advanced preparation of the area-defense sites.

The Committee report on July 14 of that year stated:

Present circumstances do not justify a diversion of our resources from the primary task of defending the deterrent to the less urgent objective of providing a defense against the evolving Chinese Communist threat.

But by this time most participants in the debate were deeply entrenched. The debate raged through another four weeks on the Senate floor, with the Safeguard proponents winning by only a slightly more comfortable margin, 45-53, on August 19.

In the meantime, according to the only thorough public report on SALT, John Newhouse's *Cold Dawn*, the Administration had proposed to the Soviets in Vienna in late April, 1970, that ABM deployments should be limited to the defense of each side's national capital. The Soviets accepted the proposal in less than a week, and, although there were later shifts in position regarding ABM, the ultimate resolution of the ABM issue in SALT I (two sites for each side, one at the national capital) had been fixed in basic terms by April of 1970. History reveals no alternatives, so it will never be known whether or not the continuing threat of an American ABM deployment provided the essential leverage that produced the SALT agreements. But few would argue that the Soviet party and military bureaucracies were not motivated to some extent by a wish to limit Safeguard, whatever its technical limitations. As Newhouse puts it:

To the Russians, the Sentinel-Safeguard components—radars and missiles alike—were not only far more sophisticated than their own, but a base on which the Americans might build something that would actually work.

It can be argued that Safeguard was an effective bargaining chip, but it was a hard one to cash.

The signing of the SALT treaty and interim agreement in Moscow, in May, 1972, did not halt, and in fact hardly tempered, the debate over strategic policy and arms control. President Nixon's speech to the Congress announcing the arms-control agreements came on the evening of Thursday, June 1. The following Monday, four days later, proposals for one hundred and sixty-eight million dollars in increased spending on strategic weapons were made public by the Secretary of Defense. Critics protested angrily against using arms-control agreements as the occasion—and even as the rationale—for increasing strategic-weapon programs. The Secretary argued that the increases were essential in order for Defense to be able to support the SALT agreements. This dispute percolated along throughout the summer.

The familiar controversy over the relative merits and demerits of assured destruction and damage limitation surfaced particularly in connection with two programs sought by the Administration: an ABM site for Washington, D.C., and an improved re-entry vehicle for the counterforce mission. The Washington ABM was characterized by Senator Jackson on the floor of the Senate, on June 1, as "useless and a waste of the taxpayers' money." For many, the counterforce re-entry vehicle raised the same fears as a nation-wide ABM—the suspicion that we were shifting to a strategy of trying to fight a nuclear war and relaxing our emphasis on deterring one. The *Washington Post* editorialized on August 14, "[t]his is not like one of those nonsensical disputes on the subject of arms and arms control to which the Congress occasionally gives way. It is serious—dead serious—business."

The funds for the Washington ABM defense, the improved re-entry vehicle, and several additional SALT-related programs were deleted by the Senate Armed Services Committee "without prejudice," when it reported the Defense Authorization Bill on June 29, on the grounds of lack of data and the late arrival of the formal request. The other SALT-related items were restored to the bill, in whole or in part, during the Conference between the House and Senate. The national-capital ABM and the improved re-entry vehicle were not.

There was also extensive controversy that summer over the arms-control agreements themselves. Some maintained that the interim agreement on offensive weapons was worse than no agreement at all, because it halted no programs and because, as the Secretary of Defense had demonstrated, it had the apparently perverse effect of even encouraging further strategic spending. The most politically effective criticism, however, came in connection with the Jackson amendment to the Resolution authorizing the offensive-weapons agreement. The amendment proposed that further SALT agreements "would not limit the United States to levels of intercontinental strategic forces inferior to the limits provided for the Soviet Union." The debate surrounding the amendment contained strong criticism of the first round of agreements, especially the agreement on offensive systems, as having given too much away for too little.

At first the Administration seemed to be of several minds about what to do. But in time it took the stance that: *a*) it did not agree with the criticism of the agreement on offensive systems voiced by many of the amendment's supporters; *b*) the amendment itself changed nothing; and *c*) the amendment should be supported. This finely honed position, although perplexing to the lay observer, had dual advantages from the Administration's point of view. It did not repudiate the just-negotiated agreement, but it still sent the Soviets the message that, being second in number of offensive launchers, the next time we would try harder and that, perhaps contrary to their expectations, Congress would help. Those in the Senate who fully supported the SALT agreements, who felt that numerical disparities in launchers were unimportant, and who wanted to send the Soviets no such message were left to oppose the Jackson amendment alone and to be defeated 56-35.

The debate on strategic systems and SALT picked up further steam in 1973 with the controversy over the Trident submarine. The initial decision had been made in September, 1971, by the then Deputy Secretary of Defense, Mr. David Packard, to maintain a schedule that would develop the Trident I missile to be retro-fitted into Poseidon submarines. Work on the large Trident submarine was, according to this earlier decision, to be continued for possible deployment later in the nineteen-eighties.

This decision was reversed toward the end of 1971, and the accelerated construction of the submarine itself was proposed by the Administration; this meant more overlap—"concurrency"—between development and construction, and it increased immediate strategic spending. There was much criticism of this acceleration decision in the Congress during 1972 and 1973. Critics emphasized the concurrency and the high funding required during the early years, as well as the alleged irony of accelerating a primary strategic system simultaneously with the signing of the SALT agreements. Some critics suspected that the Administration had begun with a decision to increase strategic spending in order to show resolve and had only then determined that Trident was a good horse to start; their opposition was, by that measure, increased. Supporters of the decision argued, however, that submarines were the most secure part of our deterrent forces, that the aging Polaris submarines needed to be replaced by a quieter and more modern fleet of boats, and that vigor must be shown in some strategic programs for bargaining leverage in SALT. The acceleration was approved in 1973 by a one-vote margin in the Senate Armed Services Committee and, after a lengthy debate, by a two-vote margin on the Senate floor.

The strategic debate, along with a large number of other matters, was overshadowed in 1974 by the constitutional crisis spawned by Watergate. The preparations for the possible impeachment and trial of the President continued until his resignation August 9, by which time the authorization bill for the Defense Department had become law and the appropriations process was well advanced. Even though the mood prevailed at the Capitol in the spring and summer that the decks should be cleared and that those disputes, wherever possible, should be avoided that might show us to the world as being divided on fundamental issues, there was still a reasonably healthy battle over the question of our basic nuclear strategy. At issue was seventy-seven million dollars to increase the yield and improve the accuracy of Minuteman ICBMs and to develop a maneuvering re-entry vehicle (MaRV). After being struck from the budget by the Research and Development Subcommittee of the Senate Armed Services Committee and restored by the full Committee, the Senate defeated a move to delete the funds by a vote of 49-37.

At the end of 1974, the communiqué signed at Vladivostok by President Ford and Secretary Brezhnev pointed toward a ten-year agreement on strategic offensive weapons fixing launchers at 2,400 and MIRVed launchers at 1,320. Supporters of the type of agreement likely to emerge from the negotiations stressed the equal numbers and the Soviets' willingness to compromise on their earlier position that American "forward-based" nuclear systems and the nuclear arms of America's allies justified numerically larger Soviet forces. Critics particularly emphasized the high levels of offensive weapons implicitly sanctioned by such an agreement, the failure to press for immediate mutual reductions in strategic forces, and the large Soviet advantage in total missile throw-weight.

From this sketchy and selective history, it is possible to identify five more or less classic positions in the convoluted arguments over nuclear strategy and arms control; their representatives might or might not answer to the following—at least reasonably descriptive—names: Assured Destroyer, Damage Limiter, Compleat Controller, Cost Cutter, and Political Container. The members of these species have cross-bred, of course, but the strains still exist in sufficient purity that the debate on these matters often resembles a jumble of monologues. One participant will begin from the premise that a certain weapon system is not needed by the United States, because it does not further his own favorite objective, and he will then demonstrate to his own satisfaction that it is perfectly all right to negotiate it away in exchange for very little or to halt it unilaterally. Another will begin from the premise that the system is badly needed, regardless of the consequences, and will in turn demonstrate conclusively that there is no reason for it to be involved in the bargaining process or, if it is, only on impossible terms. The goal of negotiated strategic-arms control thus often becomes a pawn in the domestic debate.

In most other bargaining between groups—e.g., a labor negotiation or a House-Senate Conference on a bill—the members on either side will have their differences, but they will compromise them in advance, seeking to present a united front in order to withstand and win concessions from the opposition. Moreover, there is ordinarily a specific procedural goal that both sides agree must be achieved ("We have to get a contract of some kind"; "We all know we have to get a bill out"). What would happen to the domestic strategic debate if the participants regarded it as a kind of caucus prior to negotiations similar to these other negotiations—if they decided that they might have a better opportunity to limit Soviet strategic arms as part of a bargain the more they could work out their differences among themselves and thus be seen by the other side to be patient and united? If they agreed to talk with one another at all under such novel ground rules, the domestic participants might sound something like this:

Cost Cutter: Look, I think I should start this out because I'm not sure I want to be in this meeting at all. I used to have hopes for arms control. I remember back in the sixties it was all so simple. We used to go to conferences and write papers—saving money was the main objective. Later, when we nearly beat Safeguard on that tie vote, it was the high-water mark. Then the Pentagon discovers this "bargaining chip" argument, and the more arms-control negotiations we have, the more we spend on strategic weapons so we can have something to bargain with. I've just about had it. How can we ever reorder priorities if, as soon as an agreement is signed, the Pentagon is over on the Hill requesting more funds for Trident and everything else on their wish-list?

Assured Destroyer: Now just a minute, Cost, we usually agree on most things, but you have to admit that deterring nuclear war is the most important job we do. Besides, strategic forces really do have to be modernized from time to time. Trident is a reasonably cost-effective system, although I admit the boats may be a bit large. Last year we spent less than four billion dollars on strategic R and D, procurement, and construction—that's half what we were spending in the late fifties and less than we were spending at the peak of the Vietnam War, when I was *really* paring down strategic spending. Now, sure, we're wasting some money on these counterforce gadgets, when all we need to do is make sure that we can kill at least thirty-three per cent of the Soviet population as cheaply as possible in a retaliatory strike, but. . . .

Damage Limiter: That's just plain immoral. I think. . . .

Political Container: Damage, we'll get back to you and Assured in a minute. First I want to ask Cost where he and his friends stand on recomputation.

Cost Cutter: What in the devil is recomputation?

Political Container: Just as I thought. It's a way of increasing military retired pay which would add sixteen billion dollars to the defense budget within the foreseeable future. In other words, it's a defense cost, too, and on the same order of magnitude as Safeguard and Trident.

Cost Cutter: What does that have to do with the arms race?

Political Container: Because it's just one illustration of how you need to reorder your own priorities. If you did, we might find it easier to get together on a few things. Look, in the last two decades ninety-three per cent of the increase in the defense budget has been in pay and operating costs, like retired pay. Sure, weapons are more expensive, but Defense has been making it up by not buying so many. And Assured just told us that strategic weapons are a relatively small part of overall weapons costs. You spend most of your effort on the smallest part of the problem. I suppose that's one reason we argue so much about strategic issues.

Cost Cutter: I've heard all this before, but don't blame it all on me. I can't get anybody interested in saving money if it means they have to try to understand grubby issues like recomputation. Besides, strategic weapons are just plain sexier than intractable problems like retirement pay and support costs. To be quite frank, I decided a few years ago that if I just complained a lot about the things people were interested in, I could keep up the public pressure, restrain overall defense spending, and let inflation cut the defense budget.

Damage Limiter: Well, if you'll forgive me, that's salesmanship, not leadership. It'll be your fault if we end up with a defense establishment that's all tail and no teeth. Why don't you at least go out and form a Federation of American Actuaries or Logistics Specialists or something so that the scientists and arm-chair strategists aren't the only ones who get newsletters about defense problems and sit there second-guessing the Secretary.

Compleat Controller: Damage, you're being a bit hard on my friend. In my opinion, we and the Russians and everybody else could do without a lot of these "teeth" we have now. I don't ask you to agree with that, but at least admit that it's crazy by anyone's standards to waste money on weapons intentionally—to do anything just *because* it's expensive. I have a feeling, for example, that the reason they reversed Packard and accelerated the Trident submarine, instead of the Trident I missile, in 1972 was to spend more money faster so they could convince the Russians, or themselves, or somebody, that they had "resolve."

Cost Cutter: You're exactly right, and that's the sort of mentality that makes me mad. It's short-sighted, too; it's just telling the armed services and the civilians in Defense that it's all right to waste money. Political, you're usually not quite so Strangelovian—which is more than I can say about some of these others—but I have a feeling you don't mind wasting a billion or two to send "signals" to the Russians. How do you know they're getting the message? Maybe they just think we're rich and irresponsible.

Political Container: Well, uh . . . perhaps we've done all we can now with the cost issue. Damage, I said we'd get back to you.

Damage Limiter: I don't know if anyone but Political will listen to me. These days I'm not even certain about him. But I've got to try and make you all understand why we have to have better counterforce systems. We really need to do a better job of attacking hard targets such as missile silos. In the first place it's immoral for the United States to have a policy of holding civilians hostage by terror. The President ought to have more options, if we are attacked, than doing nothing or detonating a doomsday machine. The deterrent isn't credible if it's an all-or-nothing proposition. The Secretary of Defense's proposals this past year for improvements in our counter-force capabilities. . .

Cost Cutter: . . . were at least fairly cheap, by Defense Department standards. I guess it's some improvement when you're proposing seventy-seven-million-dollar programs instead of multi-billion-dollar ones. I'm not interested in these obscure arguments on strategy. If you just want a few million dollars for accuracy and you stop wasting money on the B-1 and Trident, I'll go along with you.

Damage Limiter: I was hoping you'd see it that way. Of course, we have a long way to go. We may run into a bit more expense later on, when we deploy the new large counterforce ICBM. And if the Soviets are uncooperative in SALT, it could also involve some added cost for us to deploy a population-defending ABM after we abrogate the SALT treaty, but it would be money well spent and. . . .

Cost Cutter: Now, wait a minute. . . .

Compleat Controller: That is the most incredible thing I . . . . I . . . .

Assured Destroyer: Damage, I think you just disillusioned Cost, and I didn't think even you could make Compleat turn red like that. Frankly, I don't blame them. It's clear that your inexpensive little counterforce improvements are just a foot in the door. Let me tell you what's wrong. First of all, by deploying—or even by developing—counterforce systems, you force the Soviets to do two very undesirable things. They have to deploy more weapons because they have to worry about our striking first against their ICBMs. And, even worse, in a crisis they may feel that they have to use their weapons or lose them. Do you really want to encourage that? Suppose they misprogram an early warning radar's computer and it picks up a flight of birds or the rising moon?

Damage Limiter: The Soviets didn't learn their strategic thinking in the Office of Systems Analysis. I think they're going to deploy weapons and adopt strategic policies as it suits them, and I don't think we can control that. We have to be able to attack their silos, if they strike first, to keep them from holding our cities hostage.

Assured Destroyer: I don't really think you're interested in deterrence at all. If the Soviets strike first, they aren't going to be so dumb as to leave any ICBMs in their silos. They'll withhold their submarine-launched missiles, which your "counterforce" weapons are useless against. What are you going to shoot at after a Soviet first strike—empty holes in the ground in Siberia? I think your elaborate scenarios are just concocted to hide the fact that you've always supported an American first strike and. . . .

Political Container: Gentlemen, if I may say so, I've heard you two ring the changes on this particular argument off and on for the last fifteen years. You're still pushing each other into extreme positions, and it's partly because you like to argue so much that we never seem to be able to get together on anything. Damage is partly right. If nuclear weapons ever start going off, the President ought to have some options available to him short of all-out war. He probably wouldn't be able to stop things at that point, but if there would be even a small chance to prevent a full-scale war, it's a capability we want him to have. I might add that I particularly sympathize with the military on this issue—they're trained to destroy the enemy's forces and his weapons, not to terrorize civilians. No wonder they've never gotten along with Assured and his computers.

What I don't see is why you have to keep beating the drums for new hardware and a change in strategic policy. They can go ahead and improve accuracy if they want to—we probably couldn't keep your friends in the Pentagon from tinkering with their gyroscopes anyway. And no one is going to object too much if you have all sorts of fancy computer programs that can re-target every missile we own in three nanoseconds. Target them on air fields, depots, and submarine bases, if it takes too many of them to destroy a silo. But stop trying to bring back the sixties. Sure, it would be nice to have a first-strike capability again. We wouldn't use it, but it might help slow the Russians down next time they stir up trouble. The problem is we can't afford it, and the Russians will spend whatever's necessary to keep us from getting it. And nobody's going to abrogate the ABM treaty.

Damage Limiter: Well, maybe sometimes I get a little carried away. But, look, the Soviets are developing and deploying new ICBMs at an incredible rate, and I'm the only one who's trying to do anything about it. I was hoping that emphasizing new counterforce hardware would be a way to let them know we could make that huge investment of theirs worthless, and pretty cheaply, too.

Political Container: What you've mainly succeeded in doing is convincing Assured, Cost, Compleat, and all their friends that you have some sort of bizarre affection for nuclear war.

Damage Limiter: They didn't complain about counterforce in Congress this year as much as they used to.

Political Container: I guess that's because everyone was preoccupied with Watergate, impeachment, and such, and didn't want to rock the boat. They still had a pretty fair debate. I may be wrong, but I think the more you emphasize counterforce programs the less chance we have of getting together and convincing the Soviets that we're not always at one another's throats.

Assured Destroyer: I don't like the encouragement you gave Damage to improve accuracy and to target military installations. If we start going down that road. . . .

Political Container: I know, I know. But part of your problem is that you always focus on one objective and then analyze a subject to death. All these strategic questions could be handled that way if we were all working for a philosopher-king who knew what he wanted. We could state the objective, lay out the options, and let him choose. But there are a number of people involved in this who have different objectives and different ideas. In other words, it's too important not to be political. Somebody has to start synthesizing. We're going to have to compromise. Think of it this way: What seems to concern you most is the design of the weapons themselves, not their targeting. If we emphasize survivability, and not counterforce, in the design of our weapons, you wouldn't really insist that they be targeted only at cities, would you?

There's something else. I know I worry about these things more than you do, but I'm not very comfortable with the agreement that appears likely to result from Vladivostok. It's not so much the substantive terms that bother me—I'd like for us to have done better, but the Soviets did make some concessions, I suppose—it's that the agreement is apparently to be only for a ten-year period. What do we do when, nine years from now, the Soviets have dozens of major weapons programs in advanced development, ready for deployment, and we've done next to nothing because you've all been saying "it would be inconsistent with arms control"? Do we ask them to be reasonable and hope they don't demand something like a two-to-one numerical superiority? They think we're on the decline anyway. It's an article of faith for them, whatever the facts, but we do seem to have been confirming some of their fondest hopes lately. After Vietnam, Cambodia, and Watergate, with inflation everywhere, with our oil supply vulnerable, I wouldn't be surprised if they didn't try pushing us fairly hard sometime in the next few years.

Another thing, our strategic situation isn't so bad right now, but there are some unpleasant trends for the future. Our fixed land-based missiles are more and more vulnerable because of the Soviet ICBM buildup and improvements. Soviet submarine-launched missile and SAM developments threaten our bomber force, although the problem is probably not so immediate as for our ICBMs. Our ballistic-missile submarines are much less threatened, but anti-submarine warfare is a complicated field, and dramatic developments are at least possible. And where have you been while this has been going on, Assured? Don't you have any new ideas anymore, or do you just argue with Damage about the accuracy of re-entry vehicles?

Compleat Controller: You sound like you want to build and deploy new weapons. But the point is that we've all got too many already. How can you expect the Soviets to show restraint unless we do?

Political Container: You're our conscience in this business, but I don't think you have an opposite number over there. The Soviets may be a bit more cautious than they were a few years ago, but, detente or no detente, getting them to do something by making concessions is no easier now than it was in forty-six. Here, let me read you a Kennan theorem from that era, which I brought along. I thought it might come in handy:

Don't make fatuous gestures of good will.

Few of us have any idea how much perplexity and suspicion has been caused in the Soviet mind by gestures and concessions granted by well-meaning Americans with a view to convincing the Russians of their friendly sentiments. Such acts upset all their calculations and throw them way off balance. They immediately begin to expect that they have overestimated our strength, that they have been remiss in their obligations to the Soviet state, that they should have been demanding more from us all along. Frequently, this has exactly the opposite effect from that which we are seeking.

Compleat Controller: Well, then, you'd say there's no stopping the arms race.

Political Container: Probably not, for a long time anyway. But I think you'd still accomplish a great deal if you'd concentrate on channelizing it. If both sides negotiate and end up by pursuing less destabilizing strategic developments than they would have otherwise, you've done quite a bit. It's not the number of weapons that makes the world dangerous, it's whether someone has any incentive to use them. And you aren't going to save much money on strategic arms anyway, unless you stop all modernization, which isn't very likely. Even then, remember that stopping all strategic investment for four years, at last year's rate, wouldn't pay for the recomputation of military retired pay.

Cost Cutter: All right, all right. Don't run that one into the ground.

Political Container: The point is that we won't be able to get the Soviets to slow down or stop any of their programs—either in this agreement or a later one—unless we have something to trade, something to stop doing ourselves so that they can convince each other that they have to stop doing something, too. I'm sorry to keep quoting Kennan, but some things haven't changed much in thirty years:

No one can argue any proposition in the . . . councils of the Soviet government unless he can show concretely how the interests of the Soviet Union stand to gain if it is accepted or to suffer if it is rejected. This principle is applied with the most serene objectivity.

Cost Cutter: What's wrong with trading them Trident or the B-1?

Political Container: They're replacements for the older Polaris submarines and the B-52s. Maybe we can find a way to use cheaper bombers or submarines for replacements, but we can't agree not to modernize our existing systems unless the Soviets do, too. We need a new program.

Compleat Controller: I'll never agree to doing something just to have a bargaining chip. What's wrong with limiting accuracy and MIRVs? We have qualitative superiority in those areas, and we wouldn't need to start a program up just to trade it away.

Political Container: I've always been suspicious of qualitative limitations, because they're so hard to state with precision and to verify. And any agreement that's vague and hard to verify is one that we have to keep and the Soviets don't—they don't have Congress and a press to keep them honest. But I don't want to start up a system just to have a bargaining chip. We should only start work on something if it improves our confidence in the deterrent, and if we really want to deploy it because the Soviets keep pushing programs—such as large ICBMs—that concern us. In other words, we should only start something we definitely need if eventually no good agreement develops, whether now or ten years from now.

Cost Cutter: Well, if you have to do something, you could keep the cost fairly low by using an existing platform—say a plane, or a boat, that doesn't need to go through R and D.

Assured Destroyer: I suppose you could start putting intercontinental-range cruise missiles on a C-5A or a 747. It's not clear how, or if, that would be limited in the next agreement, but it does make some strategic sense. In a crisis, you could put them on airborne alert here in the United States. Damage will try to give them huge payloads and incredible accuracies, but we could probably keep that from happening.

Compleat Controller: You haven't convinced me that we need any new systems at all, however cheap and theoretically unprovocative. And I still don't see why you're against our debating these issues the way we always have. Let's fight it out in Congress. Why do we have to agree?

Damage Limiter: I like the idea of starting a new program, but you certainly haven't convinced me that we should be spending money on this one. I think the idea of counterforce is beginning to catch on. The budget is going to be tight enough anyway. If we do what Assured suggests, we may end up not doing anything else.

Political Container: Compleat, you and Damage and everyone else can fight this out the way we have before. It's a free country. But I'm just suggesting that we try something new, that we see if we can't agree on something, so that over the next few years we can reduce the noise level. I've already told you why I think the Soviets may start pushing on us before long. Ever since Brest-Litovsk they've been negotiating over the heads of governments and playing on their opponents' domestic divisions. If the economic situation gets worse in the West, I think they're going to start crowding us—I don't know where or how, but I do know that the more divided we are internally, the more they're going to underestimate us. They see us filtered through their own preconceptions. To them, when they calculate what they call the "correlation of forces," division on the home front means weakness. That's understandable, given the origins of their own regime. But it creates a problem for us, because the ordinary give-and-take of our open society makes us look frail, especially when we're dealing with things like nuclear strategy. I know some of you don't much like the idea of working together on this. But no one's going to exploit you—you can back out any time. All I can say is that, by cooperating, you can at least blunt the most extreme notions of the others—and all of you do have them. . . .

Compleat Controller: You mean "all of *us*" have them, don't you?

Political Container: I do forget that occasionally, don't I? Look, I know it's going to be hard for us all to agree on what we should do, much less on a single rationale. But I do think that we have a chance, if we work at it, to find some general approach that we will all be only moderately unhappy with. Maybe we have to emphasize strategic systems primarily designed for survivability, not counterforce, to do it as cheaply as possible, and to show the Soviets that we can, and will, have the ongoing programs to match them in numbers, unless they agree to reduce. If we can even begin to get behind that as a position—or something else that one of you proposes—we might convince them we have some staying power. But what we decide on is probably less important than the way we deal with one another. The main thing is to see if we can't keep talking, make some compromises, and agree on a few things for a change. That's the only way we'll gain any concessions from them on arms control. If we show a bit more unity, we might even help discourage them from doing something foolish over the next several years.

Compleat Controller: Could we also talk about how we develop an approach to discourage *ourselves* from doing something foolish?

Political Container: We can even fold that in. Now, does anyone want to leave before we start?

THOMAS C. SCHELLING

A Framework for the Evaluation of Arms-Control Proposals

This is an exploration of the different motives that can lead two countries to bargain about armaments. Its purposes are to classify the alternative preferences about possession or nonpossession of weapons that arms bargainers might have in mind and to see what kinds of bargains are compatible with different preferences, and what understandings and misunderstandings are likely.

The discussion is restricted to situations typically identified with arms control: the object is to reduce armaments on the other side and not, as in an alliance, to increase them. I discuss weapons that we should prefer the other side not to have and omit any weapons, or systems of command and control, that we might prefer they invest in for our joint safety.

To keep the analysis simple, I am assuming that the choice is binary: to have or not to have it. Some arms bargaining is in fact about all-or-none decisions, or decisions that are nearly so; ABM, biological weapons, weapons in orbit, MIRV, and many others have been approached as yes-no decisions. Other decisions are about quantities, numbers, sizes, distances, degrees, and durations; but even for these decisions, the special case of dichotomous choice can be illuminating, if not directly applicable. Often in such cases the negotiation will eventually lead to a binary choice: to adopt or not to adopt some specified limit or reduction or increment.

Alternative-Preference Configurations

The variety of preferences arises from the fact that one side, while deprecating possession by the other side, can have any one of several attitudes toward its own possession of the weapon.

First, it can prefer *not* to have the weapon under any circumstances, simultaneously preferring that the other side not have it either. Our side may have decided, for example, that ABM is a waste whether or not the other side has it, that hundred-megaton weapons or bombs in orbit involve too much risk or adverse publicity, whether or not the other side invests in these weapons, and so forth.

A second possibility is that a side prefers *to have* the weapon whether or not the other side has it. The Soviets, to take an example, may prefer to have a Fractional Orbital Bombardment System (FOBS), whether we have one or not. We may prefer to have heavy bombers, whether the Soviets have them or not. Either side may feel that way about sea-based missiles.

Now a third case: The weapon may be one that we are *not* motivated to acquire if the other side does *not*, but that we *would* invest in if the other side *did*. Although the

187

logic was not always clear, it was often asserted during the nineteen-sixties that ABM was the kind of weapon that the United States could not afford to be without if the Soviets had it, although the United States might not want to put resources into it unless the Soviets did. Sometimes the basis for this motivation is military effectiveness and strategy: a "matching" weapon may be needed if the adversary has it, but may not be worth having otherwise. Sometimes it is psychology and diplomacy: "our side" must not appear incapable of developing the weapon, too stingy to procure it, or plain inferior for lack of it, if the other side has it. Sometimes it is domestic behavior or politics: the arms-bargainer believes that political and bureaucratic pressures will be irresistible if the other side embarks on the program, but can be contained if the other side does not.

This third case is one in which there is not an absolute preference but a *contingent* one, a preference conditional on what the other side does.[1]

The second case—in which we prefer to have the weapon whether or not the other side has it—has to be subdivided into two distinct subcases: 1) While we prefer to have it, whether they have it or not, we would willingly forego it on condition they forego it also; or, 2) while we want them not to have it, we would *not* willingly forego it just to keep them from acquiring it.

The difference between these two subcases reflects the relative ranking of the middle two among the four possible outcomes. In either subcase our preferred result is to have the weapon while the other side does not; least preferred is for the other side to have it while we do not. The two middle-ranked outcomes are, then, both to have it and both not to have it. In the first subcase, we prefer both *not* having it to both having it. In the second subcase we prefer both having it to both not having it.[2]

For purposes of easy abbreviation I am going to refer to the first kind of preference mentioned earlier—the preference not to have the weapon, whether or not the other side has it, as a "NO" preference. The contingent preference—to have it if the other side has it, otherwise not—I shall call an "IFF" preference ("if and only if"). And the two cases in which we prefer to have the weapon whether or not the other side has it, I shall call "YES" and "YES!" The exclamation point goes with the stronger case, the case in which we would prefer both to have it than both not. The YES-case is, then, the one in which, if our acquisition were unrelated to theirs, we would acquire the weapon whether they had it or not, but we would prefer that both of us not have it compared with both going ahead and acquiring it.

These four cases—YES, YES!, IFF, and NO—refer to the preferences of one side (either our side or their side) with respect to some particular weapon. There is no reason why the attitudes on the two sides should be mirror images of each other, so we cannot assume that a NO preference on our side will be matched by a NO preference on the other side. There are thus sixteen possible pairs of preferences of the two sides about possession or non-possession of the weapon. Four situations are symmetrical: both sides are YES! or YES or IFF or NO. The other twelve are such combinations as YES-IFF and IFF-YES.

A Bargaining Combination: YES vs. YES

Begin with the combination of YES and YES. This configuration of preferences is familiar to students of bargaining and conflict (and, because of its symmetry, it may be generalized to include multiparty situations). It has the following interesting characteristics. First, each is *unilaterally* motivated to acquire the weapon, whatever the other has done or is expected to do. If the other side proceeds to acquire the weapon, we would elect to acquire it, too; if they *unilaterally* promise not to have the weapon, we would welcome their promise but still go ahead and acquire the weapon. But if each of us makes that *independent* choice, we both reach an outcome that is our second choice from the bottom rather than second from the top. Neither side regrets its choice as a unilateral action: had it chosen otherwise, it would have suffered the worst possible outcome, the other side having the weapon and itself not. If both should happen somehow to be obstructed in their efforts to invest in the weapon, each will come out second best, given what its preferences are; yet both are better off than if both had succeeded!

This is the classic case in which something like "enforceable contract" can lead to a bargained result that is superior for both parties to what they might have achieved independently. Though each prefers to have the system, whether or not the other does, each has a *stronger* preference that *the other not have* it. Each gains more from the other side's foregoing it than from his own side's having it. There is room for a "trade."

Trading with the Enemy

Here, then, is a case in which "trading with the enemy" is a good bargain. If we can reach agreement to abstain from this weapon, we both come out second best instead of third best. But this is an agreement that has to be enforced. If the agreement cannot be monitored—if compliance is inherently invisible—and if the consciences or legal systems on both sides will not coerce compliance, each will not only fail to keep the bargain but will expect the other not to keep it either.

Not every weapon that gives a relative advantage to the side that has it, but is costly and to no avail if both sides have it, corresponds to the YES-YES situation. A weapon that yields a relative superiority can still generate a NO preference if it makes the outbreak of war more likely or has other deplorable side effects. There are, moreover, weapons that one might prefer to have on *both sides* rather than on neither side: "invulnerable retaliatory forces" to supplement vulnerable ones might appear jointly desirable. I hesitate to name examples of YES-YES weapons because any example will be evaluated by the reader and, if he evaluates the weapon differently from me, he may not find it a representation of the YES-YES situation. But *suppose* that our side (whether or not you and I agree with this valuation) considers a fleet of warships in the Indian Ocean, or a forward-based missile system, or the deployment of a MIRV technology worth having if the other side does not have it, and perhaps even more worth having if the other side does have it. But suppose, nevertheless, that we would consider any gains more than canceled out if both sides had it. No relative advantage is achieved if both have it, greater expense is incurred, and there is possibly some greater risk of war, or some aggravation of diplomatic relations. Then we have the YES-YES situation with a basis for negotiated "exchange," provided the result can be monitored and enforced.

Alternative Agreements and Understandings

An enforceable agreement is not the only kind of effective understanding that might be reached in this YES-YES case. Perhaps one side can make a credible promise that it will abstain *if and only if* the other side does. The second side then knows that its decision will determine whether both have it, or neither, and it can safely abstain. (A "credible promise" is equivalent to incurring some penalty for possessing the system if the other side does not, a penalty sufficiently severe to change the promising side's preference order from YES to IFF.)

A third way that restraint might be induced lies in each side's announcing that it will abstain so long as the other does. If both sides know each other's preferences and perceive that an enforceable agreement would be in their joint interests, they may perceive that a sufficient method of "enforcement" is simply each side's readiness to go ahead if the other does. Enforcement is by reciprocity. This requires that each be able to detect whether or not the other is proceeding with the weapon—and to detect it in time not to suffer by being a slow second.

An interesting "credible promise" that might be available to the United States government would involve using conditional legislative authorization. Suppose the Congress authorized procurement of a weapon system contingently—that is, authorized appropriation of funds and procurement to take effect only upon certification that the other side had unmistakably embarked on a comparable program. (In earlier times the British Parliament legislated contingent automatic procurement authorizations for naval tonnage, thus signaling to the other side—France, in the late nineteenth century, Germany in the early twentieth—that British procurement would be determined by the other's procurement.)

Two Qualifications About Agreement

Before leaving this case of YES-YES, two observations should be made. First, while a weapon characterized by YES preferences is a clear opportunity for reciprocated restraint, which can be achieved with or without a formal enforceable agreement so long as the choices can be monitored, it is not true that both sides, even with full understanding of each other's preferences, ought always to be willing to agree on restraint. Because either side can deny the other something it wants—at the cost of denying the same thing to itself—it may perceive a bargaining advantage with respect to some *other* weapon, that is, it can make an agreement on this weapon that is contingent on the other one.

Second, because neither side can be sure of the other's preferences, this YES configuration can occur without its being plain to both sides what each other's preferences are. Other preferences can in fact obtain while one of the parties is mistakenly thinking that the situation is YES-YES. The consequences of mistaken estimates will be discussed below.

Reciprocated IFF

A second configuration familiar in the study of bargaining is the symmetrical IFF-IFF situation. This describes the weapon that each wants if and only if the other side has it. It differs from the preceding case in that either side is not merely willing to forego the weapon on condition that the other do likewise, but has no incentive to obtain it unless the other does. There are two outcomes that are "conditionally satisfactory." As long as neither has it, and neither has reason to expect the other to acquire it, neither is motivated to obtain it. If both have it, neither is willing to dismantle it unilaterally. But if either side confidently perceives the situation to be IFF-IFF, it can confidently abstain or dismantle a weapon in the knowledge that the other side will do likewise. Neither expects the other to jump the gun secretly and race to be the first to get the weapon: the other side does not even want to be the only side to have it. Such a weapon is valuable only in the role of "counter-capability" to the other's possession of the same weapon.

This IFF-IFF situation is an easy case for arms control. It is necessary only for the two sides to act in *concert* with each other and to *reassure* each other. If both confidently perceive what the situation is, there should be no problem. Of course, if each believes the other's preferences are in the YES! configuration, each may consider it a foregone conclusion that the other side will have the weapon, see no value in negotiating, and proceed with the weapon itself. Without negotiations, they may never discover that they committed symmetrical errors in imputing wrong preferences to each other. Furthermore, there can be a tactical advantage in pretending that one's preferences are IFF when they are NO, if the other side's preferences are YES: it offers some inducement for the other's restraint. And, as when both had YES preferences, either side may consider it a bargaining advantage to threaten possession of the system, though its true preferences are IFF, to induce restraint on yet another system that may have been coupled with this one in negotiations.

Finally, as mentioned earlier, a YES configuration may be deliberately converted into an IFF decision by formal legislative commitment to contingent procurement. (I leave it to the reader to consider the likely behavior in an IFF-IFF configuration where there is absolutely no way for either side to monitor the other's possession.)

The NO-NO Configuration

Ordinarily this would be a trivial case—a weapon that neither side wants, whether or not the other has it. There must be an infinity of ridiculous weapons that nobody is interested in having, even if the other side is foolish enough to procure them. In isolation from other weapons, this is merely a logical category, empty of significance, that completes our matrix of permutations. But in a wider context, as part of a logrolling scheme, one side might *pretend* that its preference was not NO but YES!; or it might, in aggressive bargaining, *threaten* to acquire the weapon despite its own preference not to have it. So the NO-NO case does not necessarily preclude bargaining.

The IFF-YES Configuration

This situation, if clearly recognized, leads easily to the same result as IFF-IFF. It is equivalent to a YES-YES situation in which one side has arranged a credible promise to abstain provided the other side does. The one with the YES preference knows that its own choice will determine whether both sides will have the system or both not. Since it prefers that both do not, it can abstain.

Problems arise if the IFF motivation is wrongly perceived, or if YES is wrongly perceived to be YES! by the IFF side. Misperception can lead both to believe that the inevitable outcome lies in both sides having it. The IFF side then acquires it, confirming the mistaken belief of the YES side. If the YES side believes that the IFF motive is YES!, it may not even initiate the bargaining that would be invited by a symmetrical YES situation. And, again, either side may perceive a bargaining advantage in coupling this weapon with another, exploiting the threat in declaring an intention to acquire this one, pretending its motivation is YES!.

A frustrating situation can occur if possession of the weapon cannot be monitored. As in the symmetrical YES case, the YES country would prefer to own this weapon even if the IFF country does not; if possession cannot be monitored, the IFF country must assume that the YES country will procure it. Anticipating that, the IFF country procures it also.

Thus, with monitoring, the combination of IFF and YES can be as benign as symmetrical IFF; without monitoring, it can be as frustrating as symmetrical YES.

YES-NO

If motives are transparent and if there is no coupling with any other negotiable weapon, the outcome in a YES-NO case is that the YES country will go ahead and the NO country will not. But if the NO country can successfully *threaten* to acquire the weapon or *pretend* an IFF or YES motivation, it can induce the YES side to forego it. Alternatively, if the NO country is unable to misrepresent its motives or to threaten credibly that it will procure the weapon, it can introduce another weapon for logrolling purposes: it offers a concession on the latter, or threatens to obtain it to induce the YES country to abstain from the first.

NO-IFF

This case does not differ significantly from NO-NO

The YES! Configuration

Considered on its merits, the symmetrical YES! situation is the trivial counterpart to the symmetrical NO case. There is no bargain that we would be interested in that is confined to this weapon alone. While each prefers the other not to have it, neither is willing to abstain from obtaining it merely to induce the other to do without.

Bargaining arises only if this weapon can be coupled with another. Thus among our sixteen permutations, seven preclude successful bargaining unless the weapon can be coupled with some other weapon or some other issue. The ramifications of this point are many.

First, it can be a bargaining advantage to pretend that one's motivation is YES!. If the coupling of the two weapons were not possible, such a pretense would merely preclude agreement. But if one country's motivation is YES! on a particular weapon and the other's is YES on some other weapon, the latter can refuse to bargain (i.e., pretend a YES! motivation) on the second weapon in order to couple the two and overcome the first side's absolute preference for the first.

Second, the very possibility of a YES! preference can interfere with arms bargaining by being anticipated. It used to be commonly alleged, for example, that the Soviet Union's attitude toward active defense made no bargaining on ABM possible: The Soviets would rather have an ABM matched by ours than forego it on condition that we do likewise. Had that been a firm belief, but a wrong one—say, that instead the situation was symmetrically YES (or IFF-YES or NO-YES)—then we would have missed an opportunity to bargain away the ABM. If both sides are YES and believe each other to be YES!, discussion of the subject may seem so unpromising that the bargaining possibility is never discovered.

A third consequence of the YES! preference, when the other side's preference is YES, is that a misunderstanding may spoil prospects for bargaining on other weapons. Suppose our preference is YES and we believe theirs is also, but theirs is in fact YES!. Believing a bargain possible, we propose negotiation and are rebuffed; or we enter negotiation and discover that the other side insists on coupling this weapon with another that we believe irrelevant or inappropriate. We believe them to be holding out, jeopardizing a good bargain to obtain concessions on other issues. They may be quite unable to convince us that their preference is really YES!, i.e., that they are unprepared to forego the weapon merely on condition that we forego it. We are unlikely to believe them if they tell us this, because it is precisely what they would have told us if, indeed, they had been "just bargaining."

Misperceptions

Before we leave these permutations, some further results of misperception are worth noticing. Suppose both sides are IFF, but believe each other to be YES: neither believes his own abstention will induce the other to abstain, but both believe agreement may be possible if they negotiate. To avoid appearing to be NO, which might leave the other side (believed to be YES) free to obtain the weapon with impunity, one side may exaggerate its interest as YES. Though, in principle, agreement is possible, there is no guarantee that such negotiations will succeed. Each may overstate its case, become greedy and be inept, bog down in endless argument, or become domestically committed to the system. The negotiation having failed, each believes the other will go ahead, and so proceeds to acquire the weapon itself.[3]

Even NO configurations on both sides, if each believes the other to be YES, can lead to unnecessary negotiations to prohibit systems that neither side wants anyway. And if the negotiations fail, one or both may have been deluded into, or committed to, programs in which, in the absence of bargaining, neither would have had any interest.

Natural Coupling, Tactical Coupling

Most of the foregoing discussion has been concerned with motivations, perceptions, and tactics in relation to a single weapon—ABM, strategic bombers, sea-based missile systems, or MIRV, for example. Some of the discussion has referred to the coupling of two or more weapons or issues in a bargain. There are two quite different kinds of coupling, and they might be called "natural" and "tactical."

"Natural coupling" occurs when two weapons are complementary. For example, a "natural package" might be an agreement about *their* ABM and *our* offensive missiles, and not an agreement forbidding ABM on both sides (there being nothing about the other side's ABM that makes us want ABM). Or, we might argue that MIRV technology on our side is "naturally coupled" with ABM on the other side. We may argue that, if they proceed with ABM, we shall double our missile force, or MIRV our land-based missiles, and we may propose, therefore, to abstain from some *offensive* capability if they abstain from some *defensive* capability. We do this on the grounds that we have a "natural" *IFF-preference relation between our offensive capability and their defensive capability.* Similarly, we might take the position that there is "natural coupling" between our sea-based system and their anti-submarine (ASW) system. "Tactical coupling" refers to the coupling, for bargaining purposes, of two or more systems in which we and the other side have quite different interests. *They* may be concerned about forward-based bombers, *we* about ASW. The two have no strategic relationship; there is nothing intrinsic to ASW that compels us to do something about forward-based bombers. But there may not be a symmetrical agreement about forward-based systems that makes sense to both sides. And perhaps we have no system that quite corresponds to the particular ASW system that we deprecate on their side. So we—or they—propose that we restrain forward-based bombers and they restrain ASW.

This is what is commonly called "packaging" or "logrolling." It is different from natural coupling. In natural coupling, there is a YES or IFF relation between a weapon on the other side and one on ours. In tactical coupling, there is a weapon of concern to us that does not seem promising for separate agreement, and another of concern to them that also does not seem promising for separate agreement; by combining the two, we may reach an agreeable pair of restraints.

Bargaining Chips

The idea of a "bargaining chip" seems to involve some weapon or plan or intention that one side has that is of greater concern to the other side; it is therefore eligible to be traded away. To be "traded away" means to be yielded or abandoned on condition that the other side also makes some appropriate concession.

The term is also used to describe some project that a side merely *pretends* interest in, expecting a negative interest on the other side sufficiently compelling to make a trade possible. "Bargaining chips" are not peculiar to arms negotiations; they are common in tariff bargaining, diplomatic bargaining, and industrial relations. Because the term covers so wide an array of tactics, hardly any generalization can be offered about the wisdom or propriety of playing with bargaining chips. But in identifying the situations to which the term can apply, it is useful to notice several different intentions that a country may have for a weapon, some of which involve this notion of "bargaining chips."

1) At one extreme is a weapon that a country is so interested in having that it would not be likely to bargain it away—a YES! interest. Of course, if the other side has a sufficiently strong interest in opposing it and is willing to make important enough coupled concessions, almost any weapon is likely to be negotiable. Still, some weapon plans are expected not to be part of any agreement or even to be discussed with a view to agreement. These will not be categorized as "bargaining chips."

2) A second category consists of projects that a side is strongly interested in, but still considers to be within the realm of bargaining because the other side's negative interest may well outweigh the first side's positive interest. This kind of YES project is within the arena of bargaining and is recognized as negotiable—not brought to the table only to be traded away, but nevertheless subject to negotiation. This, as I perceive the current usage, would also usually not be called a "bargaining chip."

3) The third category covers YES-projects that a country ordinarily would carry out but that are clearly of much more interest to the other side. These are the projects that are "taken to market," or "brought to the bargaining table." There is nothing contrived or fictitious about them; they are genuine plans, but they are recognized in advance as strong candidates for trading.

4) Fourth are the "pure bargaining chips"—arms that one side has no genuine interest in, but that make a difference to the other side. These are weapons, NO or on the borderline of NO, that one side could obtain with little effort and/or at slight cost and that represent threat or nuisance to the other side. They are not bona fide intentions, but they become trading assets in their potential threat to the other side.

If these "pure bargaining chips" are of no value to the side that puts them forward, why is the other side compelled to make concessions to have them put aside? There are at least two reasons: One is that the side putting forward the bargaining chip may successfully *pretend* a strong interest. The second is that it may more brazenly *threaten* to carry out the project unless the other side pays a price. Depending on one's standards of behavior, this mode of bargaining may or may not be characterized as "blackmail," or by some similar pejorative that identifies the motive and deprecates the tactic.

5) Finally, a country may project a NO-weapon that it would deplore acquiring, hoping that the other side deplores it sufficiently to bargain for its elimination. The side putting it forward wants not only to win something for abandoning the weapon, but also to protect itself from having to acquire it. This case, too, can be characterized either by pretense or by blatant threat. Sometimes the ethics of this tactic is judged according to whether it is employed cold-bloodedly for gain or is used to oppose—that is, to be bargained away against—something deemed improper that the other side proposes.

Absolute and Contingent Chips

In negotiating, a side may put forward a projected weapon that it expects to trade away, but without linking it to some *particular* concession on the other side. Alternatively, it may put forward a contingent project with an IFF motivation—a project that will go forward if and only if the other side proceeds with a particular project of its own. This automatically links the bargaining chip with the particular exchange that is intended—with a matching project on the other side. If the United States pretends a strong interest in ABM because it believes the Soviets would pay a price to get the United States to abandon it, the proposal would be a bargaining chip of the general or absolute variety. But if the United States proposes ABM as a natural response to a Soviet ABM, or as a natural response to some Soviet offensive-weapon capability, implying not that we are YES toward ABM but IFF, with a clear indication as to which of the other side's weapons the IFF refers, the project becomes a "matched" or "contingent" bargaining chip.

Thus the contingent is always coupled, "naturally" or "tactically," with some weapon on the other side. It may then be that no further bargaining is needed. With the absolute bargaining chip, the bargaining itself is essential—one pretends a YES or a YES! motivation and waits to be induced to abandon it. In the contingent case, the chip is matched with something in particular, and if that something on the other side is abandoned, by reciprocal announcement or unilaterally, the result may be achieved without negotiation.

IFF and YES Bargaining Chips

A bargaining chip can be introduced in two quite different ways. Suppose the United States is only marginally interested in ABM, or even reluctant about it, but resolved on a tactic of pretending an interest or incurring a commitment, subject to progress in SALT. At some stage, American negotiators will have to suggest that the ABM program is *negotiable* and *contingent*. (There may be a pretense that it is not, but a pretense that is merely designed to raise the bargaining price.) Inasmuch as there may be political and bureaucratic forces in favor of ABM, as well as against it, the United States may find itself able to seem committed without having to pretend very hard.

Now there are two quite different commitments that the United States can appear to undertake. One is to proceed with ABM if the Soviet Union does, and not otherwise. The second is to proceed with ABM unless *agreement* prohibiting ABM is reached with the Soviet Union. If successful, these two may come to the same thing; but the risks and procedures are different. If we commit ourselves, as a bargaining tactic, to match Soviet ABM, there may be no need to reach formal agreement.

If instead we pretend a YES motive, we may commit ourselves to proceed unless an explicit agreement is reached. This tactic runs the risk that aborted negotiations leave us obliged, in consequence of a bluff, to carry through with a program that we did not want to proceed with. But if the bargaining chip takes the IFF form, it is the other side's *behavior*, not the successful *negotiation*, that gets us off the hook.

The Motivational Context of Bargaining Chips

If the other side's motivation is known to be IFF, we do not need to employ the bargaining-chip tactic. We need only reassure it of our NO, and its IFF leads it to abstain. The "bargaining chip" is pertinent when the other side's motivation is believed to be YES. If the bargaining chip succeeds, the results are acceptable so far as a particular agreement is concerned. (We might in the longer run prefer not to establish too many precedents for playing with chips.) We fail if the other side's motivation is YES!. In that case, if we bluff an intention to proceed, we will be caught bluffing and will have either to back down or to proceed with a program we do not want.

There is another danger. If we overplay our chip and pretend that our motivation is YES! in order to exact a higher price, the other side may believe us! It may not even bother to bargain, and we will end up committed to a program whose only purpose was to be traded away.

These risks of failure suggest that an IFF chip is safer than a YES or YES! chip. To become committed only on condition that the other side proceed with some *action*, and not committed in the absence of formal *agreement*, incurs less risk. A satisfactory result does not depend on a successful negotiation. If each side is IFF but thinks the other is YES, using a bargaining chip might result, if negotiations fail, in both sides being committed to go ahead. But if both sides are committed only to an IFF re-action, aborted negotiations can—may not, but can—leave both sides willing to wait and see.

The Internal Effects of Bargaining Chips

There are two ways that bargaining chips are used: one is as a pretense, the other as a commitment. There are many ways a government can become committed to a course it clearly does not care to undertake, even where it is evident that the commit-ment has been incurred for bargaining purposes. A legal way, mentioned earlier, is to pass legislation that obliges the government, in certain contingencies, to do what it might not ordinarily wish to do (and to have Congress go home for the fall season, leaving the Executive branch with its hands tied). There are also other ways.

Now, many kinds of bargaining require sufficient privacy so that a pretense appears plausible, or a commitment appears not to be rigged. But it is difficult for a democratic government to pretend an interest in, say, ABM for the benefit of a diplomatic audience abroad, without deceiving the domestic audience as well. The Soviet government usually need not broadcast an embarrassing public contradiction of the position it has taken in negotiations, but the United States government often cannot avoid it. Bargaining chips are probably an ineffectual tool for a government that cannot bluff in private. From this comes the anomaly that in the last few years the bargaining-chip idea has become a subject of popular discussion precisely because the Executive branch has put forward positions that it explained at home as being "bargaining chips." There is nothing tactically wrong with this, so long as the govern-ment can reasonably become committed, whether or not its hypocrisy is transparent. There is nothing tactically illogical in proposing to the home folks that one really wouldn't want ABM under any circumstances, but needs to become committed to it—provided one can become convincingly committed. But the pretense that typically makes bargaining chips valuable is often unavailable to a government that must ex-plain aloud to a large audience that it didn't really mean what it said to its bargaining partner. And a democratic government risks losing some credibility at home—as the United States government probably did in making this argument so blatantly during the SALT negotiations.

Precisely because the cold-blooded pretense is not easily available, a government may have to go through the motions of seeming to be genuinely intent on a program, though part of the motive for the program was to provide a bargaining chip. The danger is that in the process the government becomes genuinely committed, so com-mitted that it forgets it did not intend to go ahead, or so committed that it has to go ahead. It may become so committed that bargaining power within the government shifts to those who wanted the weapon in the first place. A government may believe it has kept open the option of backing out of a commitment if the bargain does not come off, only to discover that it has lost the option.

The Symmetry of Bargaining-Chip Analysis

What has been said about "our side" and bargaining chips can usually be said about "the other side" as well. The other side's interest in some weapon—a YES interest or an IFF interest—could be genuine, pretended, or contrived. (By "contrived" I mean that, without necessarily pretending a genuine interest, the other side adopts a *policy* of proceeding with a weapon if we do, or of proceeding in the absence of negotiated agreement, or of proceeding unless we abstain from some other weapon, or negotiate an agreement about some other weapon.)

One difficulty in judging the other side's position with respect to a given weapon is similar to the difficulty of identifying our own side's position. Within a government there are strong interests in favor of a weapon and strong interests opposed to it. Within a government there may be optimism about negotiation, or pessimism. Within a government there may be a belief that the other side is already committed to procurement, so that an IFF-motivation is a reason for proceeding with the weapon and not with negotiation. Within a government there may have been a tentative decision to proceed without full commitment, and no decisive determination yet of the strength of the interest in the weapon. To an observer who is not part of the government, there will be similar difficulties in judging the positions of both sides, although the United States and the Soviet Union clearly have governments that vary in their ability to pretend, to adopt conditional policies, to display or to disguise indecisiveness, to make up their own minds or to remain undecided, even to be incapable—when legislative as well as executive decisions are involved, or when allies have to be accommodated—of making up their minds or knowing what their own policies are.

Domestically Oriented "Bargaining Chips"

Bargaining chips can be used to influence *domestic* decisions. One way is to initiate development or procurement of a weapon on the ostensible grounds that, even if in the end it should not be procured, it enhances our bargaining position. Then, by confusion, commitment, or default, the program goes forward unless the other side manages to "obstruct" it with an agreement. Anyone who can sabotage the agreement can convert a bargaining position into a weapon program.

Another tactic is the opposite: A government that has decided against a weapon in which there is popular interest, either in the Congress or elsewhere, or which it has promoted in the past but has changed its mind about, may need an excuse to abandon the weapon. Converting it into a "bargaining chip" and reaching agreement can legitimize a decision that could not so readily have been taken unconditionally. Negotiation of the Non-Proliferation Treaty probably provided instances of both of these tactics abroad.

An Arms-Control Judgment on Weapons

The foregoing classification has at least a limited value—if only a limited value—in explaining, providing guidance for, and clarifying the reasons why a person interested in sound strategy (including arms control) might favor or deplore a particular weapon program, or favor it only conditionally. But this classification is abstract, and it is uninformative to the extent that it does not relate either to the strategic characteristics of weapons, or to budgetary, or to diplomatic or domestic political considerations. It is not conclusive or comprehensive. Still, in clarifying and communicating one's attitude toward a weapon, even this classification can prove useful.

People have opposed MIRV for Minuteman, using a number of motivational permutations. There were those who felt that MIRV was positively bad on military-strategic grounds or military-industrial grounds, whether or not the Soviets had MIRV, but who also believed that the Soviets were not going to have MIRV anyway—a NO-NO configuration. There were those who believed it was not only bad on military-strategic grounds but, worse, would induce the Russians to acquire it themselves, although they wouldn't if we didn't—a NO-IFF configuration. There were people whose configuration was IFF-YES, who believed we should declare a willingness to abstain so long as the Soviets did, and others who, with the same IFF-YES configuration, felt that we should choose the negotiation of a MIRV ban. There were those who felt our own position should be IFF, but believed the Soviet position to be NO and felt it would therefore be a mistake to go forward; others felt it was IFF on both sides, and we would force the Soviets to obtain it if we did so ourselves. Others have felt that our position was IFF, but the Soviets' was YES: we should make clear to the Russians that we would if they did, although it was not necessary to negotiate. Some undoubtedly felt that the Russian position was YES! and that there was no possibility of negotiating a MIRV ban, while others agreed that the Soviet motivation was YES! and that MIRV could be successfully coupled with other weapons in a larger package. And there were still other views.

Evidently these represent different opinions of what our own preference should be, what the Soviet preference is, and what the diplomatic prospects are. This classification does not explain on what grounds one arrives at a NO, IFF, or YES preference. What this classification does do is clarify *arms-race considerations* in one's position toward a particular weapon: that is, it clarifies one's position on whether we unilaterally want the weapon, unilaterally do not want it, conditionally want it, think our acquisition will affect the other side, think an enforceable agreement might be negotiated, or think this weapon might usefully be coupled with another.

This classification will not be much help in clarifying a position that is based primarily on broader diplomatic considerations or domestic political ones. When the time came to vote on ABM in the Senate, the issue may have been the war in Vietnam, the military-industrial complex, the Nixon Administration, executive-legislative relations, the size of the defense budget, or promises given and positions taken that constrained what one could say, or favor, or vote on. But to the extent that one rests his position on what is usually called the "arms race," on the interplay or interaction of development, procurement, and deployment of strategic weapons on both sides, this classification will be useful.

REFERENCES

[1] I ignore the logically possible case that we want it if and only if "they" do not have it. It arises in other contexts, but seldom in disarmament negotiations.

² If the reader is curious about what the logical possibilities are, we can identify the four possible outcomes in terms of which side, or sides, has the weapon: We Only, They Only, Both, and Neither. If we have
"strong" preferences among these four situations—no ties among them—there are 4 x 3 x 2 possible ways to
rank these four outcomes. But if we restrict our study to weapons that we prefer the other side not to have,
We Only is always better than Both, and Neither is always better than They Only. This restriction reduces
the number of alternative rankings to six. Two of these are the two subcases just discussed. There are also
two subcases for our preference not to have it, irrespective of whether or not they do; but the difference
relates to whether, if one side were to have it, we would rather be the side to have the weapon we do not
want, and that kind of choice rarely arises in arms negotiations. Then there are the two contingent cases: we
want it if and only if they have it—case 3 in the text—and we want it if and only if they do not have it, a
situation that can arise in other contexts but that is unlikely in arms bargaining.

³ I consider it likely that each side was IFF on ABM but believed the other side to be YES, with a suspicion that it might be YES!, and therefore both believed that only a negotiated agreement could prevent it.
Had the negotiations failed, both might have gone ahead with systems based on misperceptions—misperceptions that would have appeared to be confirmed and aggravated by the negotiation itself.
(Here is a case in which the fiction that the "U.S. Government" had a "preference" can only be shorthand
for a retrospective prediction about policies that probably emerged from a multitude of interests and positions in different parts of the executive and legislative branches.)

GEORGE W. RATHJENS

Changing Perspectives on Arms Control

WHEN THE ABM TREATY and the Interim Agreement on Strategic Offensive Arms were concluded in Moscow in 1972, they were widely welcomed as the beginning of a program to limit, and then reduce, the strategic arsenals of the superpowers. But subsequent developments have done little to justify this optimism: The hopes that seemed to motivate the arms-control efforts of the fifties and sixties have been much eroded. The efforts in the Conference of the Committee on Disarmament seem increasingly sterile.[1] Concern grows over the proliferation of nuclear weapons, especially in the light of the Indian nuclear explosion and the realization that dramatic growth in nuclear power is now imminent. Doubts thus increase about the viability of the Nuclear Non-Proliferation Treaty, as it comes up for review.

Especially troublesome is the situation with respect to strategic arms. Over the last two years the feeling has developed increasingly that the results of SALT I, particularly the offensive-weapons agreement, are unsatisfactory: the offensive-weapons programs of the two superpowers seem to be moving forward virtually unabated and, in the view of some, are even being fueled by arms-control efforts—intragovernmental agreements reached to secure support for the SALT I accords and new weapons programs initiated in the hope of improving bargaining positions for further international negotiations. More significantly, cynicism about the prospects for substantive strategic arms limitations has become widespread, and the efforts to maintain hope by periodic expressions of optimism and the promulgation of occasional minor agreements (such as that to reduce the number of sites permitted each side under the ABM treaty from two to one) have hardly been noticed. Not surprisingly, the immediate reaction to the agreement in principle, reached at the Vladivostok summit meeting, on limiting strategic-force levels has been restrained. Some cautious optimism (generally from Administration supporters) and some mild disapproval (from those who fear that the agreements will do little to slow the arms race) can be observed, but for the most part the attitude seems to be one of wait-and-see; it reveals little evidence of great expectations.

The fact that we may be in for a period of heavy going in arms control is perhaps nowhere more dramatically illustrated than by the efforts, announced at the June, 1974, summit, to extend the nuclear test-ban treaty to limit underground weapons testing. The proposal was widely seen as a transparent effort to convey an impression of continuing momentum in Soviet-American arms control when nothing was being done about the central effort, that is, SALT II. In fact, the terms of the proposed agreement have been severely criticized on substantive grounds by most of those in the United States who heretofore had been in the forefront of efforts to limit nuclear-weapons testing.[2] These ought not to be viewed as isolated problems. They are rather symptomatic of more fundamental difficulties. We shall find the framework within which arms-control efforts must be considered much more complex and confusing than the one that characterized the previous quarter-century's efforts.

The Consensus of the Fifties and Sixties

Certainly during the fifties and well into the sixties something approaching a consensus could be found in the United States on the nature of the military "threat" we faced and the arms-control efforts that should be made to reduce it. The Soviet Union was seen as threatening in three ways: First, there was the possibility of a direct attack upon the United States; secondly, there was fear of an attack on Western Europe; and finally, there was the likelihood that the Soviet Union would support satellite states or dissident groups, should they come into conflict with American clients. Although lip service was paid to the potentials of a Chinese "threat" to the United States and of an unrestrained nuclear proliferation, the American defense posture was determined, or in any case rationalized, almost entirely in terms of a response to Soviet-related "threats."

There was a widespread conviction that arms-control efforts should concentrate on nuclear weapons, partly because the nuclear threat seemed so direct and overwhelming in its destructiveness and partly because it was believed to be more susceptible to containment and reduction through arms-control efforts than were the possibilities of either a massive non-nuclear attack against Western Europe or conflict in the Third World. Nuclear weapons-delivery systems, particularly those appropriate to intercontinental conflict, were large in size and limited in number—hence, countable and controllable with relative ease; and it was hoped that much could be done on a bilateral basis, involving only the United States and the Soviet Union. A further consideration in favor of concentrating arms-control efforts on strategic nuclear weapons was grounded in a belief, which gained substantial currency in the United States at least, in nuclear "sufficiency" or "enoughness," i.e., a belief that little could be gained from acquiring strategic forces in excess of levels sufficient to inflict massive damage on an adversary. Hence it was felt that, if agreements could be reached that would insure the viability of each power's strategic retaliatory forces, much of the incentive to increase offensive force levels would be removed and the balance of power would remain stable in crises. Neither power would stand to gain much from a "first strike," and neither need fear such a strike by its adversary. Thus it was hoped that genuine arms-control progress could be made by imposing constraints selectively—i.e., primarily on developments that might threaten retaliatory capabilities.

Because of the enormity of the damage that appeared likely in the event of a thermonuclear war, it seemed appropriate to many to try to reduce that possibility independently of whatever else might happen in Soviet-American relations. Strategic arms control should not be linked with either local conflict, or other differences between the superpowers, or the interactions of each with other states.[3]

There was also a consensus on the order of priority for the three generally accepted objectives of strategic arms control. Reducing the risk of war, particularly the likelihood of its breaking out in situations of crisis, commanded first priority. Retarding the arms race was next, partly because of concern about costs, but more importantly because of the belief that massive strategic-weapons programs would contribute to tensions and would increase the likelihood of the occurrence of instability in crises. Because the force levels available to both sides were so great, and because the technical problems of limiting damage to industry and population seemed so formidable, the third objective—of reducing damage in the event of war—was generally last on the list (particularly after about 1964) both for arms control and for strategic arms planning generally.

The fifties and sixties were also characterized by a belief in the power of negotiation for limiting and reducing strategic arms. This belief seemed plausible because of the mutual realization that the strategic forces of each side were far more than adequate to destroy the other, and because of the relative simplicity of the kinds of measures that were envisaged. Faith in negotiation was fed by the occasional small successes of the period: the partial nuclear test-ban treaty, the outer-space and seabed treaties, and others, culminating in the strategic arms limitation talks, which seemed so promising when they began in late 1969, and which resulted in agreements two and one-half years later that were generally well received, at least initially.

Finally, there was some agreement on the criteria for measuring the success of negotiating efforts and on the kinds of impediments that had to be taken into account in efforts to reach a settlement. Almost any agreement that involved constraints would be judged a success so long as it did not result in a comparative advantage to the adversary. Because of the very natural tendency to view the adversary's activities conservatively, i.e., in the worst possible light as regards one's own interests, each power seemed to the other to be seeking advantage for itself, whether that was in fact its intent or not. This became particularly evident in the later stages of SALT (probably more so when dealing with limits on offensive forces than on ABM systems). Thus, despite protestations to the contrary, the approach to negotiations, again especially in the later SALT talks, was largely from the perspective of two-person, zero-sum game theory, i.e., where each of two competing parties strives to deny advantage to the other, and where any absolute gains by one side are reckoned very much as equivalent losses by the other. Because concern was expressed, at least in the United States, about the adversary's realization of advantage through clandestine violation of agreements, verification problems were generally considered to be of critical importance in arms control (reflected, in the case of SALT, in the designation of the senior American analytical group as "the Verification Panel").

Simplifying somewhat, it can be said that the American arms-control efforts of the fifties and sixties, including the establishment of the Arms Control and Disarmament Agency, rested almost entirely on three simple and generally accepted ideas: suspicion of a single adversary—the Soviet Union; fear of a nuclear holocaust involving it and the United States; and belief that, through negotiations, this threat might be reduced.

Changing Views on the Assumptions Underlying Policy

We now find the consensus on these points shattered, not as the result of a single development, but rather as a consequence of a number of changes that have occurred over the last half-dozen years. Views in the United States about what constitutes the "threat" now diverge widely. At one extreme, there is what might be called "the

Department of Defense position," little changed from that of a decade or more ago. It assumes that the Soviet Union is a generally implacable adversary, likely to exploit any American weakness or any schism in the West, and ready to stir up, or at least capitalize on, instability and local conflict in the Third World. The 1975 Defense Posture statement reflects this position even more starkly than have earlier statements. It suggests that, with direct American military involvement in Southeast Asia almost ended, it is now time to settle down for the long haul. It is clear from the tone of the document that the assumption behind "long haul" policy planning is a continuing adversary relationship with the Soviet Union extending into the indefinite future. This is strikingly apparent in the justification of decisions to cope with the Soviet "threat" by developing a variety of weapons, many of which will not be operationally important until the nineteen-eighties.

But there are others who, to quote Thomas Schelling, find it "more and more difficult to remember why we consider the Soviet Union our chief enemy." The extreme of this opinion maintains that the Cold War is over, that the Soviet Union, like the United States, has more to gain from stability than from conflict, that both have learned that attempts to impose their wills in the Third World involve costs that are incommensurate with likely gains, and that, even if there were gross disparities in military strength, neither would benefit by using that strength militarily or politically against the other. More cautious commentators limit themselves to discounting Soviet "threats" so long as the Sino-Soviet confrontation remains unresolved.

There are still other gradations to the spectrum of opinions identifying what the "threat" actually is. Initiation of nuclear war by accident or miscalculation is held to be a very serious possibility by some commentators, and it is significant that some of the recently announced changes in American strategic doctrine—for example, greater emphasis on flexible response—are being rationalized by Administration spokesmen in part as being a response to this possibility. Increasing concern, particularly in the arms-control "community," arises over the nuclear-proliferation problem. Many would view it as more serious than the Soviet "threat," particularly when they link it with the risks of miscalculation and accident. But the superpowers have never been willing to try very hard to slow down or stop proliferation, nor are they likely to do so now. The 1975 "Posture Statement" illustrates the point for the United States: in a hundred-thousand-word document, one brief paragraph plus a subordinate clause relates to this issue. Finally, conflict over resources is likely to be a major problem in the decades ahead, pushing ideological differences into the background; and, if this happens, the United States may find itself at odds with many of its traditional allies— the oil-producing states and other oil-consuming, market-economy states in particular.

It is not the purpose of this paper to dispute the emphasis given to each of these various "threats." A great deal has been written on the subject elsewhere, and much more will be written in the future. Our objectives are more modest: to stimulate an exploration explicitly devoted to the relationship between defense policy and arms-control choices, on the one hand, and assumptions about "the threat" and other factors, on the other.

We have already noted the wide divergence in the United States on assumptions about "the threat." Perhaps equally important with respect to arms control are the widely divergent opinions about the dynamics of weapons acquisition and arms-control negotiating processes and about the prospects and importance of improvement, outside the military field, in our relations with the Soviet Union (and other countries). We now turn to these questions before considering specific weapons and arms control, as well as other military and foreign-policy options.

The United States has on occasion during the post-war years exercised restraint in its weapons programs in the hope that it would be reciprocated by the Soviet Union; the most noteworthy examples of this are the nuclear-testing moratorium of 1959-60 and the cutback in the military budget of 1964. But unilateral restraint in weapons development and procurement and, even more, unilateral disarmament have been viewed with disfavor by most of the American "establishment." Throughout the fifties and sixties most discussions of arms control and disarmament were linked inextricably with the negotiation of agreements or treaties that would involve obligations for reciprocal restraint by at least the Soviet Union and, in some cases, other nations as well. This view has become so ingrained that, when the terms "arms control" and "disarmament" are used, many understand them to refer solely to efforts that involve negotiations. This was reflected in the act establishing the Arms Control and Disarmament Agency, for it was clearly intended in the legislation that this Agency would devote itself primarily—if not exclusively—to issues that were, might be, or had been the object of efforts to achieve international agreements affecting arms.

More recently, interest in limiting weapons programs through internal processes has been increasing—witness Congressional opposition to such Administration proposals as the Safeguard ABM and Trident missile-launching submarine programs. Especially since SALT I, doubts have been raised about the efficacy of international negotiations as a viable means of achieving what most people think of as arms-control objectives; none of the agreements reached so far, it is argued, has prevented any nation from doing anything militarily significant that it would have done in the absence of agreement. Moreover, not only have the effects of agreements on arms control been questioned, but doubts have also been raised about one of the other major claims of proponents—that positive international political effects have been achieved that are important and lasting. Furthermore, as noted earlier, one of the effects of the negotiating process has been to stimulate the acquisition of arms, many of which might not have been procured in the absence of negotiation. Finally, it has become increasingly clear, many believe, that domestic factors—bureaucratic politics and pressures from labor and industry—are of such critical importance to weapons development and procurement decisions that little can be done to control the arms race by negotiation at the international level; at best the effect of agreements may be simply to channel resources into different and possibly, but not necessarily, less worrisome weapons programs. Those who have been most strongly committed to arms control have been most shaken by these doubts.

Some who have generally favored a strong military posture and who have been wary of arms-control agreements have had their concerns reinforced, particularly by the SALT I agreements. There is a feeling that the United States "got taken" in the Interim Offensive Agreement and, at the extreme, some even question whether the United States can bargain with the Soviet Union at other than a disadvantage, given the differences in the political systems of the two nations and the growing disenchantment of the American public with all military programs.

One other factor, the attainment of "parity" in strategic strength by the Soviet Union, has made the negotiating of strategic arms-control agreements a more troublesome enterprise for the United States than it seemed to be a few years ago. As Jack Ruina has pointed out, when the United States had a commanding lead in strategic arms, calling a halt to their deployment was generally considered acceptable. Almost all Americans could agree that a "freeze" perpetuating the American advantage would be a good thing, and internal arguments were about details, not about fundamentals. When it is disputable, as it now is, which nation is ahead, how exploitable superiority is, and what can be expected in the absence of negotiated agreements, it is a great deal harder to achieve an American consensus on the desirability of any specific negotiating position or on the desirability of negotiations at all.

But there is another side to this coin: it has probably never been very realistic to expect the Soviet Union to accede to any agreement that would freeze it in an inferior position with respect to major weapons or important areas of technology. Thus, to some of the dedicated believers in arms-control negotiations, the opportunities for concluding far-reaching Soviet-American agreements may be greater now that parity has been reached than they were in the past. The traditional arguments for trying still apply: first, agreements can be important in reducing apprehension about an adversary's exploiting hitherto neglected niches in the panoply of technological possibilities—the outer-space and sea-bed treaties are often cited as examples of agreements that have produced this effect; second, even aside from agreements that might be reached, negotiations are valuable as a means of maintaining contacts that can lead to better understanding of an adversary's fears and intentions; and third, agreements can foreclose significant weapons development or procurement. The ABM treaty is usually cited as an example of this.

The third major issue relevant to arms control on which significant divergence in American thinking can be found is detente. It is hard to be against a relaxation of tensions, but, if it is assumed, as it quite commonly is, that detente also implies some degree of cooperation and increasing interdependence, there is room for questioning Secretary Kissinger's enthusiastic espousal of both the necessity and feasibility of detente—room that is being exploited by his critics.

In classifying the positions, it is perhaps useful first to divide the universe into those who do not believe in detente and those who do. Most of those who are skeptical are so because they have been disappointed with the role played by the Soviet Union in the Yom Kippur War and with its continuing arms build-up, and they are doubtful that relaxation of tensions can go much further. Moreover, developing extensive trade and technology transfer is discounted because there seems to be so little that the Soviet Union can offer. Natural resources, especially oil and natural gas, no longer seem so easily accessible; thus there is increasing doubt, in the United States if not in the other market-economy countries, about becoming dependent on the Soviet Union to any significant degree for critical materials. And cooperation in the international arena is likely to be minimal because of continuing competition between the two powers for political influence and the interest of each in not jeopardizing relations with its allies. This group includes those who welcome greater trade with the Soviet Union, but are skeptical that it will develop and concerned that there will be an adverse Soviet reaction when that country comes to realize that detente is not going to be the solution to all its economic and management problems.

Others, including many who accept these views about the unlikelihood of constructive relations between the superpowers, see little point in devoting very much attention to improving relations. They find few grounds for armed conflict in any case, particularly if, as seems likely to many, ideological differences will be relatively less important in the next decade or so than they have been in the past.

Those who are more committed to detente can, for our purposes, be divided into two groups. Some are enthusiastic about it because they feel that interdependence and cooperation are important, indeed may be essential, to minimizing the possibility of conflict and providing the solution for a host of international problems. Many in this group discern a strong link between detente and arms control: each will reinforce the other and severe limits are likely to be placed on the progress of one if none is made with respect to the other. This might be called the Kissinger view; it is presumably shared by at least some of the Soviet establishment.

Others, and most of Secretary Kissinger's critics appear to fall in this group, feel that the two powers may have quite different interests in detente, but they see in these different interests opportunities for linkages and bargaining. It is widely believed that trade and the transfer of technology and managerial techniques will benefit the Soviet Union much more than it will the United States. The effect of the excess of Western exports to the Soviet Union over imports from it is seen as subsidizing Soviet military programs by allowing a greater allocation of scarce Soviet resources to that industry. On these grounds, it becomes reasonable to insist that the Soviets restrain their weapons programs as a *quid pro quo* for our continuing and expanding technological transfer and trade. Some, notably Senator Jackson, have also linked concessions on trade—"most favored nation" treatment and favorable credit arrangements—with the issue of Jewish emigration.

Finally, still another position on the linkage between detente and arms policy might be called the "traditional arms-control" view, although it is shared by many in the "defense" community. This view holds that the threat of nuclear war is really in a different class from all other interactions between the two countries and that it should therefore be dealt with independently of these other interests. Detente is discounted, not because it is a vacuous concept but because arguments about it, attempts to exploit it, concerns that it might be jeopardized, or hopes that it might be strengthened might detract from the more immediate and crucial business of what to do with strategic arms.

Four Policy Questions

Having identified at least some of the cross-currents in American thinking to which weapons and arms-control decisions are likely to be sensitive, we turn to an examination of a selected group of those issues.

Flexible Response with Strategic Forces

One issue of particular concern now is the resurgence, after a decade of quiescence, of interest in the possible selective and flexible use of strategic weapons. What is sought, according to Secretary of Defense Schlesinger, is the capability of using American strategic forces against the Soviet Union to inflict damage sufficient to offset any gains the Soviets might realize through an attack on the United States or its allies, while avoiding unacceptable escalation. A related argument for pursuing an expanded-options policy, which is not so commonly made and which, judging from Schlesinger's remarks, has presumably not been a factor in his thinking, is that having a greater range of options or threatening to acquire it may increase a nation's bargaining strength in international negotiations.

Those opposing an expanded-options policy base their opposition on three arguments: 1) that the attainment of capabilities for destroying adversary military targets (particularly "hardened" ones, such as underground missile silos), which Mr. Schlesinger advocates as a component of his "options" policy, will encourage both superpowers to attempt a disarming "first strike" in time of crisis; 2) that by making "nuclear war fighting" more credible, it will be made more likely; and 3) that the pressures for a strategic arms race will be increased by both "first strike" fears and the desire to avoid an "options gap." The first of these three arguments can be discounted on technical grounds, including those of the growing importance and low vulnerability of missile-launching submarine forces. The second seems more plausible; certainly, the likelihood that nuclear weapons will be used will be increased, given some provocation—this is the intent of the policy change. However, the likelihood of the Soviet Union's initiating a non-nuclear attack against the United States or its allies will presumably be decreased—that, too, is the intent. Thus, if the changes in policy and capabilities have the effects the Secretary claims for them, the direct impact on the probability of nuclear war will be indeterminate.

The case against the Schlesinger proposals must depend mainly, then, on the arms-race argument, and on the derivative argument that one of the consequences of an escalated arms race may be an increase in tensions, and consequently, perhaps, also in the likelihood of war, nuclear or conventional. The outcome of weighing these arguments against those made for the policy change depends mainly on one's views regarding some of the assumptions discussed earlier. If one discounts the action-reaction theory of the arms race, i.e., the belief that weapons development and acquisition decisions by the United States and the Soviet Union are to be explained largely as reactions to each other's actions, then the simple arms-race argument against Secretary Schlesinger's proposed policy changes is much weakened. On the other hand, if one discounts the likelihood that Soviet-American arms-control negotiations will be productive, the second of the two arguments for the policy change—the "bargaining chip" argument—loses its validity. Perhaps more important than either, if one discounts the seriousness of Soviet "threats," the major argument that the Secretary makes for his "expanded options" policy is also much weakened.

Up to this point, the discussion has been within a bilateral framework. By bringing in other considerations, the balance among arguments can begin to shift. Changing policy and developing weapons that enable the use of strategic nuclear forces with greater selectivity and less collateral damage will have the effect of making nuclear war more "thinkable," and not just against the Soviet Union. Given capabilities for "surgical strikes," a President will be more likely than has been the case in the past to accede to arguments from advisers to use nuclear weapons in a variety of situations. Such use—or even the belief by others that the likelihood of such use is increasing—will be a stimulus for others to acquire nuclear weapons, either as a deterrent to the United States or for selective use against others with inferior capabilities. In short, by narrowing the gap that separates nuclear from conventional conflict—and surely Secretary Schlesinger's proposals move us in that direction—we may end up by providing further impetus to nuclear proliferation.

Thus, whether or not an "expanded-options" policy for the United States is desirable depends to a great extent on the relative weight attached to the Soviet "threat," on the one hand, and the dangers of nuclear proliferation, on the other. As noted earlier, we are very far from having a consensus on this question. Debate about an expanded-options policy may at long last lay to rest the bugaboo of a "first strike," and that would be helpful. But beyond that, answering the "options" question requires a solution to more fundamental problems.

Damage Limitation

The desirability of "damage limiting" as an objective in the structuring of strategic forces is similarly debated. Damage that the United States might suffer in a nuclear war could, in principle, be limited by active defense against aircraft or missiles, civil defense, or by the destruction of adversary missiles and aircraft before launch; at various times the acquisition of capabilities to accomplish all of these objectives has been seriously considered. However, since the mid-sixties American strategic arms policy has been dominated by what might be called the "orthodox arms-control" position, according to which developing these capabilities should command low priority.[4] On occasion they have even been regarded as positively undesirable. The position has its basis in two firmly held beliefs: first, that effective damage limitation would be a losing game technically—any such efforts could be offset relatively easily by adversary improvements in offensive capabilities; and second, that the Soviet Union would, in fact, improve its offensive forces as a reaction to whatever the United States might do (and vice versa). Thus "damage limiting" efforts, by either power, would be likely to lead simply to higher and higher levels of arms on both sides with no real improvement in security for either. The ABM Treaty can be viewed as a testament to the persuasiveness of this argument, and the opposition in the United States to the development of multiple warheads of ever greater accuracy, which might be used in "counterforce" attacks against Soviet missiles and aircraft, has also been based largely upon it.

However, the view that Soviet weapons decisions are only minimally influenced by American ones, i.e., the rejection of the "action-reaction theory" of the arms race, undermines one of the major tenets of the "orthodox arms-control" position, and the case for restraint on the part of the United States in the development of "damage limiting" capabilities is greatly weakened. Moreover, when one takes the nuclear proliferation problems seriously, as has not been common in the past, the case will be strengthened for these capabilities, less from the possibility that other countries would be dissuaded from acquiring nuclear weapons were the United States (and/or the Soviet Union) to mount major efforts to develop "damage limiting" systems than from prudence. "Damage limiting" capabilities would then become hedges against possible nuclear attack occurring from accident, miscalculation, or aggression—contingencies that will become increasingly likely as more and more nations acquire nuclear arms.

Strategic Arms Limitation

Turning to current arms-control negotiations, and specifically to SALT, at least four different attitudes can be identified that now command significant support in the United States. The wonder is that there are not even more, when one considers all of the combinations of views regarding "the threat," the utility of negotiations, and detente that are possible. Prior to Vladivostok, there seems to have been what might be characterized as two "establishment views," one associated particularly with Secretary Kissinger and the other with three "defense" spokesmen—Secretary Schlesinger, Paul Nitze, and Senator Jackson. They had in common serious concern for the continuing growth in Soviet strategic offensive strength. As a consequence, there was little argument on the immediate objective of SALT II, namely, the negotiation of an agreement that would impose limits on strategic offensive forces that would be more acceptable than those negotiated at SALT I, including limitations on large missiles with multiple warheads. There also appeared to be agreement that the United States had to have a vigorous weapons program underway, or at least in prospect, if it was to bargain effectively at SALT II.

Beyond this, the positions diverged. In the "defense" view, hope of achieving meaningful arms control through negotiations was attenuated by skepticism about its likelihood. This view maintained that the United States should match the Soviet Union in military strength, whatever the outcome of negotiations—this is the doctrine of "essential equivalence." Skepticism was also voiced about the importance and durability of detente. The Kissinger position appeared to be more complex. Threats other than those involving the Soviet Union were not so completely discounted; detente and interdependence weighed more heavily. The Secretary argued, "There can be no peaceful international order without a constructive relationship between the United States and the Soviet Union." This argument, coupled with seemingly greater optimism about negotiations, or perhaps greater conviction about the necessity of making progress through them, required that more emphasis be given to improving relations with the Soviet Union and relatively less to whether any agreements that might be concluded would be in strict balance at any given time. Secretary Kissinger has said "the balance cannot be struck on each issue every day, but only over the whole range of relations and over a period of time." This meant that "linkages" were seen differently from the two perspectives. In the Kissinger view, and this seems also to be the view of the Soviet leadership, SALT has been seen as part of a larger process, with the effect on detente, broadly construed, apparently counting heavily.

The differences in attitudes were reflected to some degree in the comments following Vladivostok by the Secretaries of State and Defense, with the latter taking a somewhat "harder" line on the continuation of major programs, while the details remain to be negotiated, and on the question of building up to the Vladivostok-permitted limits.

In the negotiations on details and in considering other limitations and reductions, it is likely that there will continue to be differences. From the Kissinger perspective, some military imbalances could be acceptable (assuming they could be sold domestically), if, from a broader perspective, negotiation seemed likely to contribute sufficiently to improvement in Soviet-American relations. In contrast, "defense" judgments about the acceptability of various positions are likely to be based almost exclusively on military considerations—on the effect on the relative strategic balance. There will be little interest in "linkages." Indeed, there will probably be active opposition to any trade and technology transfer that is likely to favor the Soviet Union, although, on the assumption that the Soviet interest in trade and technology transfer, and in detente generally, is greater than that in this country, it might possible, at least theoretically, to exploit that interest and obtain somewhat better terms on strategic arms agreements than might otherwise be possible.

The "traditional arms controllers" will presumably approach further strategic arms negotiations, as would those with a "defense" perspective, concentrating almost entirely on weapons programs and eschewing linkages. However, they will be less concerned with balanced agreements and much more with maintaining "stability." Thus, the concept of "sufficiency" can be expected to play a greater role, and the acquisition of "bargaining chips" will be played down. One can expect particular emphasis on maintaining the viability of deterrent forces, and—discounting the argument that they are neither in any jeopardy nor likely to be—the "traditional arms controllers" can be expected to give high priority to preventing the attainment of yield-accuracy-number combinations for missile warheads that might make possible a "first strike" by either side against adversary missiles. In the same vein, they might also push constraints on anti-submarine warfare capabilities that could conceivably threaten submarine-launched ballistic missile (SLBM) forces. And they would give less weight than "defense" advocates to trying to preserve technological superiority and more weight to trying to prevent "destabilizing" developments by negotiated agreements.

Finally, some feel that SALT may not be worth pursuing for the reasons mentioned earlier: arguments for "bargaining chips" may lead to the acquisition of weapons that would not otherwise have been procured; the negotiations may divert attention from threats some believe to be more serious—nuclear proliferation and world economic crisis; and agreements reached may simply divert arms efforts into different channels.

But if not SALT, what? That depends on one's views of the Soviet "threat," of the "action-reaction theory," and of the arms race. If one discounts these, or if one believes in "nuclear sufficiency," there is a strong case for unilateral restraint and for organizational reform directed toward reducing weapons-acquisition pressures. Concern about proliferation or economic pressures may also dictate moving in these directions, even if some increase in risks vis-à-vis the Soviet Union is implied.

Mutual Balanced Force Reductions in Europe

As with SALT, one can reach very different conclusions about the question of force postures in Europe, depending on the assumptions one makes with respect to the "threat," the utility of negotiations, and detente. The Western approach to Mutual Balanced Force Reductions (MBFR) has so far been predicated on a "defense" view of the threat, i.e., the view that the NATO force posture should be designed to cope with a deliberate Warsaw Pact attack. But a quite different view might prevail if it is assumed that Soviet interest in the stability of Europe dominates any interest the Soviets might have in conquest. Then the major "threat" is more likely to be civil war, and more likely to be in Southern Europe or the Balkans than in Central Europe.

Thus, the balancing of NATO and the Warsaw Pact forces may be less important than the structuring of these forces to prevent events from moving too rapidly following an outbreak of violence. To some this would suggest emphasis not on balanced force reductions, but on deployments of both weapons and troops and the establishment of command, control, and consultation arrangements that would insure the opportunity for diplomatic containment and the reduction of a conflict that neither side wants. Those suspicious of Soviet intentions want a hedge against intervention by the Soviet Union should events seem not to be going its way, but even in such a case, the emphasis in MBFR talks might center on achieving delay in intervention rather than on balance in forces *ab initio*.

Another position on MBFR has some adherents, analogous to the fourth position mentioned in the discussion of SALT II, namely, belief that the major effect—if not intent—of the negotiations is to give one or both powers an excuse for maintaining forces in Europe. Finally, there are those who argue that the negotiations may have divisive effects on NATO. For those holding either of these views, the adverse effects of prolonged negotiations may well offset the advantages of any agreements that might eventually be reached.

Policy Challenges

The resolution of a host of other questions will depend on the uncertainties we have been reviewing (e.g., questions relating to specific weapons—whether the United States should go ahead with its new strategic bomber and submarine programs—as well as others relating to doctrine and arms-control proposals), but the discussion thus far will suffice to demonstrate that progress in treating such issues will be very difficult if we do not first achieve a greater consensus on more fundamental questions. Without this consensus, we will continue programs and policies that will be divisive in their effect on American politics; and we will be sending signals that reflect our confusion to adversaries, allies, and others. One of the worst effects is likely to be a return to the tenacious belief that, if in doubt, "it is better to err on the side of safety"—in other words, without a consensus on rationales for weapons choices, force levels, approaches to arms control, and the reactions of others to what we do, we had best built up our strength. Obviously it is therefore important to resolve these uncertainties. Recognizing this, Secretary Kissinger has called for a national debate on detente and related questions, and he has warned the nation in increasingly pessimistic terms of the perils we face. But the country has been so preoccupied with inflation and recession that debate of the breadth he has called for has not developed. Furthermore, if Zbigniew Brzezinski is right in his observation that we may be at the beginning of a period of "introversion" in foreign policy, it may be a very long time before a consensus will be reached on many of the fundamentals on which military and arms-control policy should be based.

Resolution could perhaps be accelerated by strong executive leadership. However, as a consequence of the prolongation of our military involvement in Southeast Asia long past the point when it commanded widespread domestic support, and of Watergate, not to mention the seeming inability of either the last Administration or the present one to cope with economic problems, the nation is not likely to put much trust in the White House, notwithstanding our penchant for giving the President very wide latitude in foreign and military affairs. The likelihood is further diminished by Mr. Ford's not having been elected to the Presidency and the Congress's large Democratic majority.

In the light of this, and with the country now preoccupied with economic problems, there is a special challenge for the academic arms-control community. The two-fold nature of the challenge should be obvious from our discussion: 1) to make explicit the relationship between the arguments for and against various proposals affecting arms and the controversial assumptions that underlie the analysis, and 2) to explore the validity of those assumptions. This means that the community of interest must become broader than it has been in the past. A greater role must be played by those concerned with foreign-policy issues and the analysis of bureaucratic behavior, while those committed to basing solutions to problems on a very few simple principles— such a powerful approach in the pure sciences—may become frustrated and contribute less. The simple principles are just not there, or at least are not widely accepted.

So much for the challenge to the academic community. What can be said for the bureaucracy and the nation's political leadership? First, we will have to be less ambitious and more cautious about playing the leader on the international scene, for we can hardly expect others to follow when we speak with many voices, as we inevitably shall for some time. Second, it is becoming increasingly unlikely that the Congress can be made to support military programs at levels that the present Administration seems to feel will be required for the foreign policy and arms-control negotiations it would like to undertake. This is partly a consequence of the erosion of confidence in Executive leadership already mentioned—we are not likely soon to have another Gulf of Tonkin resolution—and partly preoccupation with other problems.

The fact that the country will be less willing than at any other time since World War II to provide military capabilities for contingencies that are not already apparent and about which it might later have doubts may have special significance for arms-control negotiations. To the extent one believes in the importance of "bargaining chips" in negotiations, the American position will depend increasingly on the mobilization base and linkages involving the country's economic strength and less on weapons already in existence or firmly committed.

Finally, we would suggest that the country rely less on the Defense Department than it has in the past for the development of doctrine and policy regarding weapons use and for analysis of weapons choices—and for that matter, of arms-control proposals. As we have seen, preferences depend on what the "threat" is perceived to be, on the way one understands how bureaucracies behave, and on a host of other factors, about which there are now great divergencies of opinion. It is unlikely, in the absence of radical change, that the Defense Department will reflect these divergencies in any analyses it might undertake. The same can be said of the Arms Control Agency and of the Department of State. More of the burden must fall where responsibilities are broader—in the White House and on the National Security Council staff, in particular. But this will hardly suffice, for in any Administration, selection processes and defense mechanisms will operate to limit the framework for analysis, and this is likely to prove much more troublesome than it has in the past when we were closer to having a consensus. In particular, any Administration wishing to develop support for a "position of strength" in foreign policy—including arms-control negotiations—is likely to try generating support for its policies by exaggerating "the threat," particularly when the country is divided. For this reason, other groups in our society, including the Congress and its various committees and caucuses, must assume more of the responsibility for analysis and decision.

REFERENCES

[1] The fact that the activities of the Conference of the Committee on Disarmament (CCD) are virtually unknown outside the very small circle of disarmament experts is a measure of how little it is accomplishing. During the sixties, most of the important arms-control and disarmament negotiations took place in this forum and its predecessor, the Eighteen Nation Disarmament Conference, but, with the Strategic Arms Limitation Talks and the negotiations relating to force reduction in Europe under other auspices, the CCD has become relatively unimportant, although it continues as the principal forum for involving non-NATO, non-Warsaw Pact powers in arms-control and disarmament discussions.

[2] The objections to the agreement are these: It would permit underground testing of weapons up to 150 KT even though compliance with a much lower threshold could probably be verified without on-site inspection (the issue over which efforts to achieve a comprehensive test ban foundered in 1963). The agreement would not become effective until 1976, and during the interval larger underground weapons tests would be conducted—indeed, on an accelerated scale to meet the deadline. "Peaceful nuclear explosions" in excess of 150 KT would probably be permitted under the agreement, and these might also be used to continue weapons development. Additionally, inclusion of provisions for such explosions are seen by some as a stimulant to nuclear proliferation.

[3] These views, like those relating to "sufficiency," were articulated in their clearest form in what might be called "the orthodox arms-control" community. In the world of *Realpolitik* they were subject to great stress with various reactions. To the dismay of some of the most committed arms-control proponents, concern about possible repercussions in NATO and elsewhere led the United States to delay the SALT talks for a "decent interval" following the Soviet intervention in Czechoslovakia in 1968. The fact that the Soviet Union did not find it necessary to refrain from active SALT negotiations at the time of the American bombing of Hanoi and Haiphong in 1972 was a contrasting example (and a somewhat surprising and encouraging one to many arms-control advocates).

[4] Some critics would prefer to argue that weapons-acquisition decisions have been *rationalized* rather than determined by appealing to the orthodox arms-control arguments.

Notes on Contributors

GRAHAM T. ALLISON, born in 1940 in Charlotte, North Carolina, is professor of politics at Harvard University and the author of *Essence of Decision: Explaining the Cuban Missile Crisis* (1971).

LES ASPIN, born in 1938 in Milwaukee, Wisconsin, is Congressman from the First District of Wisconsin and a member of the House Armed Services Committee.

HARVEY BROOKS, born in 1915 in Cleveland, Ohio, is Gordon McKay Professor of Applied Physics, Dean of Engineering and Applied Physics, and member of the Faculty of Public Administration at Harvard University, and the president of the American Academy of Arts and Sciences. His publications include *The Government of Science* (1968).

BARRY CARTER, born in 1942 in Los Angeles, California, is an attorney in private practice in Washington, D. C.

ABRAM CHAYES, born in 1922 in Chicago, is professor of law at the Harvard Law School. His publications include *ABM, An Evaluation of the Decision to Deploy an Anti-Ballistic Missile System* (with J. Wiesner; 1969) and *The Cuban Missile Crisis, International Crisis and the Role of Law* (1974).

PAUL DOTY, born in 1920 in Charleston, West Virginia, is Mallinckrodt Professor of Biochemistry and director of the Program for Science and International Affairs at Harvard University. His publications include many articles on subjects in biochemistry, molecular biology, science policy, and arms control.

RICHARD A. FALK, born in 1930 in New York City, is Albert G. Milbank Professor of International Law and Practice at Princeton University and Senior Fellow of the Institute of World Order. His publications include *This Endangered Planet* (1971) and *A Study of Future Worlds* (1975).

F. A. LONG, born in 1910 in Great Falls, Montana, is Henry Luce Professor of Science and Society and professor of chemistry at Cornell University. His publications include a number of articles on science and technology.

FREDERIC A. MORRIS, born in 1950 in Tulsa, Oklahoma, is a student at the Harvard Law School and in the Public Policy Program of the Kennedy School of Government, Harvard University.

G. W. RATHJENS, born in 1925 in Fairbanks, Alaska, is professor of political science at the Massachusetts Institute of Technology, and a contributor to *SALT: The Moscow Agreements and Beyond* (1974) and *Nuclear Arms Control: Process and Impact* (1974).

THOMAS C. SCHELLING, born in 1921 in Oakland, California, is professor of political economy at Harvard University. He is the author of *Strategy of Conflict* (1960), *Strategy and Arms Control* (with M. H. Halperin) (1961), and *Arms and Influence* (1966).

MARSHALL D. SHULMAN, born in 1916 in Jersey City, New Jersey, is Adlai E. Stevenson Professor of International Relations, Columbia University and the author of *Stalin's Foreign Policy Reappraised* (1963) and *Beyond the Cold War* (1966).

JOHN STEINBRUNER, born in 1941 in Denver, Colorado, is associate professor of public policy, Harvard University and assistant director of the Program for Science and International Affairs. He is the author of *The Cybernetic Theory of Decision: New Dimensions in Political Analysis* (1974).

R. JAMES WOOLSEY, born in 1941 in Tulsa, Oklahoma, is an attorney in private practice in Washington, D. C., and a former general counsel to the United States Senate Committee on Armed Services.

215